Conversations with

Literary Conversations Series

Peggy Whitman Prenshaw
General Editor

DATE DUE

Conversations
with Richard Wright

Edited by
Keneth Kinnamon and Michel Fabre

University Press of Mississippi
Jackson

Copyright © 1993 by University Press of Mississippi
All rights reserved
Manufactured in the United States of America
96   95   94   93   4   3   2   1
The paper in this book meets the guidelines for permanence and durability
of the Committee on Production Guidelines for Book Longevity of the Council
on Library Resources.

Library of Congress Cataloging-in-Publication Data

Wright, Richard, 1908-1960.
    Conversations with Richard Wright / edited by Keneth Kinnamon and
Michel Fabre.
        p.   cm. — (Literary conversations series)
    Includes index.
    ISBN 0-87805-632-7 (cloth). — ISBN 0-87805-633-5 (paper)
    1. Wright, Richard, 1908-1960—Interviews.   2. Afro-American
authors—20th century—Interviews.   I. Kinnamon, Keneth.
II. Fabre, Michel.   III. Title.   IV. Series.
PS3545.R815Z474   1993
813'.57—dc20   93-13938
                                                                         CIP

British Library Cataloging-in-Publication data available

Books by Richard Wright

Uncle Tom's Children: Four Novellas. New York: Harper, 1938.
Native Son. New York: Harper, 1940.
Uncle Tom's Children: Five Long Stories. New York: Harper, 1940.
Native Son (The Biography of a Young American): A Play in Ten Scenes. With Paul
  Green. New York: Harper, 1941.
Bright and Morning Star. New York: International Publishers, 1941.
12 Million Black Voices. With photo-direction by Edwin Rosskam. New York: Viking,
  1941.
Black Boy: A Record of Childhood and Youth. New York: Harper, 1945.
Cinque Uomini. Milan: Mondadori, 1951.
The Outsider. New York: Harper, 1953.
Savage Holiday. New York: Avon, 1954.
Black Power: A Record of Reaction in a Land of Pathos. New York: Harper, 1954.
The Color Curtain: A Report on the Bandung Conference. Cleveland: World, 1956.
Pagan Spain. New York: Harper, 1957.
White Man, Listen!. Garden City, N.Y.: Doubleday, 1957.
The Long Dream. Garden City, N.Y.: Doubleday, 1958.
Eight Men. Cleveland: World, 1961.
Lawd Today. New York: Walker, 1963.
American Hunger. New York: Harper & Row, 1977.
Richard Wright Reader. Ed. Ellen Wright and Michel Fabre. New York: Harper &
  Row, 1978.
Early Works: Lawd Today!, Uncle Tom's Children, Native Son. New York: Library of
  America, 1991.
Later Works: Black Boy (American Hunger), The Outsider. New York: Library of
  America, 1991.

Contents

Contents

Introduction

Southern writers may have very different backgrounds and very different ways of responding to interviewers. William Styron once confessed
that "a certain amiable garrulousness" was characteristic of his southern
background and accounted for a great deal of his prolixity. When approached by people able to ask interesting questions, he found himself
"responding at length out of the sheer pleasure of the intellectual inter-
change that ensued."

Some writers may be chronically withdrawn, but most like to hear
themselves talk; and when the questions or arguments are provocative
enough, the dialogue can be lively, even exciting. Such was surely the
case in Paris at the Café Tournon on the Left Bank in the 1950s, where
expatriated African American writers and artists congregated for hours
at a time. There Richard Wright, along with Ollie Harrington and
Chester Himes, was one of the most brilliant storytellers and talkers,
but such conversations have gone largely unrecorded. As a result, one
dazzling aspect of Wright's verbal personality does not appear in the
"conversations" collected here.

Nor do Wright's interviews resemble those of his contemporary and
fellow Mississippian William Faulkner, who often intentionally de-
ceived interviewers to protect his privacy. Although Wright was
reserved about his adult private life, he spoke freely about his past,
considering it representative of the lives of those inarticulate Southern
blacks to whom he also gave voice in *Black Boy* and *12 Million Black
Voices*. Nor did he avoid explaining his literary intentions and strate-
gies. In the early phase of his career, before his expatriation, he wanted
to clarify his work for American white readers, whose prejudices often
impeded their understanding of black writing. After going to France, he
was always conscious of the need to explain the unfamiliar social background of his literary works to French or other European interviewers.

Although Wright could be entertaining in relaxed conversations with
friends and although he occasionally achieves grim racial humor in his
writing (as in "Man of All Work" and "Big Black Good Man"), the

reader will not find much levity in the interviews collected here. The tone is usually serious, often didactic, as Wright deals earnestly with writing, politics, race, and social issues. In *White Man, Listen!* he records his answer to a question as to whether his ideas would make people happy: "My dear, I do not deal in happiness; I deal in meaning." In his interviews as well as in his fiction, this maxim holds.

This is not to say, however, that such seriousness emanates from a somber or stern personality. Having read the fiction before approaching its author, many white interviewers, both American and European, expected to encounter a bitter or aggressive or sullen or even hostile man. Instead, they were received hospitably by a pleasant individual who radiated charm through his sparkling brown eyes, his soft voice, and his resonant laugh as well as through his words and gestures. In 1938 Marcia Minor noted in the Communist *Daily Worker* Wright's "clear brown eyes narrow[ing] with mirth in his oval shaped face" and his "boyish charm." In the bourgeois *New York Sun* two years later an interviewer pointed up the contrast between *Native Son,* "fast, forceful and full of violence," and the "good-natured, soft-voiced young man" who wrote it. An interviewer in Mexico City called him "strong and cheerful." Other interviewers in the early and mid-1940s noted such characteristics as these: "mild-mannered, soft-voiced" (Wilder), "poised, logical, good tempered" (McCullough), "melodious voiced" (*PM*), "affable, poised, quick to smile, almost gay" (Rolo).

As his expatriation began, first tentatively in 1946 and then permanently the following year, French journalists were equally charmed by Wright's personality. In the first of two interviews she conducted with the author, Jeanine Delpech found him to be "a lively person with a jolly smile under his big, round glasses." Michel Gordey also interviewed Wright twice over the years. In the first Gordey expressed the contrast between preconception and reality felt by so many. Imagining "a man with clenched fists and set jaws, locked in bitterness," he instead felt immediately "the calm, the kindness, the reason radiate from this middle-sized, dark-complexioned man with soft, intelligent eyes behind rimless glasses." In an interview a year later Gordey mentions the "deep, throaty laughter of his, childlike and clear-ringing." Many European interviewers were similarly impressed. Raphäel Tardon heard "a great laugh, broad and free" (1946). Peter Schmid called it "a clear, free laugh, without bitterness" (1946). Lucienne Escoube ends her 1946 interview concerning film censorship and spiritual malaise in the United States with these words: "At this point, Richard Wright smiled a smile that contradicted the pessimism of his pronouncements. Large, strong, his face expressed poise, health. And when he laughed, one could not imagine that anyone who laughed in that way was not, at bottom, a firm optimist." Nor did Wright laugh only in interviews with white Europeans. In "Black Boy in France," published in *Ebony* in 1953 and probably the best contemporary account of Wright as expatriate in Paris, fellow black expatriate writer William Gardner Smith reports that Wright "has a broad sense of humor and laughs raucously, soft brown eyes twinkling behind rimless glasses." Without detracting in the least from the genuineness of Wright's risibility, though, one may suggest that it was not seldom what Langston Hughes and many others have called laughing to keep from crying. Indeed, one of his last interviewers in 1960, the Englishman Peter Lennon, commented that "he laughed most readily when mentioning some particularly illogical and unjust act of discrimination against the Negro in America."

Because interviewers were alert to personal characteristics, interviews with Wright provide what is seldom apparent in his works, a vivid sense of Wright's mature personality and character, quite consistent over the years, in addition to a record of his opinions and ideas. The Wright that emerges from these interviews is a pleasure to know. His very first interview in Paris was given on the platform of St. Lazare Station moments after his arrival on 9 May 1946. The interviewer was the enterprising, not to say insistent, Maurice Nadeau, who was to review Wright's books and interview their author again in the years ahead. Not seeing Wright at first among the passengers arriving from Le Havre, Nadeau writes, he "was about to turn back when a big, resonant laugh made me turn around suddenly. Squatting down, his face hidden by a wide-brimmed hat, the bottom of his ample overcoat spread out on the platform, a young man was playing with his little daughter. 'Julia!' he cried." Nadeau introduced himself and began to ask questions, despite his realization that "his daughter interests him more than I do." Tired from his trip, eager to see the streets of Paris as he is driven to his hotel, telling Nadeau "that this is not a good place to talk," Wright, a former newspaper correspondent himself, nevertheless gave Nadeau the interview and the scoop. Asked an indiscreet question, Wright deflected it and "took little Julia in his arms and headed toward the exit without saying any more. I had the impression that my question had been rude. He noticed my embarrassment and came to my aid" with an honest answer. The interview ends with this sentence: "With his daughter in his arms, Richard Wright rushed off, but not before giving me a big pat on the back, punctuated with a peal of tremendous laughter." Nadeau's last interview with Wright took place several months before his death. "One well knows," the first paragraph ends, "Richard Wright's welcoming warmth, his great ease in conversing now in English, now in a halting but pure French, his gaiety, the congenial aura his persona exudes. Yet he is just recovering from a disease caught during his recent travels in Africa." Whether the tired traveler of thirty-seven or the ailing author of fifty-one, Wright charmed Nadeau, as he did so many of his inter-viewers, with the warm congeniality of his personality.

Most interviews with Wright were conducted by print journalists, not by scholars, critics, or editors of literary quarterlies. Spatial considera-tions were paramount, resulting in terse questions and brief answers. Furthermore, from the late 1930s to the late 1950s tape recorders were seldom used, let alone video equipment. Interviewees seldom had a chance to expatiate. Another restraining factor was the popular taste that newspaper interviewers had to satisfy. The occasion of an interview with Wright was often the awarding of a literary prize, the publication of a book, the production of a play or a film, a newsworthy political event, or his arrival in France or Argentina or Spain or Scandinavia. His residence in France yielded some of the longest and most thoughtful interviews, concerned not only with his fiction but with racial and politi-cal developments in Africa and Asia as well as Europe and America. His early recognition of the importance of the emergence of the Third World transcended the usual fixation on the East-West rivalry, but Wright spoke trenchantly on the latter topic as well. Other common themes and concerns emerge, but one is impressed also by the intellec-tual give-and-take occurring when a knowledgeable interviewer posed provocative questions.

Since half of Wright's career was spent in France, with travels to three other continents after taking up residence in Paris in 1947, numer-ous interviews included herein have been translated into English. For some interviews in foreign languages (usually French), Wright prepared written answers to questions submitted to him in advance or was given the opportunity to correct and change oral interviews before publication.

In such cases we have used Wright's written English responses to questions in other languages when they were readily available in the Wright Archive at the Yale University Library, noting in the source headnotes that we have translated only the questions. This procedure obviously provides greater fidelity than translating back into English responses that appeared in print in *L'Express,* say, in French translation from a written English text. It should also be noted that unless otherwise indicated, all items are presented in their entirety. We have eliminated extraneous material from radio panel discussions. Throughout the collection obvious typographical errors have been silently corrected.

As the term "conversations" suggests, more is included here than formal interviews; discussions on radio programs, either with a single interlocutor or in a round-table format, are also included, as is an essay constituting a kind of self-interview on the relation of *Black Boy* to his reading. The present volume constitutes a representative record of conversations with Richard Wright that were printed or broadcast. Although an author cannot be held responsible for what he says in an interview in quite the same way that he is accountable for what he writes and publishes, *Conversations with Richard Wright,* chronologically arranged, does provide valuable glimpses into the author's development and character as well as his thinking and his reactions to events, racial and national or international, over nearly a quarter century of his public career.

Finally, the editors wish to acknowledge with gratitude the cooperation of Ellen Wright in making this book possible. Keneth Kinnamon wishes to thank his colleagues John DuVal, Raymond Eichmann, and James Horton for help in translating a few passages from French and Portuguese. The editors are grateful to their wives, children, and grandchildren in ways far too numerous to mention here.

Chronology

1908   Richard Nathaniel Wright born 4 September on Rucker's
Plantation, some twenty miles east of Natchez, Mississippi,
the first child of Nathan Wright, a sharecropper, and Ella
Wilson Wright, a schoolteacher

1910   Brother Leon Alan Wright born 24 September, second and
last child of Nathan and Ella Wright

1911   Ella Wright leaves farm with her children and goes to
Natchez to live with her family. They are later joined by her
husband.

1913   Wright accidentally sets fire to the house of his grand-
parents, the Wilsons. Later Nathan and Ella move with their
children up river to Memphis.

1914   Father leaves his family to live with another woman.

1915   Wright matriculates at Howe Institute.

1916   Mother becomes ill and the children are placed in an
orphanage. After spending the summer in Jackson, she
moves with her sons to Elaine, Arkansas, to live with her
sister and brother-in-law, Maggie and Silas Hopkins.

1917   Uncle Silas, a relatively prosperous builder and saloon-
keeper, is murdered by whites. Aunt Maggie, Ella, and the
children flee to West Helena, then move back to the Wilson
house in Jackson, and finally to West Helena again.

1918   Wright begins school again in September.

1919   Mother's deteriorating health culminates in a stroke, leaving
        her paralyzed. The children are separated, Wright going to
        live with an uncle and aunt in Greenwood, Mississippi.
        Unhappy, he returns to Jackson.

1920   Wright attends Seventh-Day Adventist school taught by his
        Aunt Addie, but is rebellious.

1921   Attends the public Jim Hill School, where he excels
        academically and gains friends

1922   Works at various jobs after school and during the summer;
        reads much pulp fiction

1923   Attends Smith Robertson Junior High

1924   Writes first short story, "The Voodoo of Hell's Half-Acre,"
        published in the Jackson *Southern Register*

1925   Graduates from Smith Robertson as valedictorian, but
        refuses to deliver a speech prepared by the principal; leaves
        Jackson for Memphis

1926   Works at optical company and begins more serious reading

1927   Spurred by reading Mencken, Wright begins to read the
        American naturalists; moves in December to Chicago.

1928   Begins working in the Chicago post office

1931   Publishes the short story "Superstition" in a black magazine

1933   Joins the Chicago John Reed Club and writes proletarian
        poetry; joins the Communist Party

1935   Continues publishing poetry, tries unsuccessfully to sell his
        first novel (*Lawd Today!*), expands his acquaintance among
        left-wing writers, and joins the Federal Writers' Project

1936   Active in black South Side Writers' Group; publishes the
            story "Big Boy Leaves Home" in *The New Caravan*

1937   Moves to New York and writes for the *Daily Worker* while
            continuing to work with the Writers' Project. His "Fire and
            Cloud" wins first prize of $500 in contest sponsored by the
            magazine *Story*.

1938   *Uncle Tom's Children* appears and receives good reviews.

1939   Wright marries Dhima Rose Meadman, a white ballet
            dancer.

1940   *Native Son* is published, becomes a best-seller, and receives
            many favorable reviews. *Uncle Tom's Children* is reissued
            in an expanded edition. First marriage fails.

1941   Marries Ellen Poplar, a Communist organizer from
            Brooklyn and the daughter of Polish Jewish immigrants.
            The play *Native Son,* written by Wright and Paul Green, is
            produced on Broadway by Orson Welles and John House-
            man. Wright collaborates with Edwin Roskam in *12 Million
            Black Voices*.

1942   Daughter Julia born. Wright withdraws from the Communist
            Party without publicity.

1944   Public break with the Communist Party announced in "I
            Tried to Be a Communist" in *The Atlantic Monthly*. "The
            Man Who Lived Underground" published in *Cross Section*

1945   *Black Boy*, a Book-of-the-Month Club selection, is pub-
            lished in March, receives excellent reviews, and becomes a
            best-seller.

1946   Travels to France in May as an official guest of the French
            government, is received eagerly by French intellectuals, and
            stays until late December

1947   Encountering racism again in New York, Wright, Ellen, and
          Julia return in August to Paris, where they become
          permanent expatriates.

1949   Second daughter, Rachel, is born in January. Wright writes
          film version of *Native Son* and travels to Chicago and
          Buenos Aires for filming.

1951   Film *Native Son* shown in Buenos Aires, New York, Venice
          and elsewhere

1953   *The Outsider* published in March to mixed reviews; travels
          in the Gold Coast

1954   Travels in Spain; publishes *Black Power* and *Savage
          Holiday*

1955   Visits Spain again; attends the Bandung Conference

1956   *The Color Curtain: A Report on the Bandung Conference* is
          published in March, having appeared in French three
          months earlier.

1957   *Pagan Spain* and *White Man, Listen!* appear.

1958   *The Long Dream* is published in October, but reviews are
          mostly unfavorable.

1959   *Daddy Goodness,* adapted by Wright from Louis Sapin's
          Papa Bon Dieu, is produced in Paris. Wright tries his hand
          at haiku.

1960   *The Long Dream*, adapted from the novel by Ketti Frings,
          has only a week's run on Broadway. Wright dies of a heart
          attack on 28 November.

1961   *Eight Men,* a collection of stories, is posthumously pub-
          lished.

1963   *Lawd Today*, originally entitled "Cesspool" when it was declined by several publishers in the thirties, is published.

1991   The Library of America publishes in a two-volume edition *Lawd Today!*, *Uncle Tom's Children*, *Native Son*, "How 'Bigger' Was Born," *Black Boy* (*American Hunger*), and *The Outsider* in versions approved by Wright, restoring cuts and various changes made by publishers and others.

Conversations with Richard Wright

Author! Author!: Prize-Winning Novelist Talks of Communism and Importance of "Felt Life"

May Cameron/1938

From *New York Post*, 12 March 1938, p. 7. Reprinted by permission.

Whatever else Communism in America may have to answer for, you may chalk up to its credit the development of one superb writer. For without his years of work and study in the John Reed Club of Chicago, Richard Wright probably wouldn't have written the four unforgettable stories in *Uncle Tom's Children*, winner of the $500 prize offered by *Story* magazine for the best manuscript submitted by workers on Federal Writers' Projects.

You will look long and far behind the lines in *Uncle Tom's Children* without finding anything resembling doctrinaire politics. However, the Communist ideology, as I gathered it, suddenly pointed to a better way of life and it struck home in the heart of a Negro boy slowly fighting his way up from the Deep South.

The first day he went to school, Richard Wright told me, he learned that because he was a Negro many jobs and professions and ways of living were forever closed to him. Born on a Mississippi plantation, Wright lived in many Mississippi towns before his father deserted his mother and the remaining family went to Arkansas to try making a living in a dozen other towns. Apparently almost from the time he could toddle he worked at a thousand odd jobs, house boy for white folks, porter, dish-washer, ticket taker, and so on, just to keep body and soul together.

A few years under the care of his religious grandmother left Richard Wright steeped in the language of the Bible—he says he has never known a Negro who didn't read the Bible—and, considering the simplicity, directness and clarity of his prose, this seems to me worth remembering. He ran away from home at fifteen because:

"The compulsion of Negro life in the Deep South is to get up and travel, to get North. Other Negroes came back and tell you that a Negro in the North is treated like a human being and, if you want certain

3

things, you get up and travel hundreds of miles. Remember that even today in the South a Negro can't be treated like a human being. There are definitely two separate worlds, the white world and the Negro world, and the two never meet. Even the practice of lynching is an extreme measure of fear, used to drive the Negro back his 'proper' distance."

Memphis was the first stop North where this odd-job boy managed to save a little money and to hear more tales of Chicago, the logical destination, he explained, for most Negroes living in the Deep South, a city that is to the Mississippi Valley what New York is to the Atlantic seaboard. In Memphis, too, he began reading because his interest was caught by an editorial of H. L. Mencken's about an Alabama Negro artist who had been refused admission to his own exhibition simply because he was a Negro. Richard Wright bought Mencken's book, *Prefaces*, and proceeded to read every book that Mencken, no matter how casually, mentioned.

From reading Mencken in Memphis, Richard Wright branched out in Chicago to Henry James and Dostoievsky, to Hemingway, Malraux, Faulkner, Sherwood Anderson and Dreiser, writers of "the more or less naturalistic school," although he lays no claims to being, or even wanting to be, a "naturalistic" writer.

"I wanted to show exactly what Negro life in the South means today, the total effect, a kind of common denominator. I've used what I've lived and observed and felt and I've used my imagination to whip it into shape to appeal to the emotions and imaginations of other people, for I believe that only the writing that has to do with the basic issues of human living, moral, political or whatever you call it, has any meaning. I think the importance of any writing lies in how much felt life is in it: It gets its value from that."

As to a Deep South Negro boy's dream of being treated like a human being in the North, Richard Wright's experiences, especially since he became a prize-winning writer, may be illuminating. Since many of his letters commenting upon "a nigger winning a $500 literary prize" are pretty much the same, it seems best to pick out one of them, a letter, he said, full of deep indignation and hurt.

Alberta, a young Negro cook for a wealthy family in Connecticut, hurried to prepare dinner one night with a copy of the Negro newspaper, *Afro-American*, announcing Richard Wright's prize under her arm. A guest of the house wandered into the kitchen and got interested in the Negro newspaper.

"Will you read this thing about this nigger Wright?" he called out. "Won a $500 prize in literature. I wouldn't read another thing that Sinclair Lewis ever wrote. Niggers are made to work and suffer, not to write books."

[And for the information of the Connecticut objector, Sinclair Lewis was the one dissenting judge of three. He preferred another book. The other two judges, Lewis Gannett and Harry Scherman, threw their hats over the moon in enthusiasm.]

Uncle Tom's Children—watch for the critical fireworks—will be published by Harper's in two weeks.

An Editorial Conference

Harry L. Shaw, Jr., Donald Thompson, James
Magraw, et al./1938

Transcript of part of a radio discussion of the New York Federal
Writers' Project broadcast on WNYC on 13 April 1938. Reprinted
by permission.

Shaw: How about *American Stuff*? The anthology, I mean—or
American Stuff Magazine, for that matter? After all, most people have
pretty definite ideas about literary publications in general, and belles
lettres in particular. I know that you and James Magraw were on the
editorial boards of both of them, but how did it work? Bluntly, I mean,
was there a hushed, dignified atmosphere, or did you get out publications like this right in the midst of the project floor, which is probably
the noisiest place in New York outside of an evening paper city room?

    Thompson: If you mean did we strike esthetic poses, no. This work,
of course, wasn't really a project job. The writers—hundreds of them,
all over the country—had written the pieces they submitted at home,
after hours on their projects. The editorial services were volunteer; and
usually the board got together after hours at night, or weekends, in
somebody's smoke-filled hotel room. It wasn't easy work selecting fifty
or so pieces from all the material which flooded in from project writers
all over the country, and we usually walked out of the hotel without
speaking to one another; but it was something that needed doing, and
that we wanted to do, so we probably enjoyed it. There were better moments, too. I'm sure that Mr. Magraw, here, remembers the Saturday or
Sunday afternoon when we all, for the first time, agreed on a manuscript. Do you remember, Jimmy, when Richard Wright's autobiographical piece, "The Ethics of Living Jim Crow," came in?

    Magraw: I certainly do. I don't think I had agreed with you or
anybody else for two hours before Wright's piece came up. As I recall,
I had been reading some pretty heavy epic poems and I suppose I'm
allergic to epic poems. Anyway, "The Ethics of Living Jim Crow" did
change things. I may be wrong, but I think you and I even bought the
sandwiches.

6

Thompson: I'm not sure of that. Anyway, the pleasure we got out of running across that piece at the time became even greater when, only a few weeks ago, Richard Wright's book, *Uncle Tom's Children,* won the *Story* Magazine-Harper's prize. Lewis Gannett, Sinclair Lewis, and Harry Scherman were the judges there, but we at least are entitled to some claim of prior discovery. I could probably say a lot of things about Richard Wright, but it all seems pretty unnecessary, since he's right here with us this afternoon.

How did you come to send "The Ethics of Living Jim Crow" in, Mr. Wright? I mean, had you written it before the call was sent out to Chicago for anthology material, or did you write it especially for the book?

Wright: I wrote "The Ethics of Living Jim Crow" experimentally, really. The theme, of course, was one which I was even then putting in book form, so it was probably the only sort of thing I could have done at the moment. When the call came for anthology material, I didn't have to look far for a subject.

Thompson: I see. Speaking for *American Stuff,* it was a good editorial break that we did catch you at a moment when you were spending your off-time on *Uncle Tom's Children* rather than, let us say, a history of Panama Canal. Do you mind my asking, by the way, was *Uncle Tom's Children* also autobiographical?

Wright: Yes, with liberties, of course. It's not that I have any great brief for autobiography as a literary form. It's just that I decided that my own experience had a significance which went beyond the personal and that, frankly, I'd be foolish not to use it to paint the scenes which I felt I had to paint in any event. I used what I lived and read and observed and felt, and I used my imagination to give it a form which would make it appeal to the emotions of other people.

Thompson: Well, in this case, I believe you have plenty of evidence for feeling satisfied in your use of the form. I don't know whether this is a proper question or not, but I was told that of the three judges selected by *Story* Magazine and Harper's for their project contest, two liked your book immediately, but one, though he liked it, didn't cast his vote at the time. Did you hear about this?

Wright: I believe I did hear something of the sort. But, after all, there were a *lot* of good manuscripts entered in the contest—more than five hundred, I believe. I haven't read Meridel Le Sueur's book, or Fred

Rothermell's, or Stephen Griggs', but there's a pretty good chance that if I had I would have voted for them rather than my own.

Thompson: How about your work on the New York City Project, Mr. Wright? I understand you're really carrying a double load now working on both the Guide and our survey on "The Negroes of New York."

Wright: I just submitted a final draft of the Harlem essay and at present I am struggling with the Harlem locality story.

Thompson: You mean the locality story for volume two of the Guide, the one covering Manhattan?

Wright: Yes.

Thompson: I am afraid you have been so busy on the Guide that it may be unfair to ask you about the racial survey, but what are your general impressions of a book of this sort judging from what you have seen of "The Italians of New York" and the preliminary copy of "The Negroes of New York"?

Wright: The most amazing thing about these stories, to my way of thinking, is that they were never done before. I have read I don't know how many studies, both factual and fictionized, of the American Negro and many of them used New York as a locale, but the fact remains that the average American's conception of Negro culture and life as it exists in New York is probably derived from not very accurate novels, or Hollywood representations of the urban Negro as a man who is either shabby and comical or one who is an exceedingly prosperous conductor of a popular swing orchestra.

Thompson: The aim of the racial studies is, of course, a little more serious than that. How true a picture as far as you can tell at this moment will be painted by our book on the New York Negro?

Wright: I believe that the picture can be made a true one. First of all we intend to show Harlem without makeup. Our aim will be to show how the Negro in Harlem, despite his handicaps, strives to find for himself a dignified place in America's largest city.

We intend to go behind the scenes and show that phase of Harlem which the casual visitor or tourist does not see.

Thompson: Of course Harlem is the largest concentration of Negroes in New York, or for that matter, the world. But every Negro in New York does not live in Harlem. Are you covering the other parts of the town too?

Wright: Yes. Though the emphasis will be on Harlem, the book will treat Negroes living in other parts of the city.

Thompson: Judging from the copy already in, there seem to be some exceedingly interesting facts about the professional categories especially. Do you have any figures, Mr. Wright, about the professional workers in Harlem?

Wright: By and large, New York is a haven for the Negro professional worker. More Negroes engaged in professions live in Harlem than in any other Negro community in America. I would say that roughly there are some five thousand of them, with law and medicine leading.

Thompson: Does that include the theatrical profession, music and radio?

Wright: Yes, it does include the theatre and even motion pictures. But there are very few gainfully employed in radio.

Thompson: I know there was motion picture production in the South, but I hadn't heard of a studio producing Negro films in Harlem. How long have they been going?

Wright: The Micheaux Corporation has been in existence for years. They have produced more than thirty pictures to date.

Thompson: Does the work you're doing for the project during the week leave you too flat for night and weekend jobs of your own?

Wright: *American Stuff* and *Uncle Tom's Children* were breaks that way. The New York Writers' Project does keep me pretty busy, but I hope I still have something to say and, if the nights are long enough, I may get it said.

Thompson: How did the southern reviewers receive *Uncle Tom's Children?* Have the reviews come in yet?

Wright: Yes. On the whole, their reaction was surprising. In a certain sense it can be said that they accepted the book. In contrast to northern reviewers, they admitted that the material was true and they were not skeptical. After all, they should know. The tone of the press in Texas, Virginia, Alabama, North and South Carolina was particularly interesting. They admitted the validity of the life pictured in *Uncle Tom's Children.*

Thompson: Incidentally, I noticed the other Sunday that one of your reviewers compared you with Ernest Hemingway. I have a profound admiration for Mr. Hemingway but I do think that we may have enough

Hemingways now. At latest count, I believe, there were something like thirty scattered around the country, with other parts to be heard from. Just to get a load off my mind, would you mind telling me just who, if anybody, is your favorite modern writer?

Wright: I like the work of Hemingway, of course. Who does not? But the two writers whose work I like most today are André Malraux and William Faulkner. I think both of them in their respective fields are saying important things.

Thompson: Why Faulkner?

Wright: Well, as a fellow Mississippian, I know that Faulkner's books deal with a phase of the real South. He is the only white writer I know of living in Mississippi who is trying to tell the truth in fiction.

Thompson: And Malraux?

Wright: What Faulkner is to a small area, Malraux is to the progressive movement all over the world, that is, an interpreter. Faulkner shows how human beings are stunted and degraded in Mississippi, while Malraux shows how millions all over the world are trying to rise above a degraded status. I value Malraux higher than I do Faulkner because of the quality of heroic action Malraux depicts in his novels.

The American Writer in a Democratic Society

Carl Miller/1938

Transcript of a broadcast of the Radio Division of the WPA Federal
Theatre in the series "Exploring the Arts and Sciences" on WQXR
in New York on 24 June 1938. Reprinted by permission.

Miller: This evening—through the cooperation of the Committee for
the Public Use of Arts and the League of American Writers—"Exploring the Arts and Sciences" presents a young Negro author who has
recently attained distinction among the younger generation of American
writers.

If literature be of the substance of life, then our guest speaker, Mr.
Richard Wright, is better qualified than almost anyone I have ever
met—to speak on that aspect of literature which is most directly related
to life itself—and that is, the relationship of the writer to the world in
which he lives. Mr. Wright shares with all really great writers, past and
present, that profound sense of experience which one can derive only
from the varied pattern of adversity, oppression, struggle, and tri-
umph—in short, the whole range of heroic human efforts.

A native of the South, Mr. Wright has worked as an errand boy,
laborer, Postal clerk and newspaper reporter. Except for a few years of
elementary schooling, he is entirely self-educated and by his own efforts
has launched himself on a literary career of considerable promise. He
has written short stories and articles for various current periodicals and
was awarded a prize of five hundred dollars by *Story* Magazine for his
first book, *Uncle Tom's Children,* a volume of four long stories describing the lives of the negroes in the deep South.

I am happy to introduce Richard Wright, young Negro author and a
member of the National Council of the League of American Writers,
who speaks on "The Place of the American Writer in a Democratic
Society."

Wright: With some measure of justification based on historical fact,
the general public regards writers as strange creatures. The lives of
writers today and in the past seem to support this attitude. Recalling at
random a few well-known figures, the attitude at first glance seems

11

correct. Bryon's life was one long torment, envied by nobody, perhaps, except adolescents. Dean Swift, one of the great lights of English letters, died insane. Coming closer to home, who would envy the life of Edgar Allan Poe with all of its straining and isolation? And a few years ago Hart Crane leaped into the ocean, ending a life which from the vantage point of even our own today seems hideous.

And then there was the lot of the Russian writer before the October Revolution. To recount their struggles would be to tell a long history of human horror, exile, pain and persecution.

Those few writers who did succeed followed one of two paths: they either found patrons, or they banded themselves together into informal groups and waged war upon their society, which, curiously enough, was sustaining, and at the same time tormenting them. All of this has had its effect upon the men who write our novels and poems. The greatest single effect, I think, has been to produce in writers a lack of confidence in themselves and doubts as to their value to society. In order to justify their work they spoke vaguely of posterity. Even many young writers today, writers whom I know, poets and novelists of talent, find it impossible to identify themselves wholeheartedly with their times.

This lack of confidence, this gnawing doubt, manifests itself in the writers by their retreating from the world in which they live and spinning webs of obtuse theories to justify that retreat. They cultivate themselves in isolation and call it culture.

Ten years ago many young writers did not think overmuch on these facts. If they were seriously interested in their work, they took it for granted that it was a thankless task. In order to survive, they sought patrons, and the assistance of friends or relatives.

In 1929, when millions of people lost their jobs, many writers fell heir to a new experience of privation, the reality of which was denied by many, or if not denied, underestimated. It was claimed that writers had always been poor, and that poverty stimulated their best work. But many failed to see that this privation was not only economic but cultural. The small reading public and the patron who supported little magazines vanished suddenly. Theatres suspended production; art galleries closed; and publishing houses pruned their lists. The very physical face of the nation began to alter; breadlines came; packing box colonies sprang up on the edge of cities. Amidst all this, writers, accustomed to a well-ordered world, began to doubt the reality of the "unique" existence of the man of letters. They had led extremely individualistic lives and the sudden change left them bereft of bearings, direction, and perspective. They became a part of that vast mass which they'd been taught to regard as being alien to their interests. These writers felt, and rightly so, that what they were undergoing was important and somehow they wanted to express it. Here they were faced with a problem, the enormous complexity of which they did not at first understand.

Miller: Well, Mr. Wright, can you tell us what effect the depression had on young writers?

Wright: Left without patrons or the support of a circle of wealthy readers, the young American writer found himself face to face with the masses of his own people, with nothing to stand between him and them. He did not know how to approach them and they did not know how to approach him, since they regarded him as traditionally belonging to another race of men.

Writers caught in the situation were confronted with two possible courses of action. First: They could refuse to consider seriously the mass of people with whom they had become identified and take up the cudgels against their regarding them as an enemy; or they could accept the destiny of the people as their destiny, and then make an attempt to shape the future. Those who took the former course moved toward what we today call the conservative position; those who took the latter course moved toward the liberal position.

Miller: And then what happened after this division in the attitudes of writers?

Wright: The first and normal reaction of the writers who moved leftward was to make an attempt to understand the nature of the society in which they lived. They tried to understand and explain society in the most accurate and realistic fashion possible. This new realism revealed to these writers a highly dramatic picture of a world which was primarily occupied with the conflict of interests. It was a world which compelled active participation. This world-picture unified the personalities of many of these writers, organized their emotions, and buttressed them with an obdurate will to cast their lot with that of the great masses of people with a view to social betterment. Active participation wrought a still deeper change in their personalities. They found that as they became active agents in this picture, that is, when they addressed

their artistic productions to the people they helped to crystallize new
social attitudes.

Miller: Can you tell us just exactly what were the practical results of
the writers' active participation in the rough and tumble struggles of the
world?

Wright: They found, to their surprise and elation, that they could
lend their pens in an artistic manner to accelerate the growth of trade
unionism, the struggles of sharecroppers, and aid the cause of racial
minorities. They found further that they could assist in creating in the
minds of many people this newly-gained picture of theirs which in turn
would inspire them to meaningful activity. They found, still further, that
when they had grasped this dynamic concept of society that they now
had a new sense of dignity, and had acquired a new heritage from the
Depression.

As a result of this new tendency in literature the American people
have reaped a rich harvest. Beginning on their own, the activities of
these writers—together with artists, musicians, actors and dancers
developed into our national arts projects. For example, we have a
writers' project, supported by the Government in every state of the
union. To date they have published some 150 volumes of all kinds, with
hundreds more to come. Many of these works deal with subjects as yet
untouched by American writers, such as studies of various racial minorities, as well as local geography.

These projects have given employment to more than 3,000 writers of
varying talent, enabling them to stand on their own, allowing them to
produce work which is socially useful to the public at large.

Aiding in this process of cementing the relationship between the
writers and the masses of people has been the activities of the Public
Use of Arts Committee which was instrumental in getting the Welfare
Council to sponsor the Federal Writers' Project in the production of a
book called *Guide to Housing*. At present the Public Use of Arts
Committee is engaged in a campaign urging the use of fine arts in the
subways for purposes of decoration.

A third organization which has aided the writers in establishing
relations with their country and the world at large is the League of
American Writers, an organization committed to a struggle for the
maintenance of democratic institutions, a struggle against war and
fascism, for the support of progressive trends in all branches of national

life, and for the preservation and extension of minority cultures. The League also aids writers in maintaining contact with writers of foreign countries.

All of this constitutes in a large measure a new role for the writer, a role which some might think is less glamorous than that of the old one. True, writers so engaged do not depend upon surprise and novelty alone to reach a reading public. But what is lacking in traditional glamor is more than compensated for in the new feeling of identification with their time, their place, and their people. Compare the relationship of Gorky to Russia and that of Dreiser to America, and the vast difference can readily be seen. Gorky was loved by the masses throughout Russia; even towns and streets being named in his honor, because he was not only a writer in the ordinary sense of the word, but an active participant in the happenings of his day. Dreiser, though in a measure accepted by America, is still isolated from the meaningful and important currents and processes of American life. I say this not to cast disparagement upon the work of Dreiser, for I value it above perhaps the work of any American writer, but to illustrate my point.

By living actively in his own times the life of the people, sharing their fears, hopes, defeats, and triumphs, the writer does not write from note-books of bulky material or write under the guidance of elaborately spun theories as direct grooves of expression; but from his heart, the most indelible note-book of all, the seat from which all lasting ideas spring. In his new role the writer will still be able to say, when asked why he writes: "I write to express myself, but it is a social self I am expressing, for I am a member of society."

Miller: Thank you, Mr. Wright.

An Author Discusses His Craft

Marcia Minor/1938

From the *Daily Worker*, 13 December 1938, p. 7. Reprinted by permission.

The boy walked up to the desk and quietly handed the librarian a slip of paper bearing the titles of books. With the books under his arm, he marched out again . . . Sometimes a book called for on the paper was not in the library. Then the boy left, to return later with another item on the booklist.

"That's the way I used to get books out of the library in the South when I was a boy," explained Richard Wright, the brilliant 30-year-old Negro writer who has just been awarded second prize in the O. Henry Memorial Award short story contest for his long short story, "Fire and Cloud." "A white friend loaned me his card. When a book I wanted wasn't in, I would never ask for another. Oh, no! I would go out, change the list, and come back again."

It is not surprising to see the lengths of stratagem to which the boy went. Reading was to him an "intellectual outlet" in an unpromising environment from which he later ran away. Today, as the author of a prize short story of the prize-winning book of short stories, *Uncle Tom's Children,* he still reads—whenever he can find the time. This profitable pastime, of which he was nearly deprived in his native South, underlies his study of literary technique.

"I take an author, study his works carefully, go into his life with the same thoroughness, follow the way the facts of his life are related to the fiction he created. I have done this with Dostoevsky, Chekhov, Conrad, Turgenev."

Like Dostoevsky, author of the unforgettable *Crime and Punishment,* Dick Wright has not necessarily lived through the episodes he depicts, the scenes of brutalized torture and all the various forms of exploitation of Negroes in his stories. His coming novel, of course, is not autobiographical.

"The chief character is drawn into committing a crime . . . oh, what a crime!" Dick drew his head between his shoulders shelteringly,

16

chuckled like a mischievous schoolboy "and then he murders another person to cover it up."

This book, which must be ready for spring publication, occupies much of his mind and time. He works over it, condensing and polishing, even on the subway. He always has it with him in a portfolio.

Through endless discussions, contacts, political understanding, Richard Wright has absorbed the life he describes with his typewriter. In the course of his travels, since the time he left home, he has made his living variously at many of the typical occupations from which Negroes are forced to choose—as peddler, porter, bootblack, waiter, houseboy, bellboy, newsboy, ditch digger. He reports as the most unpleasant a job in which he disinfected hospital floors with strong-smelling stuff and then scrubbed the floors on his knees.

"In Chicago I came in contact with the labor movement. That gave me incentive." For five months he was Harlem correspondent of the Daily Worker.

He feels that it is the function of the Marxist creative writer to give flesh and blood reality to what might otherwise remain, for many readers, just political abstractions.

His clear brown eyes narrow with mirth in his oval-shaped face. He looks complacent in a nice way. The comparatively easier life of the successful author has affected him only for the better. He was pleased to have good fortune come his way, but not at all set up about it.

"With all the turf-digging," he smiled, "I was too tired in those days to write in all the punctuation. I was always looking for shortcuts. I decided to eliminate the apostrophes. Later, I thought they might be left out altogether. Whit Burnett told me the Columbia professors were interested in my phonetic developments. I looked solemn and agreed it was very interesting." Whit Burnett is editor of the magazine *Story*.

Nevertheless, Dick does use dialect with conscious intent. A purpose which has a clarity beyond regions though its flavor is unimpaired.

"In my dialect," outlines the man who is a master of its use. "I want everything to be clear and yet have the reader conscious of it as dialogue and aware that whites and Negroes are expressing themselves in the same language."

One of Dick Wright's most difficult problems, as he sees it, is to convey a sense of complexity of a character in his emotional and mental life, though he uses simple words in dialect. This is so important a problem in his works because certain excruciating experiences must be registered in a sensitive person's consciousness. Dick believes a scene is more effectively conveyed through some one's consciousness than directly. A whole lynching comes in flashes to the title character in "Big Boy Leaves Home," as the youth cowers at a distance in a dangerous retreat.

To have a basis on which to build a complex character, the author conceived of the position of the chief character in his prize-winning "Fire and Cloud."

"I wanted a character simple and direct in speech, but who in calling has a wider relationship to the Negro and the white people." He drew the character of the liberal and cautious Negro minister who develops into a defier of all authority. This minister forsakes security to lead the hunger march of workers, black and white, threatened with the end of relief and with starvation. A group of Communists among the hungry helped him reach the logical decision.

Richard Wright's detachment as a writer comes at least partly from the fact that he conceives of a story he wants to tell "in terms of a character, and through the character unfold the situation. The situation is weighed in terms of a character."

As Dick talks to you, many little arrows in his conversation veer in a certain direction as the underlying element in his boyish charm and his weight as a writer—his ever-present curiosity. Once on the train, he relates, he met a judge, a little worse for drink, who boasted of the big way Cleveland citizens did things in comparison with the New York pikers. Dick plans to look him up when he goes to Cleveland just to see if it's true what they say about that city's generosity.

He passed on the street the curtained store window of a political meeting. At the sound of foreign voices issuing through the door as he half opened it, he mournfully wished he knew Spanish. "I'm always interested in the insides of rooms as I pass in the street. Now, there's a room. Inside, maybe, are a man and a woman. Perhaps they have been long married and—"

"Oh, that's dull."

"Oh, no. That's when it begins to get interesting—when the bonds begin to be felt."

When Dick wrote *Uncle Tom's Children* he had a hope for his purpose in writing it—"that the person who reads it, especially the white

reader, would get from it a sense of a people, often defeated, who remained strong with a strength which, if released and organized, would
be a rallying pole for democratic forces; that these people, whose
bodies, homes and personalities are violated and yet can still fight,
brighten the outlook of democracy and give it hope."

Guggenheim Prize to Richard Wright

New York Amsterdam News/1939

From *New York Amsterdam News,* 1 April 1939, pp. 1, 15. Reprinted by permission.

After he had captured the *Story* Magazine prize, an O. Henry short story award, all in 1937, Richard Wright, brilliant young writer, was revealed this week as the sole Negro recipient of a prized Guggenheim fellowship for 1939–1940.

The author of *Uncle Tom's Children,* regarded as one of the best books published in 1938, told The Amsterdam News in an exclusive interview on Monday that the winning of the $2,500 fellowship means that he is now able to "work for a solid year free from economic care and worry."

At present employed by the Federal Writers Project, which he explains has "supported me long enough for me to submit to the Guggenheim Committee *Uncle Tom's Children,* and plans for two more books," the writer, who has just turned thirty, will not actually start on his fellowship until June, remaining in his present position until that time.

The Guggenheim book will contain three themes, the first dealing with the plight of women in urban centers; the second, with domestic workers; and the third, the role of religion among women today. The time will be the present and the locale, Harlem and Brooklyn.

"I want to stay in New York for six months while I put the novel on paper," Mr. Wright commented, "and then I want to go away to revise it."

He has not yet chosen his destination. "The European situation," he said, "might make it impractical to leave this country."

Mr. Wright, who was known to be a Communist by members of the Guggenheim Committee before he was chosen as one of its fellows, revealed that he had been a member of that party for the past six years.

"Every Negro," he declared, "who hopes for freedom in America, can best serve his own cause by supporting, in every instance, the forces of democracy against fascism and reaction."

"My parents were poor, laboring people," Mr. Wright, who was born in Natchez, Miss., said.

"By the time I was 15, I had lived in a dozen or more small southern towns."

Running away from home at that age, he washed dishes, dug ditches, swept streets, sold insurance, and clerked in the Post Office. He never went to high school, getting his education "catch as catch can," wherever he happened to be at the time.

"I entered the labor movement in 1933," he explained, "as executive secretary of the Chicago John Reed Club, in which capacity I served for two-and-a-half years."

He first began publishing in 1933, poems, sketches and stories which appeared in the old *Partisan Review,* the *New Masses, International Literature,* the *Left Front* and the *Anvil.*"

None of his writing to date, he revealed, has been autobiographical.

"It is," he explained, "imaginative material shaped by my experiences."

Can We Depend Upon Youth to Follow the American Way?

George V. Denny, Jr., et al./1939

From *Town Meeting,* 4 (24 April 1939), 3–29.

Moderator [George V. Denny, Jr.]: Now you have heard our topic for tonight—"Can We Depend upon Youth to Follow the American Way?"—and perhaps many of you are wondering about that phrase, "the American Way," so widely used nowadays. I take it that by that phrase we mean the democratic way—the idea of "giving everybody a chance to share in making the rules," as a speaker said on our program devoted to the American Way last season. What we emphatically are *not* talking about, therefore, is one-man or one-party rule.

Now it is true, isn't it, that all the great anti-democratic movements abroad have been fundamentally youth movements—the violent reaction of youth that had no place to go in the world. And here in this country, out of our twenty-one million young people, we know today that there are about five million who are both out of school and out of work. Yet these young people are among the builders of tomorrow. What kind of a tomorrow are they going to build? Are they ripe for a Hitler, as is sometimes said? Or is the democratic way too deeply ingrained here?

To try to find a partial answer to these questions, we have here on the patform of Town Hall tonight six speakers—all young enough to discuss our topic authoritatively. Of these, two will deliver the principal addresses. The first will be Mr. Joseph Cadden, executive secretary of the American Youth Congress, winner of the gold medal presented each year by *Parents Magazine* to the young person who has rendered the greatest service to the cause of American youth. The second principal speaker will be Mr. Roswell Perry Rosengren, president of the United States Junior Chamber of Commerce in 1937–38, now an attorney in Buffalo, New York. Mr. Rosengren was selected by the official Who's Who of the Young Men of America as one of the ten outstanding young men of 1937 between the ages of twenty-one and forty—a list which included, among others, William O. Douglas and Thomas E. Dewey.

22

Then we have a panel of four other young speakers: Miss Barbara
Allen, editor-in-chief of the *Vassar Miscellany News*; Mr. Richard
Wright, whose literary talent, as exhibited in the prize-winning novel,
Uncle Tom's Children, has won him a John Simon Guggenheim fellow-
ship; Mr. Charles C. Glover, III, chairman of the *Yale Daily News*;
and Mr. George Strayer, president of the Iowa Rural Young People's
Assembly.

This panel of four will comment extemporaneously on what the other
speakers have said, and its members are free to ask the other speakers
questions. You can see that there is going to be plenty of chance for
a lively discussion. And now I take pleasure in introducing our first
speaker of the evening, Mr. Joseph Cadden, executive secretary of the
American Youth Congress.

. . . .

Moderator: Thank you, Miss Allen. Now Mr. Richard Wright, what
do you think about this whole matter?

Mr. Wright: Mr. Chairman, I speak here tonight in a dual capacity:
as a Negro youth and also as a young writer. I would like to speak about
both of these briefly, about the writer and his view of the problem of
youth first. For two thousand years, we of Western civilization have
lived by great hope, the fundamental assumption of which is that human
personality is inviolate and that which sustains it is equally so. The
invention of machines and the rapid rise of industrial civilization gave
that hope a great buttress. Until 1929, the majority of the people in
western countries—Italy, Germany, England, America, and a few other
countries—thought that that hope—the realization of personality and
security of personality—could come true. But the depression in 1929
caused a grave doubt to enter our hearts. Many of us viewed the depression as something transitory, but we were horrified at the sudden and
brutal way in which all that we hold dear in human life was swept into
obscurity. We voted in a liberal administration to patch up things. It was
a wise and right impulse. WPA, AAA, CCC, et cetera, were voted in.
Of all the groups the United States Government has tried to save in this
tragic situation, youth was in a position both appealing and moving.

I agree with Mr. Cadden's remarks about the expansion of opportunity, the urgency of that expansion, and the creation of jobs; but while
that is in process, hope must be kept alive in the hearts of youth. You
have heard about two phrases, one of which I want to bring up tonight,

and one of which we have heard a great deal—"rugged individualism."
I would like to substitute for it the phrase "rugged personality." There
are some rulers in Germany today whose description could fit "rugged
individualism." There was a man in America—Lincoln—whose description could fit that of the "rugged personality." We created five
cultural divisions of the WPA—five art projects—to keep alive the
spirit of the tradition of the human race, to link the present with the
past, and to link both the past and the present with the future. These
projects are trying to keep alive in the hearts of youth the dream of a
free and equal mankind, a dream which, if allowed to die, will open the
gates to the ruthless and brutal tide of fascism.

I would like to speak briefly now in another capacity—the Negro—
and give you some sharp figures. Unemployment among Negroes is
twenty-five per cent higher than among whites. For the twelve million
Negroes who live in America today, there are but four thousand doctors.
For the nine million Negroes who live in the South there are but a
hundred lawyers. This means that professional and educational opportunity for Negroes is virtually non-existent, and, because of their poverty Negroes find it almost impossible to attend those few universities
that do admit them. There are in America today about one million
Negro boys and girls of high school age who are not in school. If the
American Way is to be preserved, this picture, which is an extreme
picture, represents in a broad sense the state of American youth. It must
be altered. If the heritage of our culture is to be preserved, extended,
and enriched, new instrumentalities of social and political action must
be found. Liberal government must pursue the task of aid in this direction in an even more determined manner. The test of the American
Way, in a sense, is embodied in the fate of the Negro in America.

Moderator: Thank you, Mr. Wright.

Negroes Have No Stake in This War, Wright Says

Angelo Herndon/1940

From the *Sunday Worker*, 11 February 1940, p. 7. Reprinted by permission.

Richard Wright, author of *Uncle Tom's Children,* and outstanding young Negro literary figure, declared yesterday that the Finnish situation is being used by the big imperialist powers as a smoke screen for involving the whole world in war.

Wright is one of numerous noted literary and cultural figures opposing aid for White Guard Finland. Others have included the distinguished Negro actor-singer Paul Robeson, Will Geer, famous actor and others.

"England and France" Wright said, "who oppress more people than all the other imperialist powers of the world, have been for the last 20 years financing and building fortifications in Finland with the ultimate objective of using Finland against Russia."

Discussing the independence which the Soviet government granted Finland in 1917, the famous Negro author, a native of Mississippi and winner of a Guggenheim scholarship and of a WPA short story contest said:

"It is unfortunate that there still are some people who do not realize that the Soviet-German pact threw panic and fear into the British and French ruling circles and upset the balance of power. What the pact really meant was that peaceful relations between Germany and the Soviet Union struck a blow against the imperialist war intrigues of Chamberlain on the continent.

"I think the Soviet-German pact is a great step toward peace. Only enemies of peace and Russia can see it is anything else."

Wright has no illusions about the sudden switch of President Roosevelt from the New Deal to an active policy of war and hunger.

Wright expressed great disappointment over the fact that many so-called liberals who are supposed to have minds of their own, are becoming dupes and suckers of the Hoover-sponsored-aid to Mannerheim campaign.

"The presumption that 'poor little Finland' needs American aid is simply Hoover's traditional way of offering himself as a tool of Wall Street and political reaction.

"If Hoover has the first spark of humanitarian feeling, it would be very simple if he would use some of it by turning his attention to the plight of Negroes, the youth, migratory workers and the working folk of city and country who are trying to maintain a decent standard of living in our own so-called democracy."

Wright remembers the last World War and the role of hundreds of thousands of Negroes who laid down their lives for something which turned out to be a fraud. To him, and to millions of Negro Americans, it is a grim, bitter memory.

"But," he points out, "there are certain wars in which Negroes have fought and should fight—wars for democracy and freedom. Negroes fought heroically in America's Revolutionary War against English rule and they were justified in doing so, for that was a war for democracy and independence. They fought with the union forces against the slave-holding Confederacy for freedom and citizenship rights. Again they took up arms in the first World War under the smokescreen slogan of making the 'world safe for democracy'!

"I believe the Negroes who fought in that war realize today that they were misled in giving their lives in the interest of imperialism. The present war is an imperialist war too, with the added gravity of the only workers state—Russia—being singled out for imperialist aggression."

Wright does not share the opinion that it is necessary for one or the other side of the warring imperialist powers to win the war. He believes it is a war between two thieves who have fallen out and want to settle their imperialist quarrel with the blood of the common people.

Warning against leaders who always rush to jump aboard whatever boat comes along, Wright declared:

"The masses of Negro people should be ever watchful and on guard. They should watch the policies of their leaders who seek to make them feel that they have a stake in the present war.

That the Negro has no stake in this war is borne out by the fact that England and France oppress more Negroes and colonial peoples than all the Empires of the world combined. This war is not to free or protect the interest of small states, but to protect the vast colonial holdings of the imperialist powers."

Negro intellectuals, he said, have a definite and heavy responsibility
in the present confused situation.

"They should propound to white America the causes of the Negro's
plight; they should seek to steer the Negro masses into close collaboration with white workers and genuine progressives in the fight against
war. In these confusing times the role of every true Negro intellectual in
America should be that of an instrument of clarification for the Negro
masses."

With great intellectual tenacity and a lucid literary style of writing,
which few writers of the present have accomplished against a background of jim crowism, racial and social oppression and other barriers
erected at every turn of life, Richard Wright's literary achievements
here reflected the cultural genius of his people. Always modest and
congenial, he represents in the literary field, as well as outside of it, the
new forward strides of the Negro.

His new book *Native Son,* which will appear March 1 as a selection
by the Book of the Month Club, deals with the disastrous and tragic
consequences of residential segregation.

Commenting on the book, Wright said: "it is not a sentimental picture
of Negro life. It accounts for human behavior and personality in terms
of environmental factors."

Wright is at present working on another book and expects to have
it finished soon. Occasionally he takes a trip to the city from his work in
the country and actively supports the fight for Negro rights and
working-class activities.

Negro Hailed as New Writer

New York Sun/1940

From *The New York Sun,* 4 March 1940.

Richard Wright is a Negro who has had slightly more than eight years of schooling, who was a bad boy, who has been on relief, on WPA, a street cleaner and a ditch-digger, and who is now being compared to Dostoievski, Theodore Dreiser and John Steinbeck. He is the author of *Native Son,* a good novel about a bad Negro, which has just been published and is the March selection of the Book-of-the-Month Club.

The thirty-two-year-old author, whose book is fast, forceful and full of violence, is a good natured, soft voiced young man. He came to town today from his home in Crompond, N.Y., near Peekskill, and from his bride of eight months, a former dancer, to be interviewed. He seemed slightly amused by the whole thing.

Wright said he had finished *Native Son* almost a year ago and that since then he has written a 960-page first draft of a new novel dealing with the plight of Negro women, especially domestics in Manhattan and Brooklyn. He's going to be pretty busy on the novel, so he doesn't know whether he'd go to Hollywood even if Hollywood asked him.

"There are a lot of taboos out there writing for pictures," he said. "Negroes are segregated in flickers the same as in real life. You're not supposed to show a Negro eating with white people, and all that. I wouldn't go out there if I had to write around those Jim Crow taboos."

Wright likes the movies, though, and often goes to three pictures a day. That's one of his ways of relaxing while writing. He actually writes about five pages, then does something else, then writes five pages more, then relaxes some more. Sometimes he gets twenty pages done in a day that way. Another of his hobbies is photography, and he develops his own pictures.

"I sweat over my work," he said. "I wish I could say it just flows out, but I can't. I usually write a rough draft, then go over it, page by page. It's work."

Wright had had plenty of work in his lifetime. The son of a day laborer and a country school teacher, he was born on a plantation twenty-

five miles from Natchez, Miss. His parents separated when he was
about five years old. They moved around the South a lot, and when his
mother was stricken with paralysis during the world war, he was sent to
an uncle's house.

He did so much fighting, lying, stealing and school-cutting that he
was sent back to his grandmother, who said he would end on the gal-
lows. He was sent to another uncle then, who agreed. Then he was put
into a Seventh Day Adventist school that was taught by his aunt. It
didn't help him much, though, and when he was beaten he got a razor
and said he'd cut the next person who beat him.

He ran away to Memphis at 15 and got a job as porter and messenger,
and one day he picked up a newspaper which criticized H. L. Mencken.

"At that time I thought that anybody the South criticized must be
pretty good people," he said, "so I got interested in Mencken."

The Negro libraries in Memphis had few good books, he said, so he
had a white friend at the place where he worked get a card in the public
library. Then he used to borrow the card and write notes to the librarian
telling her to give books to the bearer, who was Wright. He started
reading all the books mentioned in Mencken's *Book of Prefaces,* and
finally got the urge to write.

After a few years in Memphis he drifted to Chicago, where opportunities were supposed to be better for Negroes, but they weren't so good.
He got odd and lowly jobs and about 1930 went on relief, doing WPA
jobs once in a while.

"In 1933 I became an assistant precinct captain in the Republican
primary election," he said. "I was promised a job. I didn't get it. Next
time I became an assistant precinct captain for the Democrats and was
promised a job, which I didn't get. So then I became a Red. Now I'm
what the papers refer to as a card-carrying communist."

He was a post office clerk in Chicago for a while, then in 1935 got on
the Federal Writers Project. By this time he had sold poetry and some
articles to small magazines, and at night he finished his first book,
Uncle Tom's Children, which was a hit.

He left Chicago for New York in 1937 and lived from hand to mouth
for seven months before he got on the writers project there. (He wrote
the essay on Harlem in *New York Panorama.*) Early in 1939, after he
got a Guggenheim Fellowship to complete *Native Son,* he left the project. He also did some reporting for the *Daily Worker,* which he jokingly

called Stalin's newspaper, although he said he never got any orders
from Stalin to cover anything.

Native Son was based partly on boys he had met in a Chicago rehabil-
itation school for Negro Dead End kids where he was a play instructor,
and partly on the Robert Nixon case. Nixon was an eighteen-year-old
Negro who died in the electric chair in August, 1938, in Chicago for
killing a white woman with a brick. He also was accused of attacking
and murdering other white women. The lawyer's defense scene in the
book was based partly on Clarence Darrow's defense in the Leopold-
Loeb case.

"I took the title to show that Bigger Thomas (the leading character) is
an authentic American, not imported from Moscow or anywhere," he
said.

Wright has a lot of favorite authors and still reads a lot. He even liked
one story by Gertrude Stein, "Melanctha," which was part of a book
called *Three Lives*. Wright said she was the first American author to
treat the Negro seriously. He's going to do plenty of that, too, but instead of making her wrong prose he's going to use pure Wright prose.

A Conversation with Richard Wright, Author of *Native Son*

Romance/1940

From *Romance* (Mexico City), 1 (15 June 1940), 2. Translated by Keneth Kinnamon.

Richard Wright, one of the most important young writers of the United States and author of the novels *Uncle Tom's Children* and *Native Son,* visited Mexico recently on a vacation trip. Wright is a light-colored Negro, strong and cheerful, thirty-one years of age. His second novel, a Book-of-the-Month Club selection, has sold 350,000 copies and is being translated into Spanish.

Believing an acquaintance with the most outstanding figures of North American literature to be of interest to Spanish American readers, we got in touch with Wright to ask him some questions.

First of all, we want to state that in our judgment certain differences exist between the North American writer and the European writer. Speaking in very general terms and referring to some other North American writers we have known, it can be said that they are simpler, more direct. They are in closer contact with nature, with life, with a simpler reality described in lively fashion without great preoccupations. Speaking with European writers, one has the impression that they are more "literary," more critical, more complicated, but more distanced from life, writing a literature about literature. The sensation one experiences speaking with one group or the other is therefore somewhat different. The North Americans speak of their lives and their own writings; the Europeans often theorize about literature in general.

Along with John Steinbeck and Ernest Hemingway, Richard Wright is surely one of the most successful novelists in the United States during the last few years. All three are on the crest of a gigantic, commercialized book production of such colossal figures that it frightens us Latins a bit and causes Juan Ramón Jiménez to exclaim in his "Diary of a Newly-Wed Poet":

Brentano's, Scribner's
How terrible!

Not so many, many books,
Just one book.

Such a single book, of course, is *The Grapes of Wrath,* just as such a very good book is *Native Son.*

"*Native Son,*" Richard Wright tells us, "is about the life of Negroes in the United States in their relations with whites. It is the story and the psychological portrait of a young Negro who lives in the 'black ghetto' of Chicago, unemployed, with all roads out closed and with the constant logical temptation to break the law. Finally, he meets a white girl who helps him, which surprises the Negro very much. In an accident, this girl dies and the Negro is accused of her death, is pursued, and after various sudden reversals in which the girl's own father tries to help him, he dies in the electric chair.

"It is an accusation against the society of the United States and a defense of the Negro people, who still live in conditions very similar to slavery.

"The book was written in Brooklyn," Richard Wright concludes. "It has one thousand eight hundred words [sic] and cost me eight months of work."

"What literary generation do you feel a part of?"

"The latest literary generation, the one I belong to, was formed in 1929, coinciding with the economic depression and differing from preceding generations in its great political preoccupation.

"To this generation also belong the poets Kenneth Fearing, Langston Hughes, and Archibald MacLeish; the dramatists Maxwell Anderson, Albert Maltz, and Clifford Odets; and the novelists John Steinbeck, Ernest Hemingway, William Faulkner, James T. Farrell, and Michael Gold."

"What literary influences do you recognize in your work?"

"The writers I like most and the ones the critics have pointed out to me as possible influences are Dreiser, Conrad, Sherwood Anderson, Maupassant, Flaubert, Chekhov, Joyce, Henry James, Stephen Crane, Gorky, and, especially, Dostoevsky."

We ask him if he has read any Spanish or Spanish American writer.

"In reality I don't know any," he answers us, "because of the lack of translations, but I very much want to know them, especially the poet Federico Garcia Lorca. A little while ago his *The Poet in New York and Other Poems* was published in English, translated by Rolfe Humphries."

"What are you thinking of writing now?"

"I am writing," he tells us, "a novel about the life of women in the society of the United States. I don't have a title yet. The rough draft now has a thousand pages, and I think it will be finished by the first of the year."

"In your judgment, what is the writer's mission?"

To this question he answers with these sure words:

"To create a new life, intensifying the sensibility. To work so that one understands the world, enlarging in this way life's possibilities."

Later he speaks to us of the problem of the Negro people.

"It is necessary," he tells us, "that the black community of Latin America unite with that of North America. In this way, they will both come out ahead. All black writers of both North and South America should come together and develop relations with each other."

We ask him if he knows Nicholas Guillén.

"I don't know him," he tells us, "but I really want to get acquainted with him."

We request him to give us his opinion of *Romance*.

"There is nothing comparable in America," he answers plainly. "Refugees enrich the culture of the New World.

"Finally I believe that we both have the impression that unfortunately there exists an abyss, a sad lack of relation between the North American and the Latin American literary worlds that damages all of us.

"An association of American writers is needed . . ." he starts to say.

"In this hour of grave crisis I feel that the creative writers of the Latin American world should stand shoulder to shoulder with the creative writers of the English speaking peoples in the fight for Liberty and Justice.

Salud,
Richard Wright
5/23/40
Cuernavaca"*

---

*This final paragraph appears in English in Wright's hand followed by a translation into Spanish.

Native Son to Be Drama

A. M. Rivera, Jr./1940

From *The Afro-American* (Baltimore), 3 August 1940, p. 14.

CHAPEL HILL, N.C.—"Nothing will be omitted and there will be no compromises when *Native Son* appears as a drama in the fall," Richard Wright, author of the best-selling novel, said this week.

Since July 9, Wright has been collaborating with Paul Green, famous playwright and author of *Abraham's Bosom* and the more recent *The Lost Colony* in producing a dramatic version of *Native Son*.

"Though we plan no compromises nor intend to omit any passages, some scenes will necessarily have to be stylized for the theatre and certain long reflective passages will have to be altered for dramatic effect," Mr. Wright said.

"In some instances the tragedy in the book will take the form of comedy in the stage version."

A former newspaper man himself, the thirty-one-year-old novelist stated that because of the uncertainty of everything at this stage of the operation, he could not say very much about the play version of *Native Son*.

Mr. Green added, "We have already received more attention from the press than we had expected."

Until John Houseman, an associate of Orson Welles, who is on his way to Chapel Hill now from Hollywood, reviews the script, final drafts made, and contracts signed, nothing is definite and statements are more or less premature.

Mr. Wright said he had no personal choice for the role of Bigger Thomas.

"I haven't even thought of characters and so far as I know the field is wide open," he said.

Explaining what he called a limited knowledge of the theatre, Wright said he did not plan to be very active in the staging of the novel, but that he might sit around and pass on any idea that might come to him.

"Mr. Welles and Mr. Houseman are interested in what the book tries to depict and I have confidence that they will keep the play faithful to the underlying theme of the book," he said: "There is no deadline for

scripts yet, it was disclosed, but early fall seems to be the goal set by
Mr. Wright and Mr. Green."

Probably as interesting as his two works, *Uncle Tom's Children* and
Native Son is his reason for writing in the vein that he does.

Wright very proudly explained that he is a member of a corps of writers who have for their objective the portrayal of the influence of society
on the individual.

This school of writers, according to Mr. Wright, includes William
Attaway, Arna Bontemps, Langston Hughes, Ralph Ellison, Sterling
Brown, Robert Davis, and Eugene Holmes and the movement is growing.

Accounting for the new corps of writers, Wright said that a sharp line
could be drawn separating the writers prior to 1929 and those to show
prominence since.

The depression has stripped the illusions from the minds of the people
forcing them to recognize their plight. John Steinbeck, author of *Grapes
of Wrath,* is doing much to aid our people and may be included in this
realistic school of writers. People are beginning to sense a community
of interest and the possibility of community endeavor, he explained.

"I can see no visible effect on the race problem that my book has
had," Wright said, "but I believe that if enough writers dedicate themselves to a like cause the thing will soon become a movement."

An educational campaign might point the way to a more enticing pot
at the end of the rainbow, certainly something must be done. Wright
added: In this critical period spontaneous response of the people is
needed, but one can not expect such a response today. Too many people
remember the race riots that followed the first World War, he stated.

Colored persons should ally themselves with all progressive movements, Wright advised, especially the CIO, tenant leagues and movements for better housing.

Mr. Wright said Monday that so many of his critics had voiced the
opinion that he should write something about the educated colored man
that he has decided to do so in his next work.

This new book now in the first draft, will have an eastern locale and
will be about the domestic workers. He said that he could not say much
about it because the first draft was well over a thousand pages, which
means that much alteration will have to be made.

When asked if he planned to write any biographical sketch in the
future, he smiled and answered, "When I write about myself I feel
funny."

Wright, Negro Ex-Field Hand, Looks Ahead to New Triumphs

Roy Wilder/1941

From *New York Herald Tribune,* 17 August 1941, Sec. VI, p. 4.

Soon after Richard Wright, the author of *Native Son,* came to New York City four years ago with a suitcase weighted more with manuscripts than clothes, he struck what the needle-sharp dressers back in Chicago's Negro section called "Sixty-third and Stoney Island." It meant he had arrived.

"When a Negro in Chicago gets a job in the post-office," the thirty-two-year-old Negro author explained, "that's about as high as he can get. So he tells his friends he's at Sixty-third and Stoney Island—the southern boundary of the Black Belt, the hurdle into the white man's world."

Intractable in his youth and deserted by his father, Richard Wright roamed from Mississippi to Chicago. He worked intermittently as a field hand, a porter, a bellhop, a ditch digger, a blanket salesman, a postal clerk. With no more than four years of schooling he learned to write by reading H. L. Mencken, Theodore Dreiser and Sherwood Anderson. *Native Son* catapulted him to Sixty-third and Stoney Island and beyond.

"Something told me it was easy to write," the mild-mannered, soft-voiced author of one of the nation's most violent novels recalls in telling how he got on in the world. In the telling he brushed past the dim days of his youth, the times he hungered amidst the night sounds on Southern cotton plantations, toted a razor, migrated from relative to relative in search of a home, gnawed on dry sandwiches in dingy courtrooms while his mother asked aid for her two boys.

"I figured it was easy to write," he said "And now, of all the things I've done, writing is the most satisfactory."

He was an author at thirteen, but discounts his juvenile accomplishment because he wrote only a simple story, published in a Negro newspaper. He really became of age, he believes, when he sold a story, "Big Boy Leaves Home," to *New Caravan,*—the anthology. He used the money to get his teeth fixed.

Real money came when he won the $500 prize given by *Story* magazine in 1938 for the best work done on W. P. A. Federal Writers' Project, for which he worked in both Chicago and New York (the chapter on Harlem in *New York Panorama,"* a W. P. A. Writers' Project guide, is his). His prize-winning stories were later incorporated in a book, *Uncle Tom's Children*. When he got the prize money he quit covering Harlem for the *Daily Worker* and the Associated Negro Press and started work on *Native Son*.

Half-way through the writing of that novel he won a $2,000 Guggenheim Fellowship, enabling him to finish his biography of a Negro youth in a white man's world.

Today he knows success as a writer, as a voice in the plaint of his people. Married, he lives what he calls a "proletarian existence" in a four-room apartment in Brooklyn. He works on two writing projects.

One is a novel on a migrant Negro domestic in Brooklyn and Manhattan—"a sort of feminine counterpart of *Native Son*." The other is a 30,000-word text for a book to be illustrated by photographs. Titled *12,000,000 Black Voices*—he calls it a short folk history of Negro life. It will be published in October.

The two are of a pattern of writing he plans on Negroes, focusing his immediate work on his people.

"Negro life as a whole in this country is unexplored," he reminded. "It's a virgin field for writing."

In writing he prefers to work outside Manhattan. He has tried both Harlem and Brooklyn, but considers going to Mexico, where he feels he can work more easily.

"My own stuff comes pretty slow," he said. "I live simply and I can't write unless it's quiet and simple. There are no fireworks in my life, just work day in and day out."

Usually four typewriter drafts are required before one of his manuscripts is completed. On the first he pours out what he wants to say. On the next two he polishes and cleans up his text, editing and cutting, with marginal notes in longhand. The next to the final draft he carries in a loose-leaf notebook, revising it as he rides in subways.

Wright was born fifteen miles from the Natchez, Miss., depot, the son of a sharecropper and a teacher in a one-room school. When he was a child his family moved to Memphis, where his mother became a washerwoman.

"I guess the bright lights of Beale Street were undoubtedly too much for my father," his son recalled.

The family drifted, too, for drifting was not uncommon among the Negroes of the cotton belt, and childhood became "a series of towns— roots nowhere." Uncles, first one and then another, took Wright to their farms and tried to teach him the way of the soil, as well as to keep him alive. He resented their restrictions, farming and poor living.

"My folks were dirt poor," he said, "so I packed my suitcase and hit the road. I hit Memphis on a Sunday morning, and Monday morning I had a job, making $12 a week."

Fifteen years old then, he worked as a porter and messenger in a bank building. His job in Memphis marked the beginning of his literary education, and, for him, the beginning of his life.

In a Memphis newspaper he read an editorial with the provocative title: "Is Mencken a Fool?" He did not know who Mencken was, but deducted that if a Southern newspaper could rail at a Baltimore man, Mencken must be a man of some account. He found that Mencken was a writer, and sought some of his books.

As Negroes could not get books from the Memphis public library, he borrowed the library card of a white boy, an Irish Catholic elevator operator. He presented it at the library desk with a forged note signed with the name of his friend: "Will you please let this colored boy have some books by the following authors?"

Mencken's *Book of Prefaces* was one of the books obtained. It introduced him to an understanding of other authors, and he read Sherwood Anderson, Dickens and Dreiser.

"I never could get into Dickens," he said. "He reeks with sentimentality. Theodore Dreiser, though, is the greatest writer this country has ever produced. His *Jennie Gerhardt* is the greatest novel."

From Memphis he went to Chicago, and while working in the postoffice there, as a man of Sixty-third and Stoney Island, he read T. S. Eliot, Ezra Pound, Joseph Wood Krutch and Aldous Huxley.

He said he "just sorta got into the habit of reading about that time."

His ten years in Chicago were hard years, of making a living, writing and eventually getting a temporary job in the postoffice. In the postoffice he found material for a book, written but not published, about Sixty-third and Stoney Island, about Negroes who have little chance for advancement.

"They want to become doctors and lawyers," he explained, "but few make the grade. So most of them practice the three A's—autos, alimony and abortion."

He swung his feet from a desk in the St. James Theater, where *Native Son* was playing at the time. He wore new brown shoes. Bright green socks matched by a green tie set off his ruddy brown skin. A thin gold watch chain inched across the top of his speckled tweed trousers.

He was almost among the Three A's, he said.

"Three days before I came to New York I came for but one purpose," he said, "to peddle my manuscripts.

"I got a letter saying I had been given a full-time job in the postoffice. It meant $2,100 a year.

"I took that letter, sat on my bed, and thought it out. . . . With that money I could marry, settle down, and vote the straight Republican ticket."

He destroyed the letter.

The rest of his story is on the record, *All God's Children* [sic], *Native Son,* both the novel and the play which he and Paul Green dramatized, and work on forthcoming books.

His mother and brother, an artist on the Federal Arts Project in Chicago, live in a house he bought for them. His father—"he was a sharecropper when he married and is a sharecropper still"—lives in Mississippi. He saw his father last summer for the first time in ten years. It was his first trip South in eighteen years, not to see his father, but to "re-see and re-feel the South."

"My father writes me for money," he said. "I sent him $50 recently to get him some teeth."

Untitled Typescript of Some of Wright's Answers in an Unidentified Interview

Bower/1941

Thank you, Mr. Bower.

4. My first reaction was naturally one of confusion. Orson Welles and John Houseman, the producers and stagers, warned me to keep away from the theatre until some coherence and continuity had been reached through rehearsals. I ignored their advice and hung around anyway. In fact, that was precisely what I wanted to see:—the process whereby the repetition of single lines and passages were welded into a coherent dramatic pattern.

6. No. I did not have anything to say about casting. I did not want to. Orson Welles and John Houseman had had a lot of experience with the Federal Negro Theatre in Harlem and they knew what talent was available. I have a pretty sharp sense of the difference between living characters and stage characters. What is dramatic in life may not be dramatic on the stage.

6. A:- His contribution was immense, and he is an extraordinarily talented man. The idea of framing each set within walls of dingy yellow brick, was his. And naturally the pauses, stresses, and so forth, came from him. I don't think any living person in the theatre possesses a greater knowledge of effective lighting than Orson Welles. But running through all of his directing is a high spirit of play and fun. I had the honor recently of seeing a preview of *Citizen Kane*. Running through this great film is a rather poignant and symbolic sub-theme of a boy's sled, called Rosebud. You can imagine my amazement and delight when I discovered that Orson Welles had taken the beautifully varnished sled of the white boy in *Citizen Kane,* and had thrown it into the first scene of *Native Son*. When the curtain rises on the first scene of *Native Son,* you will see in the lower left-hand corner of the stage, a crudely-made sled with the name ROSEBUD chalked across it.

8. In life Canada Lee is one of the most likeable people you'd ever hope to meet. So, Canada Lee, the owner of the Chicken Coop in Harlem, ex-jockey, ex-fighter, is not the guy one would pick to represent Bigger. But Canada Lee happens to be an actor, and I think one of the finest I've ever seen. That explains why this friendly, likeable fellow can play the role of Bigger Thomas so vividly and realistically.

10. Yes, I did have in the back of my mind the vague idea of dramatizing the novel. The offer to collaborate, however, came from Mr. Green.

12. I liked it and I was eager to try it out. I had read some of Green's plays and liked them tremendously. Especially did I like that brutal one-act play of his, *Hymn to the Rising Sun.* I think it was on the strength of that play alone, that I decided to accept Mr. Green's offer.

14. Well, as I understand it, Mr. Green had had in mind for a long time the idea of writing a play dealing with a negro character. When he read *Native Son* he felt, I think, that Bigger Thomas, though a product of urban conditions of life, could become a national symbol expressing the plight of that submerged third of our nation.

16. We collaborated pretty closely, working together daily. Our first task was that of breaking the novel down into scenes. The results of our first week's work were a tentative layout of some twenty scenes, which was later cut to ten. We would meet each morning, decide upon the contents of two scenes, and then retire to some quiet place to write. We would meet again in the afternoon to compare notes and map out plans for further work.

18. Yes, the structure of the play is Mr. Green's work. But I feel his most valuable contribution was that of helping me to compress a vast mass of novelistic material. We mapped out a division of work regarding dialogue. We would both work at a scene until we felt we had packed it with all the necessary action. Mr. Green would then compress it. After that, I would go over it, making sure that the dialogue and imagery were negro and urban.

20. One of the major changes was the pushing of many of the characters into the background. The structure and movement of a play made it necessary to regulate the action of the characters so that they merely helped to propel and project Bigger along on his course. Another change

involved Bigger's relationship with his girl, Clara. In the novel he murdered her outright. In the play he used her as a shield. Of course, in both instances, he was guilty of murder. But we felt that a new murder, coming in the eighth scene, would throw our dramatic structure out of balance. Still another odd change had to be made. In the course of dramatizing *Native Son,* I made the discovery that no less than six of the names of my characters began with the letter 'B'. For purposes of the stage, we felt that this would have created a comic impression. So we changed Bertha to Hannah, and Bessie to Clara.

22. I hope not. Of course that remains for others to say.

24. In the main, no. The story of Bigger, I feel, is the story of the promise of democracy and the actual performance of democracy as it is reflected in an individual personality. I think that point is embedded in the stage play.

26. No, there's no truth in that insofar as my attitude is concerned. If Hollywood buys the play, they will buy its violence and its meaning with it, or not at all.

28. I am working on two books, both of which are half finished. I am writing a thirty-thousand word text for a group of pictures depicting negro life in the United States. Also, I have down about a thousand pages of first rough draft copy dealing with negro domestics in Harlem and Brooklyn.

30. My short stories run rather long because maybe I'm not a short-story writer. A friend of mine once told me that my method of writing necessitated heavy themes and extended treatment. I have found that to be true.

32. Yes, but I've never made a story out of a naked, contemporary event. When I do come across such events they serve the purpose of evoking in me memories of many kindred events, all of which form the material out of which I try to construct a story.

Readers and Writers

Edwin Seaver/1941

Transcript of a radio broadcast, 23 December 1941.

Seaver: We are fortunate in having as our guest this afternoon the man who is quite possibly—and I think probably—the foremost American writer of his generation—Richard Wright. I am sure a great many of my listeners know of Mr. Wright's novel *Native Son,* or if they didn't read it as a novel, they saw it as a play in the Orson Welles production last year. This remarkable first novel, which was the Book-of-the-Month Club selection two years ago, made an impression upon the critics and the reading public such as is given to few books to achieve. However, *Native Son* was not Richard Wright's first book. His first book was titled *Uncle Tom's Children.* This was a collection of long short stories which won the *Story* Magazine prize contest for the best book of stories submitted by a WPA worker. There was a power and a fearlessness in these stories that made you sit up and take notice and you knew when you read them that here was a writer we were going to hear much more of in the future. Well, since then we've had *Native Son* and more recently *12 Million Black Voices,* a magnificent dramatic resume of Negro life in our country. I know of no other book that brings home as clearly to the white reader what it means to be a Negro. Now, to turn to this book for a moment. I understand, Dick, you got the pictures for *12 Million Black Voices* from the Farm Security Administration. Did you have to look through many to get those you finally used?

Wright: Ed Rosskam and I looked at thousands of pictures to get the 90 odd we used in the book. It is one of the most remarkable collections of photographs in existence, I think. If you want to get a comprehensive picture of our country, you should go through these files sometime. It's quite an education.

Seaver: All right, that explains the pictures. Now, how about the text? Did you think of writing the book first and then get together with Rosskam, or was it his idea?

Wright: Well, it was a little bit of both. I had thought of doing something like the text of *12 Million Black Voices* for the past five or six

43

years—hadn't thought of it as a book, however. What I wanted to do was make an outline for a series of historical novels telescoping Negro history in terms of the urbanization of a feudal folk. My aim was to try to show in a foreshortened form that the development of Negro life in America parallels the development of all people everywhere. By good luck Rosskam came along and suggested that I write the text for a group of pictures. I told him I had already been thinking of the idea and that made the whole thing come easily.

Seaver: Well, now, this idea you have for a series of historical novels. Do you mean tracing the development of a Negro family thru a number of generations?

Wright: No, that form has been used too much already and, besides, I don't think it lends itself to what I want to say, nor do I want to show one single character thru several volumes. One of the reasons why I wrote *12 Million Black Voices* in the first person plural was because I was experimenting with the kind of form I would need for this future work.

Seaver: Perhaps you had in mind something like Proust's *Remembrance of Things Past,* although I think that might be a bit too impressionistic.

Wright: It wouldn't quite do for the delineation of folk life. Frankly, I don't know quite what I want. I am hunting for some kind of cement to tie it all together. When I find it then I'll really start working in earnest. I don't expect to discover it in any book. I'll have to work it out for myself.

Seaver: Well, how long are you giving yourself to make your discovery?

Wright: I don't know, five or ten years, maybe, but when I find it I'll have the key to Negro material which will enable me to do what I think will be a life work.

Seaver: Well, how will *Native Son* tie in with this particular series?

Wright: It won't, really. The temperament of "Bigger Thomas" does belong to one of the phases of this projected work, but I think the treatment would have to be different. For instance, the religious theme is not handled in *Native Son* nor is the theme of adolescent life. The only thing that is treated is the psychological reaction of Negroes to the law and the relation of that contact with the wider contents of American life. In this new work I should want to do a more minute examination of the "Bigger Thomas" type—that is, the cultural disinherited, the marginal man living in an emotional no-man's-land.

Seaver: Well, that's certainly something to look forward to. Knowing your work as I do, I take it you haven't in mind any of the traditional approaches to the historical novel. I mean you wouldn't want to start in the beginning, back in the 17th century and work up to 1941. That would be sort of a dull way of doing things.

Wright: Oh no. I wouldn't want to start in 1619 when the first load of slaves landed here. Really, it's not important when it starts. The main thing will be to show the movement from folk life to urbanization. You could start today in some parts of the South where feudal existence and folk life remain in a pretty pure state. Or, you could start as recently as 1855 when slaves were still being brought to America. I want to show the inner complexities and scars that take place when a people are torn away from one culture and are forced to adjust themselves to another.

Seaver: In other words, it is not so much the historical picture as the emotional pattern or spiritual development.

Wright: Yes, that is one of the great dramas of our time. I sometimes think that one way of clarifying human problems today is by dividing the world into those who live in the city, those who live in the country and those who want to go to the city. In other words, the whole world is in the process of being urbanized.

Seaver: Incidentally, speaking of *Native Son,* did you come across many reactions among Negroes to the effect that you had treated them unfairly in *Native Son?* Personally, I don't think this has got anything to do with the problem of a novelist. The novelist's job is to tell the truth as he knows it but still I imagine that certain middle class elements among the Negroes objected to your choosing as your hero, an unfortunate boy like "Bigger Thomas."

Wright: Well, it wasn't quite that they thought I had treated them unfairly. You see, certain elements among Negroes conceive of literature as a cultural achievement rather than as an instrument probing for truth. There were Negroes who felt that the book didn't present the best side of the race—something that has been said over and over again. The white parallel to this reaction was, "Mr. Wright, you don't really think that we do these things, do you?" As you no doubt know from your own experience, the artist is sometimes caught out in no-man's-land. He gets pot shots on both sides.

Seaver: Of course. Still, there must have been some reactions to *Native Son* which irked you. People do get some awfully funny ideas about the writer's job.

Wright: The only reaction to *Native Son* which I resented was the one to be found in several reviews which presumed that because I was a Negro they could tell me how to write and how to feel. I did resent that. A psychological parallel of this attitude is pictured in "Mr. Dalton" in *Native Son*.

Seaver: I get what you mean. He is the benevolent gentleman, isn't he, who makes allowances for "Bigger Thomas"? By the way, *Native Son* came out of Chicago. Are there any new books being written in Chicago these days that hold a great deal of promise?

Wright: I have two in mind and I think that they hold more than promise. They have the real stuff. First is Nelson Algren, whose novel *Never Come Morning* is as hard hitting a realistic piece of writing as you will ever read. Lawrence Lipton's *Brother, the Laugh Is Bitter* is another excellent novel about Chicago. The latter deals with Jewish life and Algren's *Never Come Morning* deals with Polish life.

Seaver: Neither of these works have been published as yet, have they?

Wright: I think they'll be coming out this spring.

Seaver: What do you think of *Blood on the Forge,* a first novel by a young Negro writer named William Attaway?

Wright: The book deals with one of the major themes I have in mind. . . . the impact of industrialization on the folk temperament. I think it brings out new material and explores new fields.

Seaver: It's a bit crude, but very forceful, I think.

Wright: I'm all for Negro writers coming out and telling their stories even if they are crude. The Negro writer who treats of new subject matter has a terrible job on his hands. He has to be his own research worker, his own psychologist, he has to do the whole job himself. Dreiser could get his sociology from a Spencer and get his notion of realism from a Zola, but Negro writers can't go to those sources for background. They are hemmed in by their educational system. In fact, I think in many cases it is good for a Negro writer to get out on his own and get his stuff first hand rather than get it through the regular educational channels. A good writer like Albert Maltz, for instance, can take his city cultural background for granted. A Negro writer can take nothing for granted. He comes up against things our white writers never hear of.

Seaver: Ho do you mean? I wish you'd explain this further.

Wright: The history of the Negro is a subject of debate among scientists and anthropologists. The Negro personality is interpreted from a thousand different points of view by different sociologists. Some say the Negro is childish, lazy, etc. These ideas find their way in one form or another even into text books taught in public schools. All of this lays a heavy responsibility upon the Negro writer; he cannot trust the so-called experts in history or science, for all too often they are trying to justify the nation's attitude toward the Negro rather than give the truth.

Seaver: How does it feel to belong to a group of people about whose lives historians, scientists, anthropologists are always debating?

Wright: Sometimes it is funny; sometimes it is interesting; many times it is heartbreaking, because the ideas of these men influence the attitude of the nation toward the Negro.

Seaver: By the way, Dick, I hear you use a dictaphone. How do you like speaking your piece instead of writing it?

Wright: In the past I have used a combination of methods—dictating part of a script, writing part of it in longhand and part of it on the type-writer. I have found after long experiment that the easiest way to get a first draft is to dictate it. *12 Million Black Voices* was dictated in three days. Of course, it took months of rewriting after that. There is a tendency to be very verbose in talking and you give too much, but I would rather have the feeling that I could throw away something than not have enough.

Seaver: Do you think you could have dictated the first part of *Native Son?* You know, the alarm clock ringing and all that?

Wright: Sure, I could. I don't know, but I have a feeling that my stuff could be spoken very well.

Seaver: The play showed that. I should imagine that it is easier to dictate the dialogue than the necessary background stuff. While I think of it, Dick, I'd like to get your idea on something else. What, in your opinion, is going to happen to the realistic novel in the '40s? Will it stay pretty much as it was during the '30s?

Wright: I'm glad you asked that. Young writers all over the country are thinking and talking about that. No, I think the novel is due for change. I don't mean that realism will be abandoned. Not at all. But simple, naive realism is on the way out and you'll see, I think, greater complexity and imaginative depth in the novels that will be written during the '40s.

Seaver: Are you concerned with that problem, too?

Wright: Definitely. You see, the '30s were a period of digestion, so to speak. We know something about our country now, that is, how it actually works and the influence of that working upon personality. I look for a new surge of interest in character development in fiction. I think my new fiction will reflect that new interest in character.

Seaver: Do you think the novel will lose by this new emphasis?

Wright: No. It will be all to the good.

Richard Wright Feels Grip of Harlem Tension

Mark Schubart/1943

From *PM Daily,* 3 August 1943, p. 8.

Richard Wright, 35-year-old Negro author of *Native Son* and *12 Million Black Voices,* sees in the present Harlem disturbances not only a terrible actuality, but a promise of even more dangerous clashes to come.

Wright, who has fought tirelessly for Negro rights, both in his writings and deeds, went up to Harlem yesterday on business. Before keeping his appointment he looked around.

"I got off the 8th Ave. Subway at 110th St.," he said, "and windows were smashed and stores looted everywhere.

"I went into a stationery store run by a Jewish woman to buy a street guide. She didn't even look at the quarter I handed her. She just stared straight ahead.

"The streets were littered with debris and broken glass. I spoke to several Negroes. They had not slept all night and seemed apprehensive, as if a little slip or an accident could make things worse.

"I had the feeling that more Negro policemen could have given the crowds the confidence they needed. During my walk up to 120th St. I didn't see a single one.

"I don't think it's a race riot—though it has possibilities of turning into one. I had the feeling it was a spontaneous outburst of anger, stemming mainly from the economic pinch. The shooting of the soldier was indeed the spark that set it off.

"It was apparent that all the stores that were looted were owned by white people or Spaniards, though there was nothing that would lead me to believe that organized Negro mobs or organized white mobs were in action. It has not yet reached that stage.

"During my walk I was not molested, but I had the feeling that the people were very watchful. Most of those I spoke to seemed completely abstracted, as if they weren't conscious of what was going on. Some seemed regretful."

Asked what remedies for situations like this could be formulated,
Wright proposed:

• The plight of the Negro in the armed service should be alleviated.

• Some concerted program to relieve the economic squeeze in Harlem
should be formulated.

Negro Author Criticizes Reds as Intolerant

New York Herald Tribune/1944

From *New York Herald Tribune*, 28 July 1944, p. 11.

The Communist position on the American Negro has undergone a "distinct and lamentable regression" in recent years, Richard Wright, Negro author and former party member, said here yesterday in describing Communists as "narrow-minded, bigoted, intolerant and frightened of new ideas which don't fit into their own."

Mr. Wright's remarks were prompted by questions growing out of an article which he has written for *The Atlantic Monthly* for August under the title of "I Tried to Be a Communist."

In this article, the author of *Native Son* and other books discusses his earliest experiences as a Communist party member in Chicago, touching on the problems he faced in trying to present his own ideas to the party.

The August *Atlantic Monthly* describes the article as the first of two installments and Mr. Wright said yesterday that he would not discuss the specific details of his Chicago break with the Communists because these will be covered in the second magazine article.

Mr. Wright said that his Communist party membership covered the period, roughly, from the latter part of 1932 or early 1933 to 1940. His early association with the Communists in Chicago, he said, was broken in 1937, when he was "ejected" from the party.

On the outs with the party from about May until August, 1937, Mr. Wright said that he was reinstated in New York in 1937 and "maintained a relationship" with the party until 1940 when, he said, he left the party.

Discussing what he described as the "lamentable regression" in the Communist party position on the American Negro, Mr. Wright said that he does not know the reason for this.

"Publicly," he said, "Communists will deny that there is any substantial change in their militancy but privately they offer any handy excuse. The militancy on the Negro question has passed into the hands of right-wing Negroes. That was not true eight years ago. Most of the battles then were led by Communists."

In answer to the question as to what caused the Chicago rift between him and the Communists, Mr. Wright said:

"It was an accumulation of many things—not so much a leaving as an ejection over a difference of opinion. I had my way of expressing my conception of Negro experience in my writing. I thought it would be of value to them. They had their ideas of how I should react as a Communist. There was an irreconcilable gap between our attitudes."

Mr. Wright said that "I do not regard the Communists today as effective instruments for social change" and observed that "the Communists have a terrible lot to learn about people."

"Communists," he added, "peculiarly are too much the victims of the very society they are trying to change. This too often finds expression in intolerance and narrowness. I mean, general intolerance, in an imperious way of working.

"What it amounts to is that they are narrow-minded, bigoted, intolerant and frightened of new ideas which don't fit into their own, whether these ideas are right or wrong."

Book-of-the-Month Author Talks for AFRO

Michael Carter/1945

From *The Afro-American* (Baltimore, 13 January 1945, pp. 1, 19.
Reprinted with permission of the Afro-American Co. of Baltimore
City T/A The Afro-American Newspaper.

IS THERE A SOLUTION?—*Writer says that no existing political
party, social organization or trade union is qualified to
eradicate this fear and until the fear element is removed,
normal race relations are impossible.*

Wright, who is married to a white woman and has one
child, lives in a six-room Brooklyn apartment. He has a
library of 600 books, including 200 psycho-neurotic works.
Says he studies the abnormal in order to understand the
normal. Thinks his new book, *Black Boy,* will bring down on
him curses of colored people, liberal whites, and fascists
alike because "it's strong, it's raw—but it's life as I see and
live it."

BROOKLYN, N.Y.—"The underlying influence in all interracial relations
in America is fear," Richard Wright, author of the best selling novel,
Native Son and one of the most mature writers in America told the
AFRO. "The fear the colored man has for the white people is expressed
either in abject submission and degradation to the white man or in violent, undisciplined individual outbursts," the writer declared. "In either
case, the motive is fear."

Wright feels that no existing political party, social organization or
trade union is qualified to eradicate this fear, "and until the fear element
is removed, normal race relations are impossible," he said.

"It may be," he added, "that a loose, over-all national organization
can harness the race's energy—divert it from fist fights, bar rooms,
dance halls and meandering churches and channelize that wonderful
creative energy in constructive lines.

"It is ironically humorous that at a time when colored people in the
South are afraid to walk the streets, some whites in the North talk about
'progress' and 'tolerance,' neither of which exists on a national scale."

Trade unions alone are not enough, because "when a colored worker submerges himself in the union and becomes a union man first and a colored person second he lends himself to partisan struggles among whites and contributes nothing to the race."

Wright admits, however, that trade unions have gone further than any other organization towards securing the acceptance of colored people "but they haven't gone far enough and they don't touch upon certain areas of group life."

Wright is one of the few colored novelists (perhaps the only one) who makes a good living by his writings and royalties. His works have been translated into Russian, French, Danish, Swedish, Chinese and Portuguese.

Native Son will be produced as a play in March in Buenos Aires, Argentina.

"I've heard it only in English," he said.

Wright was born in Natchez, Miss., in 1908. He lived in the various sections of the South and finally moved to Chicago. While in that city he became a Communist and resigned from that party not long ago.

He, his white wife, Ellen, and their skillful, pretty brown skin daughter, Julia, now 3, live in a six-room Brooklyn apartment. His phone number is not listed, and is known to only a few people.

His house is equipped with custom-built furniture made by Ad Bates, famed Harlem furniture maker. Wright, his wife, and Bates designed the furniture.

His private office, where he writes, is simply furnished and contains copies of books he is reading, ten or more copies of *Native Son,* and a half dozen prints of his new book, *Black Boy,* which will be the March Book-of-the-Month Club selection.

Black Boy is an autobiographical study of the novelist's life from his boyhood in Natchez to Chicago.

"It will bring down upon me the curses of colored people, 'liberal' whites, Communists and fascists alike," he declared. "It's strong, it's raw—but it's life as I see and lived it."

Much of *Black Boy* was dictated into a dictaphone machine. Use of this device is no affectation on Wright's part. "It saves me much time," he said, "and it permits me to write when I don't want to be bothered with typing."

He does all the finished typing himself and a completed manuscript bears hardly a penciled correction in twenty pages. His workroom is similarly neat.

A keen observer of his people, Wright is obviously our greatest chronicler. Give him a piece of a conversation and he can finish it in sharp dialogue that gives you the idea that somehow he heard the original conversation.

He has strong, bold ideas on every phase of race and national life. He loves to talk and his speech is a soft, slow drawl. He calls himself "Dick Wright," but signs his name "Richard Wright."

He does not believe that colored people fully and unreservedly support the war. "Go down on Fulton Street (Brooklyn's Lenox Avenue) and talk to the fellows."

"Colored people are thinking about meat and food now and meat and food after their war jobs close," he continued. "We are a great people. We react to reality in real ways. We have been reacting to ugly, bitter pressures so long that we figuratively keep a gun handy at all times— and we are apt to go off the handle any minute."

Speaking of the South he said: "The only safe topics in the South are sex and religion. I don't know exactly why sex and colored people are always described—in some quarters—in perfectly vile terms, but they are."

"Sex is not a determining factor in race relations," he said. "It is injected in the race problem by whites to confuse the issues."

One of his unorthodox ideas on race and foreign policy was expressed as follows:

"The government should select an old, slew-footed colored man named Sam and ask for his advice on every detail of foreign policy as it affects race.

"Suppose they'd have asked Sam about the Oriental exclusion act, Sam, would have said, 'That'll make the Orientals mad and we shouldn't do it.'

"Then the government would say, 'But, Sam, we exclude you and you don't get mad.' Sam would have answered, 'Yes, sir, boss, but that's because I don't have any army or navy.'"

Yet Wright repudiates race nationalism as a dangerous unguided force which can lead to a kind of intra-racial fascism. He also says that "some whites don't like me because I've never pulled any punches."

He lets off steam—his pent-up rejection of the deal white America gives our people—by his writing. He deliberately writes in a hard-boiled, smashing style because "you need a new language to express the nature of race relations here."

Wright devised a "new language" in a short novel called "The Man Who Lived Underground," but this work was never a publisher's success. It appeared only in a collection of stories called *Cross Section*.

His library of some 600 books contains at least 200 psycho-neurotic works. "It is necessary to understand the abnormal before you can understand the normal," he explained. "That is why I collect and study these books."

He cited medical experience to establish the validity of this. "In medicine a doctor studies the abnormal growth to appreciate the normal," he said. "In racial life, so much of it is neurotic or abnormal you must understand the neurotic mind to express the problem."

He believes that pressures from the white world, frustration, and hate have made many colored people a racial neurosis.

"But the worst, or best, will come when the war is over . . . the author added. The pattern of racial behavior then will be most tantalizing."

Wright is one of the few great novelists in America. His all-inclusive vision takes in every phase of American life from "school teacher snobs in Washington, D.C., and Nashville" to "poor guys in Harlem and imigres from farms."

He concentrates on the latter because "they are the backbone of the race and it is through them—when organized and led—that salvation will come."

"I love my people," he concluded.

Misery Begets Genius

Mary Braggiotti/1945

From *New York Post*, 20 March 1945 p. 21.

Since Richard Wright at six years old was considered somewhat of a juvenile delinquent (the author of *Black Boy* was a chronic drunkard in Memphis, Tenn., at the time), and since he has developed into one of the country's most brilliant young writers and a leading fighter for his race, it is natural that he should be turning his talents now towards the subject of delinquent Negro children.

He's been sitting in on Children's Court sessions near his home in Brooklyn. Disguised as an innocent observer (he's found that people don't behave like themselves before a professed writer) he has visited city institutions and various sorts of homes for wayward children.

"The surface hasn't yet been touched in grappling with the situation," said Mr. Wright the other day. "It stems from a condition. I disagree with people who call these children hoodlums. They're emotionally deprived children who need a chance. Most of them are children of migrant Negroes from the South—from a section of the country where they lived in a social straitjacket. Their parents have never had a chance to come into the sphere of Western culture."

To see Richard Wright today you'd think that he'd lived all his life well within the sphere of Western culture. Its influence seems evident in his speech, his flow of language, his level-headed perspective. And in his appearance, too. He is smooth-faced and middle-sized, with a very slight tendency towards plumpness.

The man whose whole youth was a nightmare of habitual hunger, whose diet during his adolescent years was mush and gravy for breakfast, greens cooked in lard for dinner, can mention now in passing, with no more than an average gleam in his eye, the ten-pound roast of beef he bought, cooked and helped eat on a vacation in Canada last summer.

But through all these superficial signs you can see the fight in Richard Wright—the fighting mind and heart that made him battle the ignorance, violence, starvation, misery, injustice, bigotry and hopelessness that surrounded his childhood until he had beaten them for himself, and then turn around and try to beat them for all American Negroes.

The fight showed in him when he said with quiet and deadly certainty, "There'll be trouble after the war and I'm afraid it won't be grappled with honestly enough to stop it. I believe the country is on the verge of facing, for the next 25 years, the magnitude of the Negro problem as it never has before.

"Here's a very important point: It is generally assumed that the more concessions that are made to the Negro—the more he is appeased— the more satisfied he will be. That's a tragic mistake. The truth of the matter is the opposite, and it's understandable. The more the Negro is given—the more he's made to feel like a man—the more he's going to want to contend for what is his own.

"There has been too great a gap in this country between national progress and Negro progress. What we need is a conscious process of acceleration in the progress of Negroes—a process which will eliminate, for example, such a practice as the State of Mississippi's allowing $40 a year for the education of each white child and $5 for each Negro child."

What Richard Wright knows about the average Negro child's chances in the South, he tells in his autobiography, *Black Boy*, the Harper & Bros. publication chosen as a Book-of-the-Month Club selection for March.

Obviously Richard Wright himself was no average child. He was super-sensitive and super-intelligent. Born on a plantation near Natchez, Miss., in 1908, he moved with his parents and brother to Memphis when he was six. There his father deserted the family for another woman, and Richard's mother had to go to work. Her small sons were left to fend for themselves in the streets of Memphis.

Because he was so cute when he sat on the bar and got drunk, the boys at the corner saloon plied him daily with liquor until he became an addict. When he wasn't drinking he was teaching himself to read from books borrowed from kids on the street.

His life with his mother took him from Memphis to Jackson, Miss., to Arkansas, then back to Jackson, always looking for something better. Richard was tough as only a highly-strung desperately determined boy can be tough.

His formal education, which was intermittent, to put it mildly, ended with the ninth grade. (Until 1925, the year he left Jackson, there was no high school there for Negroes.) After a few unfortunate experiences trying to conform to the rules set down for Negroes by white employers and co-workers, Wright pulled up stakes and went to Memphis, where he worked for a manufacturer of optical goods.

An editorial blasting H. L. Mencken which he read in a borrowed Memphis paper made him want to know more about this fellow, Mencken. Any white man frowned upon by a Southern newspaper must have something, he figured. By means of a library card surreptitiously lent to him (Negroes weren't allowed to borrow library books), he read everything he could find by Mencken.

At 19 Wright went to Chicago. He worked as porter, streetcleaner, dishwasher and postoffice clerk—and did his first serious writing. He also joined the Communist party with which he later had powerful disagreements, described in two articles he wrote last year for the *Atlantic Monthly*. "I Tried to Be a Communist."

Wright came to seek his fortune in New York in 1937. He got on the Federal Writers' Project, won the Story Magazine prize, a Guggenheim Fellowship and the Spingarn Medal. His first book, *Uncle Tom's Children,* a group of four long short stories, was followed in 1940 by his best-selling novel, *Native Son* (also a Book-of-the-Month Club choice) and later by *12 Million Black Voices.*

With *Native Son's* first wave of success the budding author married Ellen Poplar, a white girl from Brooklyn. Their daughter, Julie, who will be three next month, is her father's favorite playfellow.

Wright gets up at seven and writes all morning—that is, when the mood is on him. He never drives himself.

"I don't yet think of writing as a profession," he confessed. "If I can get money for it, that's fine. But I'd rather wash dishes than write just for money."

Author Richard Wright Champion of Negro Rights

Trudi McCullough/1945

From *New Haven Sunday Register*, 8 April 1945, Sec. III, p. 10.
Reprinted by permission.

NEW YORK—(AP)—In his current way of life and in *Black Boy*, his auto-biography, brilliant Negro author Richard Wright poses a paradox.

With *Black Boy*, Wright again, as with *Native Son*, has written a Book-of-the-Month Club selection. It is the painful, often ugly story of a Negro boy—set apart by his own sensitivity and lack of compromise from his own race and barred by birth from the advantages of the white way of life—and his unrelenting effort to sever himself from his environment.

Richard Wright succeeded beyond measure but, paradoxically, with his success he has turned his efforts and prestige to working for those of the race he left behind him. He is a brilliant champion of Negro rights and recently was appointed to the board of directors of the American Council on Race Relations.

Those relations, he believes, "are riding for some pretty sharp clashes."

"Hundreds of thousands of Negroes," he says, "have been pulled off southern plantations into war plants. Chicago, for instance, is swollen and spilling over with the newly arrived population.

"When this happens a pattern occurs. It begins with the housing problem. Only a few months ago in Chicago there were some bombs thrown in protest against housing infringment. But what seemed unbelievable to many Negroes was that it was not the Negroes who were arrested but white men.

"It was the purely accidental presence of some liberal minded people in Chicago: Marshall Field, Edwin Embree (both on the Race Relations Council) that caused the council to be well established and effective there and which, in this instance and in others, has kept the situation what we call contained."

Wright is ready to admit that the situation won't be 'containable' for ever. He believes that, in the next 25 years, the magnitude of the Negro problem will have to be faced. His militancy shows when he says, "If I could get the trade unions, the church groups, all the Negroes, to go to Congress and compel the South at the point of guns to lift oppression, I would endorse it immediately and wholeheartedly." Such words are startling coming from poised, logical, good tempered Wright. To understand what motivates them, one has only to read his autobiography.

"It is generally assumed," he continues, "that the more concessions made to the Negro—the more he is appeased—the more satisfied he will be. That's a tragic mistake. The truth of the matter is the opposite and it's understandable the more the Negro is given, the more he's made to feel like a man, the more he's going to want to contend for what is his own."

By equality Richard Wright says he means the concrete advantages: Education, housing, jobs, clothes. As to association and inter-marriage, the author—whose grandmother was a white woman and who, himself, is married to Ellen Poplar, a white girl from Brooklyn—believes that is a matter of personal and mutual choice.

Author Wright points out another factor, the one made articulate by Lillian Smith in *Strange Fruit*. "If the South ever reckoned the cost and damage to its own whites from this self-imposed system of hate, it might further race relations considerably."

The 37-year-old author ha espoused and disavowed many causes in the course of sampling living and self-education. He tried and abandoned Communism because it was "not militant enough." He calls himself "far left of left" but broke with Communism when the party endorsed a cinema short on the status of the Negro in the Army. "I knew the Negro in the Army is still strictly 'Jim Crow' and that film should have been denounced."

Wright, of medium height and tending slightly toward plumpness, is cultured of diction and rich in vocabulary. At present, he has a play, a book of short stories and another novel about delinquent Negro children in the works. As he gets stalled on one, he turns to another, so most of his books are in the mill a long time.

Black Boy was written as the result of a speech before a mixed white and Negro audience at Fisk University. "Negroes talk among themselves about how they feel toward Negroes, but I believe that was the first time anyone had ever discussed the subject between both groups. The audience's reaction gave me a new sense of the value of my material and I made it into a book."

How Richard Wright Looks at *Black Boy*
PM/1945

From *PM*, 15 April 1945, pp. 3–4.

The other Monday evening we slipped uptown to see what would happen when an author like Richard Wright—whose autobiography, *Black
Boy*, is selling well and stirring up talk—got together with a couple of
book critics. The occasion was Wright's appearance on WHN's program, *The Author Meets the Critics*, which is presented in the theater of
the Barbizon-Plaza Hotel.

We got to the theater a little early and wandered backstage, where
there were five or six people standing about and chatting. WHN's press
agent introduced us to Sterling North, New York *Post* critic. North has
a full head of dark wavy hair and a high, broad forehead. His rimless
glasses, wide, earnest eyes and sober demeanor made him look like a
hard-working college student.

We also met Wright, who was sitting alone and looking preoccupied.

Then a tall man wearing a black derby and an immaculately pressed
topcoat walked in briskly. He carefully hung up his coat and hat, then
sauntered over to our group. A white handkerchief was flowing from the
breast pocket of his pencil-striped blue suit. The press agent introduced
him to Wright as John McCaffery, fiction editor of *The American Magazine* and moderator of the show.

McCaffery said conversationally, "I'm told you are tough." Wright
smiled but looked a little wary. McCaffery continued, "Oh, not in the
street fighting sense, but like a piece of metal. If someone pushes you,
you spring back." Wright's laugh was neither assent or denial.

It was almost time for the program to start when Lewis Gannett—
Herald Tribune critic—hurried in. He was wearing a black modified ten
gallon hat and was carrying a brief case. He looked like a kindly south-
western college professor.

Wright saw him, arose, and smilingly held out his hand. Gannett took
it energetically and they exchanged questions about the health of their
wives. McCaffery called to them, they went onstage, and the broadcast
began.

North and Gannett soon got into a discussion of the book's style. North said: "Mr. Wright's ability to handle language is partly the Negroes' ability to speak the language. There are speech rhythms throughout this thing that are exquisite."

"Pure nonsense and condescension," Gannett said. "There isn't any speech rhythm in that book. That's just written in plain American."

Wright's musical laugh rolled up above the discordant laugh of the audience. Without waiting for the laughter to die down, North plunged in with, "It wasn't meant to be condescension! I don't think it is any less like Negro speech as I've heard from a great many Negroes who speak *beautiful English*. Katherine Dunham for instance. Richard Wright, for another. I don't know if you know the right kind of Negro, Lewis."

Gannett opened his mouth to reply but McCaffery cut in quickly with, "This is the sort of accusation I was afraid we were going to get into. Let's leave it lay."

McCaffery steered the conversation to the author, and North said: "This is one of the few bits of criticism I intend to level at Richard's book, and that is the personal attitude of Richard Wright himself. Everyone has gone through some of the experiences he did without the bitter addition of the race angle. The working at hard dirty jobs that in Richard's case caused bitterness because there was a white overseer."

Wright sat there, smiling faintly. "For a half dozen stories," North continued, "he wrote the same story; of a black boy being chased in- terminably by a white man or men and fighting when he is cornered. Perhaps it is because of Richard's nature, which sometimes is dark and tragic. . . .

"Only in this book does he start to be analytical and with a degree of humor that did not show in *Native Son.*"

By this time the program had reached the half-way mark and it was Wright's turn to speak. Although he had no text or notes in front of him he seemed to have planned exactly what he was going to say.

"Of course," he began, "An autobiography is the story of one's life, but if one wants to, one can make it more than that and I definitely had that in mind when I wrote the book. I wrote the book to tell a series of incidents strung through my childhood, but the main desire," and he emphasized the words, "was to render a judgment on my environment. I wanted to render that judgment because I felt the necessity to. . . .

"That judgment was this: the environment the South creates is too small to nourish human beings, especially Negro human beings.

"Some may escape the general plight and grow up, but it is a matter of luck and I think it should be a matter of plan. It should be a matter of saving the citizens of our country for our country, and," he said, emphasizing each word with a tap of his pencil, "I don't think it should be put on a narrow moral plane of a good white person helping a poor Negro."

With plain but poetic phrases and his melodious voice Wright had the audience half hypnotized. He seemed to have got through to them as the other speakers had not.

"I wanted to lend, give my tongue, to voiceless Negro boys," he went on. "I feel this way about the emotionally and economically deprived Negro children of the South." He lowered his voice and as if reading a psalm quoted Walt Whitman, "Not until the sun ceases to shine on you will I disown you." He sighed almost imperceptibly. "That was one of my motives," he said. "I wanted to give voice to that, to make it known."

Later on, as Wright got into a discussion of part of the book's contents, his voice took on a rasp. "There is something serious to be said about this legend that all Negroes are kind and love animals and children. . . .

"That legend," he said, "serves to protect certain guilt feelings about the Negro. If you can feel that he is so different that he is just naturally happy and he smiles automatically you kind of exclude him, in an ironic sense, from the human race and therefore you don't have to treat him exactly like you would treat other people and you don't have to feel bad about mistreating him."

"Any such illusion, Richard, has been dispelled by reading your book," North told him.

"That," Wright said grimly, "is what I'm aiming for."

McCaffery said that race hatred was a pathological thing. Wright readily agreed but said: "It is not a hopeless situation. It calls for a high, perhaps agonizing degree of self-consciousness on the part of Negroes and whites."

"I don't think you are going to get the solution in self-consciousness," North said.

"Not the solution," Wright quickly answered, "But I feel that among those trying to deal with the problem there should be some recognition that whites do in many instances hate Negroes, that Negroes hate whites. Just to pretend that it doesn't happen and to explain the Negro race in terms of your maid is the most dangerous fallacy of all."

Not long after that, the air time was up but the program continued for a while for the benefit of the studio audience. McCaffery asked, "Do you feel a community of interest with the whole Negro race?"

Wright looked at the now superfluous microphone and said, "One of the things that makes me write is that I realize that I'm a very average Negro." He laughed a little and said in a lower tone, "Maybe that's what makes me extraordinary."

This, Too, Is America

Charles J. Rolo/1945

From *Tomorrow*, 4 (May 1945), 63–63.

"THE artist is a revolutionary figure," says Richard Wright. "The serious artist grapples with his environment, passes a judgment on it. He helps to deepen people's perceptions, quicken their thought processes. He makes them conscious of the possibility of historical change—and in that way he facilitates change. That's a big task, a self-sufficient one."

Ten years ago Wright believed that the artist had a role to play in politics, too. He was active in the John Reed Clubs, the League of American Writers and other left-wing organizations. He is convinced now, he says, that the artist is most effective when he sticks to his trade. "Writers and politicians move in a different tempo, on a different plane. Let the politician organize what the writer has set in motion. When a writer starts dabbling in politics, he gets sucked into an organization that amounts to leaving his work. He should put all of his passion into his work."

Richard Wright has done just that. All of his passion, all of his indignation against the Jim Crow system, the third-class citizenship and the *Sklavennoral* imposed on the American Negro he has put into a courageous, heartbreaking, sordid, explosive, sometimes melodramatic but unforgettable book, *Black Boy*.

Black Boy is an autobiography, a document in race relations and a moral indictment; it combines the unashamed subjectivity of Rousseau's *Confessions* with the harsh realism of Zola's *L'Assomoir* and the crusading fervor of his *J'accuse*. The tension, the bitterness, the tragedy are unrelieved, unshaded. It could hardly have been otherwise, for tension and hate and gray hopelessness were the realities of this black boy's story, which is also the story of America's lower depths.

Some reviewers have complained about Wright's "strained and feverish" manner; to their air-conditioned idealism the violence of his style is like a jet of steam from a burst pipe. "The manner," Wright says, "stems from the matter; the relationship of the American Negro to the American scene is essentially violent. He could not be kept in his present position unless there existed an apparatus of organized violence. Any attempt to deal with this situation must deal in terms of violence. I cannot deny the reality of my existence. It's what I've seen."

Richard Wright was born on a plantation near Natchez and grew up in the slums of Memphis and the small-town slums of Arkansas and Mississippi. When Richard was five, his father deserted his mother. A few years later his mother was crippled by paralysis. His childhood was a nightmare of abject poverty, hunger and fear—poverty that sent him begging for pennies in the saloons, where the grown-ups would get him drunk and give him nickels to repeat obscenities; hunger that was forever "nudging my ribs, twisting my empty guts until they ached"; fear of the beatings at home, of hostile black children, of ghosts and of the harsh religion of his grandmother, and later dread of the white world, which murdered his uncle and lynched a boyhood acquaintance, in which the slightest slip of word, or expression meant ugly "trouble."

The underprivileged black boy was by instinct a rebel, with a burning sense of the dignity of man. In the black world as well as the white he remained a stranger and alone. Even his uncle told the other children to keep away from him—"the boy's a dangerous fool." His white employers, too, sensed that he was "different"—though he learned to say "Sir" and smile with false heartiness and mask his thoughts and feelings. "I don't like your looks, nigger," one man said, and fired him. He was run off job after job.

He saw the worst side of the white man's world. When a dog bit him, its owner laughed: a dog bite can't hurt a nigger. "If I was a nigger," one boss said to him, "I'd kill myself." The foreman in an optical factory gave him and another black boy knives and tried to incite a stabbing. As a bellboy in a hotel he grew used to seeing white prostitutes lolling naked on their beds—blacks were supposed to take nakedness for granted, they weren't considered human.

Richard Wright found his first release in the printed word. When he was a small boy, a schoolteacher read to him the story of *Bluebeard and His Seven Wives,* and as she spoke, "the look of things was different, and the world became peopled with magic presences. My sense of life deepened and the feel of things was different, somehow." His grandmother beat him—any non-Bible story was the Devil's work—and told him he would burn in hell. But he had tasted "what to me was life," and thereafter he would slip into the schoolteacher's room, steal a book and try to decipher it in the barn. At thirteen he had not yet had an unbroken year of schooling, but he was reading everything he could lay his hands on—cheap pulp tales, for the most part, in the magazine supplement of a Ku Klux Klan paper. At fourteen he had his first story published in a Negro newspaper; he called it *The Voodoo of Hell's Half-Acre*. Three years later a friendly Irishman lent him a library card, and he discovered Mencken, Sherwood Anderson and Sinclair Lewis. Their books were his "gateway to the world." For the first time he learned that white men were fighting prejudice and stupidity and shams, using words as one would use a club, and instinctively he thought: "Maybe I could use words as a weapon." He bought a ream of paper and started to write.

The miracle of Richard Wright's achievement can no more be explained than Beethoven's genius or the poetic gift of Rimbaud in his teens. *Black Boy* certainly fails to account for the miracle, and Richard Wright has just this to add: "Some people see a ball game and they want to play ball; some see water and they want to swim; when I saw print, I wanted to write."

Why didn't he turn out like his own Bigger Thomas, for violence and crime were the norm of his early days?

"Well, for one thing," says Wright, "I kept out of jail; I never got caught. And when I had enough money to start north, I never stole again."

Wright does not believe that migration to the north is a solution to the Negro problem. But when the southern Negro goes north, he tears himself loose from folk-peasant ways, becomes urbanized—and in that, Wright sees a measure of salvation for the Negro. "Urbanization brings the southern Negro within the living orbit of the nation for the first time. It brings him into contact with literacy, with democratic ideas, makes him conscious of his relation to the nation.

"The war has accelerated the northward drift, and has speeded up the progress of the Negro. But it has been an unconscious process—like an express train stirring up dry leaves. What is needed is conscious acceleration. In Mississippi, for instance, the state spends $40 a year on the education of a white child, $5 a year on the education of a Negro child. If the Negro child is to overcome his cultural handicaps, he needs $60 or $80 a year."

The war, too, says Wright, "has shown up the fallacy of the old slogan, 'There's nothing wrong with the South but what jobs wouldn't cure. Today there are plenty of jobs, but the southerner's attitude toward the Negro has not improved. What the Negro wants is not just a job but the rights granted by the Constitution. That problem will be decided by hard factual thinking—not by paltry economic concessions, made by way of appeasement, or by moral paternalism. There's a danger in riding the moral horse. The well-meaning old ladies who say nice things about 'my nice colored maid' are sidestepping the Negro problem."

Although white liberals have done much to improve the status of the Negro, Wright is not too hopeful that mass pressure for racial equality will be exerted on the South by whites. According to a recent survey, Wright says, 60 per cent of the whites in America believe that the Negro is being fairly treated. The Negro, he is convinced, will have to assume the initiative.

What of the white writers crusading for the Negro?

"Their motives are admirable, but often their point of attack is mistaken. There's no need for them to make special pleas to the Negro to increase his militancy. The militancy is there, spilling over. Their task, as I conceive it, is to grapple with the deep-seated racial notions of white Americans. Lillian Smith is one who sees this quite clearly and addresses her work to her own class. White writers should combat white chauvinism while Negro writers combat Negro nationalism, and chronic distrust of the whites. Negro nationalism—the all-black community— spells social regression. There is no solution in withdrawal; withdrawal means perishing. The Negro has no culture except the culture of the rest of the country. As I see it, integration—complete equality—is the only solution, and as an artist I want to bring out the oneness of human life.

"Hollywood, unfortunately, is preserving and reinforcing the Negro stereotypes. It can't or won't grapple with high seriousness. The Broadway stage is more helpful."

As to his own work—Wright has no set plans. "I'll write whatever my imagination dictates." Now in his middle-thirties, he has behind him four books, two of them Book-of-the-Month Club selections—*Black Boy* and *Native Son*. Richard Wright's explosive talent, already widely recognized, is one of tomorrow's brightest promises in American writing.

As an artist Wright can improve on *Black Boy*. The autobiography fails in one crucial respect: it does not explain Richard Wright. The personality it presents is passive, a jumble of emotional tensions and sense impressions.

After meeting Richard Wright one is convinced that he will take a lot of explaining, even with his own pen. Outwardly the author of *Black Boy* is affable, poised, quick to smile, almost gay. When he speaks of the Negro, the tone is intense but still restrained, though the words, written down, are strong stuff. Here perhaps is a clue to this strangely gifted personality. Richard Wright left the South knowing that "I was taking a part of the South to transplant in alien soil," hoping that "it would grow differently . . . respond to the warmth of other suns, and perhaps bloom." That miracle has happened. But in Richard Wright two forces are still at war, and the North has not yet completely won its battle over the South, which has been so much a part of him.

Are We Solving America's Race Problem?

George V. Denny, Jr., Irving Ives, Elmer Carter, Richard Wright, and Jerry Voorhis/1945

From *Town Meeting*, 11 (24 May 1945), 3–22. Transcript of a radio broadcast.

Mr. Carter: "Joshua fit the battle of Jericho and the walls came tumbling down." Thus goes a rousing Negro spiritual. Today there are hosts of modern Joshuas all over the world, black and white, and the walls of fascism and racial bigotry and intolerance are cracking and tumbling down.

Let's contrast the record of the Negro in World War I and World War II. In the first World War, there were no Negroes in the Air Corps, no Negro commissioned officers in the Navy, no Negro nurses, no Negroes in the Marine Corps, and Negro army officers were trained in completely segregated officer candidate schools.

In this war Negro fliers have made an impressive record in combat in the European skies. There are a score of Negro commissioned officers in the Navy, one of whom is in command of a vessel with a crew composed of men of both races.

Negro nurses in the Army and Navy, working together with white nurses, tend the battle casualties without regard to race. Negro Marines have fought by the side of white Marines in the gory struggles in the southwest Pacific, and in America's mighty merchant fleet there are four Negro captains who command Liberty Ships, manned by mixed crews, which carry the sinews of war to our fighting men across the Seven Seas.

Despite the tradition of racial segregation in the United States Army there are six thousand Negro commissioned officers who received training, without discrimination because of race and color, in officers candidate schools, and the 761st Negro Tank Battalion, with officer personnel composed of both races, was a part of the spearhead of the Third Army which broke the Siegfried Line.

One by one, the racial inequalities sanctioned by law or custom which impede the full realization of democracy in America are beginning to disappear. The lynching evil has almost been eradicated; the record shows a steady decrease. The legislative devices designed to restrict the Negro's right to vote are being rendered ineffectual by the decisions of the United States Supreme Court.

Last year the High Court ruled that Negro citizens in the South could not be excluded from participation in the Democratic primaries, which ultimately insures a greater participation by Negro citizens in the government. The growing protest of both whites and blacks, North and South, against the iniquitous poll tax has swept it away in Georgia, and it can't last much longer in the remaining seven states.

The fight against intolerance and bigotry is not being waged by the Negro alone. In the South there is a growing revolt against the evils of segregation and discrimination. Virginius Dabney, distinguished editor of the *Richmond Times Dispatch,* in a trenchant editorial has called for the abolition of the Jim Crow car in Virginia.

Unique in the history of the South was a meeting, a few months ago, of the editors, Negro and white, of the leading newspapers published in that region, to discuss methods of removing restrictions of the franchise.

Only recently, southern college students, representing the leading white and Negro colleges of the South, convened at the University of North Carolina and sent two delegates to the San Francisco Conference, one a white student, the other a Negro.

These instances of growing interracial cooperation can be multiplied a hundred times. What greater proof, Congressman Voorhis, do you and Mr. Wright need to convince you?

It is here in America that the Negro has given the greatest demonstration of his capacity to attain to the highest levels of civilization and America, albeit grudgingly, has shown a willingness to accord to him an opportunity. If America were not solving the race problem, then neither a Paul Robeson nor a Marian Anderson could have emerged to win the plaudits of a civilized world. Nor could the genius of George Carver have been dedicated to the advancement of science and the enrichment of his country.

Nor could millions of others have acquired the skills and developed the character which have served our Nation so well in peace and in war. There have always been Joshuas in America, white and black, with a passion for human freedom and fair play. Because of their conviction and zeal, America moves forward toward a solution of the race problem. (*Applause.*)

Moderator Denny: Thank you, Elmer Carter. Now let's have the

other side of the case stated by another distinguished Negro, author of
Native Son and the current best seller, *Black Boy*. Mr. Richard Wright.
(*Applause.*)

Mr. Wright: I take issue with Mr. Elmer Carter's dangerous theory—dangerous theory of a gradual solution of the race problem. If his
theory is believed and accepted we stand in danger of letting race violence creep upon us unawares. It's true that under the stress of war the
Nation was compelled to admit Negroes to a few areas of life, hereto-
fore reserved exclusively for whites. But let us not be deluded into
thinking that these war gains will be lasting. Already a desire for normalcy has gripped the Nation. We all remember the bloody race riots
that swept the country after World War I when the Nation went back to
its peacetime habits.

Mr. Carter hints with pride that in 1936 seven Negroes were lynched
and in 1944 only two were lynched. Is Mr. Carter asking us to thank
lynch mobs for this record?

Let's get down to cases. The race problem is not being solved. Indeed, it is becoming more acute. Witness the recent outbreaks in Beau-
mont, Texas; Detroit; and Los Angeles.

What do we mean by a solution of the race problem?

It means a nation in which there will exist no residential segregation,
no Jim Crow army, no Jim Crow navy, no Jim Crow Red Cross Blood
Bank, no Negro institutions, no laws prohibiting intermarriage, no
customs assigning Negroes to inferior positions. We would simply be
Americans, and the Nation would be better for it. (*Applause.*) A flood
of creative energy would flow from the millions of Negroes and whites
filled with a hunger for a richer life.

But the contrary is true; the Nation is split. Racial segregation is our
national policy, a part of our culture, tradition, and morality. White
America feels that black America possesses no rights commanding
respect, that Negroes are to be kept firmly in an area branded as inferior. White America feels that it is right to treat Negroes wrong and
wrong to treat them right.

Tonight Mr. Ives will tell you that jobs are a solution to the problem;
that fair employment practices will do the trick. Now let's look at this
proposition. Before the war, Harlem had a slogan. They said, "There's
nothing wrong with Harlem but what 25,000 jobs won't cure."

Well, war came and Harlem got full employment. Then in August,

1943, a racial outbreak swept that unhappy ghetto. Why? They had jobs, but they did not have respect, justice, freedom of living space. They had jobs, but their sons and daughters were being kicked and hounded in the Army and the Navy and they resented it.

Let's not let the illusion of jobs blind us to the deeper cancer of race hate in this country. I'm for Federal and State FEPC, but it's merely a step in the right direction, not a solution.

Again I take issue with Mr. Carter. He tells us that there is now a nationwide campaign to raise $1,500,000 for Negro education. Now, not only is this inadequate, but the method of asking for it is wrong. It's public charity and it's shameful. Every child in America, white or black, ought to have the right to an education without somebody passing around the begging cup. (*Applause.*)

The paternalistic attitude of whites toward Negroes must stop because it lulls whites into feelings of dangerous complacency about rising racial tensions. Yes, I would deprive white people of the luxury of feeling good when they treat Negroes kindly. (*Applause.*)

I'd advocate the extension of simple and straight justice to everybody. The race problem cuts deep. Race hate in subtle guises is taught in our schools, our homes, and our churches. We see reflections of it in our films and hear it over our radios. But listen, here is something of great and decisive importance that is overlooked. Twenty-five years ago there were only a few thousand Negroes clamoring for justice. But today there are 13 million, and they resent the degradation of their second-class citizenship. Gradual solutions are out of date. They hide the present gravity of this problem which confronts the Nation for the first time in all of its tragic fullness.

Here is the truth, whites can no longer regard Negroes as a passive, obedient minority. Whether we have a violent or peaceful solution of this problem depends upon the degree to which white Americans can purge their minds of the illusions that they own and know Negroes.

Negro confidence and dignity increase day by day. The Negro realizes that his relationship to America is symbolic. He knows that the world is watching his bid for manhood. He knows that the widespread knowledge of his plight constitutes a great moral weapon; he will not hesitate to use that weapon. Unless white Americans pry their minds out of their horse-and-buggy ways of regarding Negroes, violence may be upon us. These are the facts; this is the issue. (*Applause.*)

Mr. Carter: I just want to make an observation that we are not contending that the race problem is solved. We are contending that America and a great portion of America is striving to solve it.

Mr. Wright has said there were riots in Harlem and other sections of the Nation. Well, there have been thousands and thousands of riots in America that weren't occasioned by difference of color and race. Riots have always accompanied progress—the progress, for instance, of American labor. Organized labor was accompanied by riot after riot until management and America began to respect the rights of labor, so rioting isn't conclusive. It only means that the Negro is moving forward in an atmosphere that permits him to move forward. (*Applause.*)

Mr. Denny: Thank you, Mr. Carter. Mr. Wright?

Mr. Wright: Well, here, I think is the heart of the issue. Are we reading correctly and accurately the feelings of the Negro people today? Riots do come, but we are intelligent. Let us foresee and prophesy practically what we know is impending. Now, if we read the consciousness of the Negro right today, the stop-gap measures devised impending all over the Nation are not sufficient to stop the Negroes. We want socially acceptable instruments handed to the Negro so that he can work out his destiny and he will not be compelled in a thousand individualistic instances to spill over into gratuitous violence. (*Applause.*)

Mr. Denny: Do you have another question, Mr. Carter?

Mr. Carter: Well, I want to make this observation, too. Mr. Wright has spoken about the rising consciousness of the Negro. The rising consciousness of the Negro as to his wrongs and his rights have come about through public schools and through colleges which have trained the Negro. These colleges are colleges which have been supported by philanthropy. That's true. Mr. Wright, I want to ask you the question, do you know that other colleges are supported by philanthropy, that Columbia, Harvard, Yale, all of the private colleges in the United States are supported by philanthropy. It's no disgrace to receive your education, Mr. Wright, from a college that is supported by philanthropy. (*Applause.*)

Mr. Denny: And I might add, Mr. Wright, that Town Hall is supported in large part by philanthropy. I see the chairman of our fund-raising committee right up there. (*Laughter.*)

Mr. Wright: Well, here is the issue. When the decisive sectors of a race of people must depend upon philanthropy, that is bad. It's all right for higher branches of education, specialized efforts, to depend upon it, but there should be a ceiling, a cushion, below which Negro education should not and must not fall. This, I believe, is mandatory. The Negro in the South cannot find his way to self-realization unless there is given to him, as a matter of course and not charity, elementary education even up to the high school level. I would say that if that is not given, then the Federal Government should step in and supplement state aid in all cases. (*Applause.*)

Mr. Denny: Thank you, Mr. Wright. Mr. Carter wants to comment on that.

Mr. Carter: I want to say that I agree with Mr. Wright on that subject and it goes to prove our point because the Federal Government has many measures designed to give federal aid for education in the South; that is, the representatives in the United States Congress are not blind to this. They're doing the best they can. They have bills and are considering bills to extend educational opportunity and resources—financial resources—to the South. (*Applause.*)

Mr. Denny: All right. Mr. Wright, do you have a comment?

Mr. Wright: Just a few figures. In the State of Mississippi, for every forty dollars allotted to educate a white child, five dollars are allotted to educate a Negro child. Whether it's a hook or crook, philanthropy or Federal aid, that equation should be upset and upset quick. (*Applause.*)

Mr. Denny: Thank you, gentlemen. Now out there in this audience—we've got a full house, a crowd on the stage and people standing up in the balcony. I should say about 25 percent of the audience are Negroes here and we'd be very happy to hear from both white and black in the question period.

Man: My question is directed to Mr. Wright. Recognizing the terrible and overwhelming responsibility to whites in the solution of the Negro-white problem, is there, in your opinion, anything that the Negro can do toward the solution of this problem?

Mr. Wright: Yes. I feel that the Negro has a sacred obligation and a moral duty to bring before the people of this country again and again and again the meaning of his problem. He has no say, fundamentally, in its solution. I believe that the Negro in each black-belt area can, by banding together, help his schools, help the delinquent children, help families, but the fundamental responsibility rests upon whites and I believe that Negro protests, Negro agitation, should increase and become

intense. It doesn't mean that I want Negroes to annoy whites, but it is
for the fundamental benefit of the Nation that Negroes cease keeping
silent about the facts of their lives. (*Applause.*)

Mr. Denny: Mr. Wright, I want to ask you a question here just to
clarify something. I'm sure that you don't mean this, but so that nobody
would possibly misunderstand you, because we have a way sometimes
of being misunderstood over the air, you don't mean that it's the function of Negroes to agitate to the point of violence at all, do you?

Mr. Wright: Oh, no, not to the point of violence, but I believe that
effective agitation by Negroes, in acquainting white America of their
plight, can stop violence. In other words, I believe that the facts that are
hidden and kept under cover should be brought out into the open. In
other words, before we had the riots last summer many people knew
that tensions were rising. But there was a tendency everywhere, from
far left to right, in the churches and out, to say nothing about it. Then
they burst upon us and we were appalled and it was ammunition for our
enemies.

Mr. Denny: That's right. Well that's just what I wanted to clear up,
Mr. Wright. Thank you.

Man: I'm a member of the Council of African Affairs, also member
of NAACP, and I lived and worked for more than two years with Negroes in Latin America. I believe I know something of the psychology
of the Negro.

Mr. Denny: And your question is to whom, sir?

Man: Mr. Wright. If the thieves of Europe would give back to the
rightful owners desirable parts of Africa, do you think that the American
Negro would assist in its development?

Mr. Wright: Before I answer that question, I'd like to take issue
with one phrase—a rather dubious one he used—Negro psychology.
I don't know any such animal. (*Applause.*)

I am all for the redemption of Africa from the imperialist powers and
I believe that it would help the entire world if it were taken out of the
clutches of those imperialist nations that exploit it and if the natives of
Africa were allowed to assimilate the ideals of western civilization and
the instrumentalities of our industrial life. But I do not believe that we
should in any degree feel that they should have Africa because of any
special characteristics, biological, cultural, or psychological. (*Applause.*)

Mr. Denny: Thank you. The soldier on the back row. Yes.

Soldier: My question is addressed to Congressman Voorhis. Do you advocate or would you condone intermarriage as advanced by Mr. Wright?

Congressman Voorhis: That's a $64 question, of course. (*Laughter.*) To my mind that is not the contribution to the solution of the problem. The problem—as I said in my speech—is to make it possible for every American to have the fullest opportunity to make his full contribution to the life of the Nation. In my judgment the Nation would be poorer and not richer if we lost the distinctive contribution which different kinds of people can make to it. I say that without the slightest feeling that God made one race superior to another one. I don't believe he did. I believe in the equality of all people in his eyes. (*Applause.*)

Mr. Denny: One minute. The soldier wants to talk back there first. Let's get what he has to say.

Soldier: Well, I only brought this question up because it was mentioned specifically by Mr. Wright. I was not advancing it as Congressman Voorhis tried to put it as a very good example of just what this meeting is about, this topic of tonight's discussion. I believe that's what the Congressman said unless I had him wrong.

Mr. Denny: Well, he just said—he just said—Ha! (*Laughter.*) He stated it too well for the moderator to try to restate it for him. I'll put it that way. Mr. Wright, do you want to comment at that point?

Mr. Wright: Well, inasmuch as I brought it up, I should take a little of the load off the Congressman here. (*Laughter.*) I don't advocate the solution of the Negro problem through intermarriage. I think that would be ridiculous. On the other hand, I think it is equally ridiculous to plaster the law books of 30-odd states with laws prohibiting inter-marriage. I was down in Mississippi in 1940 and I saw the streets thronged with mulattoes in a state where you have an airtight anti-intermarriage law. Now, there's something evidently wrong about that. (*Applause.*)

Mr. Denny: That shows prohibition doesn't work. The gentleman on the front row.

Man: Mr. Carter. If this is a free country, why do they put up a bill such as the antilynching bill?

Mr. Carter: I suppose the reason the antilynching bills are introduced is to stop lynching. (*Laughter and applause.*)

Mr. Denny: I think you ought to sit down now. (*Laughter.*) That's too good. Let's take another question.

Man: Mr. Wright, please explain the bitter anti-Semitism existing in

New York among our Negro friends, and what are you doing to combat
it? (*Applause.*)

Mr. Denny: That's a question off tonight's subject, but you may
comment on it. Go ahead. (*Shouts.*)

Woman's voice: No, it's not. Why?

Mr. Denny: Why? Because the Jewish problem is not considered a
race problem.

Voice: Why, it certainly is.

Mr. Wright: This is a rather ticklish subject and in my attempts to
bring it out into the open I have, in diverse quarters, been branded as
anti-Semite sometimes because I think you ought to talk about this
problem. It does happen that in many Negro areas there are many Jewish businessmen. Now, I don't want to say that their practices are any
worse or better than that of any other businessmen, but when people
operate in an environment where there is intense misery and operate as
businessmen, it adds to the general cultural blight of anti-Semitism in
the United States. Perhaps none of us are doing as much as we could
about this problem. I wish that if the gentleman had some ideas, he
would pass them along to me. I am as anxious as he is to see a certain
degree of fraternization based upon a realization of a common plight
between Jews and Negroes. (*Applause.*)

Lady: Mr. Wright, why are we called "Negroes?" Are we not Afro-
Americans?

Mr. Denny: All right, Mr. Wright. You have just twenty seconds to
answer.

Mr. Wright: This is the profoundest question I've been asked in a
long time. I don't know, but I'm not terribly concerned. It's a sociological definition, I take it, to designate me and if we were called by any
other name, discrimination would be just as bad. (*Applause.*)

Black Boy and Reading

Richard Wright/1945

From *The Lexington Reader,* ed. Lynn Z. Bloom (Lexington, Mass.: D. C. Heath, 1987), pp. 101–102. All rights reserved.

Since my book, *Black Boy,* was published, I've been interviewed many times, but I've yet to say what I really want to say about it. I don't want to discuss the events described there, but I do want to tell how I came to feel that those events possessed enough importance to compel me to write about them; how it was possible for me to feel that my life had a meaning which my Jim Crow, southern environment denied.

Living in the South doomed me to look always through eyes which the South had given me, and bewilderment and fear made me mute and afraid. But after I had left the South, luck gave me other eyes, new eyes with which to look at the meaning of what I'd lived through.

I came North in my 19th year, filled with the hunger to know. Books were the windows through which I looked at the world. I read Dostoevsky's *The House of the Dead,* an autobiographical novel depicting the lives of exiled prisoners in Siberia, how they lived in crowded barracks and vented their hostility upon one another. It made me remember how Negroes in the South, crowded into their Black Belts, vented their hostility upon one another, forgetting that their lives were conditioned by the whites above them. To me reading was a kind of remembering.

Another book shed light for me, George Moore's *Confessions of a Young Man,* which described how an English youth resisted the restrictions of a Victorian environment; and at once I was able, in looking back through alien eyes, to see my own life. There was another book, James Joyce's *Portrait of the Artist as a Young Man,* which depicted the double revolt of an Irish youth against the oppressive religious life of Ireland, an Ireland which England was seeking to strangle. I was reminded of the stifling Negro environment in the South, an environment that is exploited by the whites above it. I'll mention one more book, D. H. Lawrence's *Sons and Lovers,* which dealt with the experiences of a son of an English coal mining family, a son who sought to escape the demands of a bleak environment.

I had in mind none of these books I've mentioned when I wrote *Black Boy*. But books like these endlessly modified my attitude. The point is this: I do not believe that it is possible for a Negro boy growing up in the environment of the South today to develop that sense of objectivity that will enable him to grasp the meaning of his life. If he is to learn to live, he needs help from the outside. Lynching is a terror that has many forms; there is the lynching of men's spirits as well as their bodies, and spiritual lynching occurs every day for the Negro in the South.

I know that the scalding experiences of *Black Boy* are alien to most Americans to whom education is a matter of course thing, to whom food is something to be taken for granted, to whom freedom is a heritage. Yet to those whites who recall how, in the early days of this land, their forefathers struggled for freedom, *Black Boy* cannot be a strange story. Neither can it be a strange story to the Jews, the Poles, the Irish, and the Italians who came hopefully to this land from the Old World. Because the hunger for freedom fills the hearts of men all over this war-ravaged earth today, I feel that Negroes in America have a moral duty, a sacred obligation to remind the nation constantly of their plight, their claim, their problem. And when you hear the voice of the submerged Negro in America, remember that it is but one of the world-wide chorus of voices sounding for freedom everywhere.

Richard Wright Stresses Realism in Dealing with Fictional Negro Types

Coit Hendley, Jr./1945

From *The Sunday Star* (Washington), 11 November 1945, pp. C-3, C-7.

The treatment of the Negro in American fiction, since it parallels his treatment in American life, is a matter with which Richard Wright, author of best sellers *Native Son* and *Black Boy,* is deeply concerned as the racial question is blood and bone of his writing.

"Most American writers have refused to treat the Negro as a human being—but caricature him and type him until the majority of the white population can conceive of him as something else," Mr. Wright said in an interview while on a visit here.

This typing of the Negro in American fiction to which Mr. Wright objects had its beginning as far back as Washington Irving, who in his *Salmagundi* (1807) describes a dance in Haiti falling upon descriptions of physical features for humor. The first comic Negro has survived and grown in fiction right to Octavus Roy Cohen's Florian Slappey.

"It is the Florian Slappeys that I protest against most," Mr. Wright stated emphatically. "Mr. Cohen is a widely read writer in the popular magazines and he sticks to the oldest and most dishonest tricks of the writing trade when he types Negroes—and does the most damage."

"The Uncle Remus stories of Joel Chandler Harris fall somewhat into the folklore class," he continued, "but even there I stamp my foot down when possible."

Realistic handling of the Negro character is more frequent among the modern writers now—Erskine Caldwell in his *Kneel to the Rising Sun* treating him as a member of the working class and Lillian Smith in *Strange Fruit* reporting realistically conditions as they are among others.

Concerning *Strange Fruit* Mr. Wright is enthusiastic.

"I am glad the book was written. Lillian Smith is very good when she is dealing with the mentality of the upper class Southern whites. She falters occasionally in her Negro psychology, but the book is important not because of what it does to the Negro's feelings, but for what it tells the whites. She is a rare and noble woman to live in Georgia and do what she did."

Mr. Wright is very definite when he discusses the purpose of his own work.

"No good writer makes a deliberate effort to show something. You live and write out of your experiences. I lived mine and I write them. A white boy from a decent middle-class family might produce a *Remembrance of Things Past*. I couldn't.

"In Bigger Thomas (*Native Son*) I was not trying to show a type of Negro, but even more than that—a human being reacting under pressure, reacting the only way he could because of his environment.

"My description of Negro life is no more horrible than Karl Marx's picture of the English workingman during his time."

Mr. Wright sums it up like this:

"The Negro is learning what it means to be a man, but the white people are not conditioned to this change. The part American literature can play in the re-education of the white race is obvious.

"When the average popular writer realizes this, stops resorting to the cliché of the Negro type in his work and begins characterizing him as a full human being, literature and America will have made great progress."

Asserts Negro's Fight for Equality Benefit to Nation

Des Moines Register/1945

From *The Des Moines Register*, 15 November 1945, p. 7. Reprinted with permission from The Des Moines Register.

America still lives in a primitive world in her thinking on social questions, and the Negro in his struggle for his rights, is making a contribution to all, Richard Wright, Negro novelist, said Wednesday in Des Moines.

Wright is the author of the best sellers *Native Son* and *Black Boy*.

After generations of despair, Wright said, the Negro now sees signs of hope as his struggle, on the international scale, becomes part of a class struggle, rather than just a race struggle.

Great though this country's technical progress may be, there still remains a great gap between science and the primitive folk lore which pervades American thought, Wright maintained.

From Russia, he declared, the American Negro gains hope, and Russia and other European lands are taking increased interest in the American Negro's plight, he added.

"Despair is not the entire picture now," Wright said. "After World War I, Russia arose to send out the call to the oppressed. Until then the Negro had depended on the white American. But suddenly the spell was broken, and a new, alien ideology gripped the Negro's mind. Color consciousness had been replaced by race consciousness."

Wright delivered two addresses in Des Moines. He spoke in the afternoon at the Des Moines Women's club. In the evening, at Hoyt Sherman place, he addressed a dinner meeting of the Negro Community center.

Wright, 37, was born on a plantation near Natchez, Miss. He began work at 15. A former works progress administration writer, his works also include *Uncle Tom's Children* and *Twelve Million Voices*. He is a contributor to the *Daily Worker* and *New Masses*.

Wright said slavery came to America when Europe was coming out of the feudal world; that America's conscience was troubled and to soothe it, the myth of Negro inferiority was invented.

He said this concept was deeply implanted in the white's mind; that white children at the age of six believed it and to challenge it is to hit directly at the white's primal ideas on morality.

Stressing the danger of the "cultural lag" in a country where science develops so rapidly, Wright said the Negro's struggle for his rights is a part of a larger picture.

"We must learn to live in the machine age, or it will crush us," Wright said. "The problem is serious for 15 million Negroes and the country needs a rational theory for guidance. It is so easy to find excuses for lack of action."

He said legislation to end the poll tax and anti-lynching legislation will help out, but he said "we should enter into this struggle with a good background."

"Bilbo and Rankin (Senators Theodore Bilbo and John Rankin, both of Mississippi) and the others will think up something else and be prepared," he said. "They represent a small group that controls the destinies of one third of the republic and they take the vote away from whites as well as Negroes.

"I think Bilbo already has the next move thought out and they will not surrender so lightly that which gives them so much power over the nation as a whole."

Wright said the history of the Negro in America was reflected with great sensitivity in the poets of that race. In his afternoon talk he quoted from leading American Negro poets, showing how, in their highest lyrical expression, there always is struggle against the cruelty of slavery and prejudice.

While European Negro writers could write in harmony with the culture of their own lands, only one American Negro writer has had this privilege—the first to write, he said. That was Phillis Wheatley, the Negro girl poet of eighteenth century Boston, who grew up without the bonds of oppression on her.

There's No Black Problem in the U.S.A., but a White Problem, the Black Writer Richard Wright Tells Us

Maurice Nadeau/1946

From *Combat*, 11 May 1946, p 1. Translated by Keneth Kinnamon.

On the platform of the St. Lazare Station. The special train that had boarded passengers from the *Brazil* in Le Havre was late. The morning sun had not broken through the high, smoke-darkened glass windows. A slight, fresh breeze stirred up a current of air. An eddy of ticket-takers and hotel footmen bustling about, porters pushing their dollies while the first passengers got off the train, rumpled and chewing gum. A sudden concern: I didn't see Richard Wright. I imagined him big, strong, black, a little like the G.I.'s that stride briskly along our boulevards. On the platform some groups of people were hugging tearfully and patting each other on the back, but no one was black. I was about to turn back when a big, resonant laugh made me turn around suddenly. Squatting down, his face hidden by a wide-brimmed hat, the bottom of his ample overcoat spread out on the platform, a young man was playing with his little daughter.

"Julia!" he cried.

And the big laugh began again, making the man the object of attention of passengers departing on another platform.

"Mr. Richard Wright?"

"Yes!"

I was suddenly touched as I remembered again the long flight of Big Boy, a young black boy become a game animal for the whites launching out on his trail. If he is discovered he will swing at the end of a rope, burned while half alive. I know the story of Big Boy; it is his story, in which nothing has been changed. Another story comes back to me, that of a black preacher of a village whipped by vigilantes who accuse him of being another red.

"How long are you going to stay in France?"

Richard Wright expresses himself with difficulty in French, and I

87

don't speak English at all. Fortunately, an elderly lady who is holding little Julia by the hand intervenes.

"Two months, six months, a year, maybe forever!"

And again the big laugh that made him sway back and forth.

His eyes are animated behind his metal-rimmed eyeglasses. He takes off his hat showing his kinky hair cut short. His daughter interests him more than I do.

Richard Wright tells me that this is not a good place to talk. Nevertheless, he gives me some details about his life.

"I was born in Mississippi in the Deep South."

He pointed to the ground with his hands.

"Down there the blacks are very low too, lower than in all the rest of the United States. My father was a mill worker, my mother a schoolteacher. Not a lot of money in the house. Worked a lot, a whole lot, hard work."

"When did you begin to write?"

"When I was thirteen! But I was not famous. In 1927 I left for Chicago. Always hard work, very hard. A lot of different jobs. I write four novellas: *Uncle Tom's Children*. Down there Uncle Toms are the very nice blacks, very polite to whites."

"And their children?"

"Their children have changed. In 1939 I made use of a Guggenheim Fellowship to write *Native Son*, which was very successful. I wanted to show how the extreme poverty of a young Negro and the contempt in which whites hold him made him unhappy—not stronger, but miserable. And he finally killed. And then the whites said: 'See how all blacks are criminals.'"

I took the opportunity to ask him if the black problem in the United States was nearing a solution.

He looked at me, creasing his eyebrows slightly, then raising them suddenly, his eyes brightening.

"There is not a black problem in the United States, but a white problem. The blacks now know what they want, and they are engaged in a hard struggle, the goal of which, they know, is to become men like everyone else. In contrast, the whites don't know what they want. They have a lot of difficulties, not a lot of hope."

"Are the blacks always so mistreated, held in such low esteem? Are the whites always so fierce?"

Richard Wright pretended to take a great interest in his luggage. I put the question again. He did not reply.

"It's very difficult to say."

Now he took little Julia in his arms and headed toward the exit without saying any more. I had the impression that my question had been too rude. He noticed my embarrassment and came to my aid.

"The war did not change a lot in the relations between whites and blacks. There is a lot more employment for blacks now. Perhaps things are a little better.

"Were you drafted?"

"No, I was working."

One gets the impression that he has dedicated his life to his work: to make his brothers of color aware that they should no longer be Uncle Toms, that this revolt stirring in their hearts is the only thing in the world that matters.

With his daughter in his arms, Richard Wright rushed off, but not before giving me a big pat on the back, punctuated with a peal of tremendous laughter.

Richard Wright, Negro Author, Is Here to Make Home in Paris

Anne Perlman/1946

From *New York Herald Tribune* (Paris edition), 3 June 1946, p. 2.

Richard Wright, the American Negro author whose descriptions of the social and economic plight of the American Negro have been among the most widely-discussed literature in the United States during the past decade, has arrived in Paris to make his home here.

How long he will stay or where he will live he does not yet know. He'll stay as long as he likes it—and he'll live wherever he can find an apartment.

"I was burnt out with New York," the 37-year-old novelist said yesterday in an interview at his hotel in the Latin Quarter. "I've lived in New York on and off for the past nine years, seen the same people and the same sights, and I wanted to work in a new environment."

Before New York, Mr. Wright lived in Chicago, the scene of his novel, *Native Son,* which appeared in 1940. The play, which was produced on Broadway first in 1941, will probably be presented in French on the Paris stage next winter. The novel, which has been translated, will appear soon in its French version.

A series of short stories, *Uncle Tom's Children,* which appeared in 1938, will be published in French in two volumes, with the first appearing within the next few weeks.

The novel Mr. Wright is now writing in Paris concerns Negroes in New York. The author said he had never written a story in the same scene in which the story was laid. "I like to write about a place after leaving it. You can see it with double eyes," he says.

Although Mr. Wright, his wife and four-year-old daughter, Julia, arrived only three weeks ago, he is already embroiled in mastering French grammar.

He takes private French lessons two hours a day, can already get off a "Voilà" or a "Je vous en prie" in an off-hand manner, and is impatiently awaiting the day he can have easy conversation with the French writers he has discovered at the Café de Flore.

Besides apartment hunting and learning French, Mr. Wright found time to write a brief article for last week's *Samedi Soir* on his first impression of France. He intends to write a series of articles on the situation of Negroes in America for *Paris-Matin*. And, as he came to France at the invitation of the Cultural Relations Section of the French Foreign Ministry, he plans to deliver a number of lectures in Paris.

His first impressions of France, which he is visiting for the first time, are varied, and he qualifies them with a reminder that he has been here only a few weeks.

He commented on the high cultural development of the French, "the prevalence of literacy, the beautiful statues, the bookstores at every corner."

He remarked that so far he had "not detected the least iota of racial tension against the Negroes."

The situation of the Negro in America today Mr. Wright characterized as "not bad, but hopeless." Elaborating, he said: "The Negro eats, he has a roof over his head, he has a good time, but, beyond that, he is shut off. There is a ceiling on any aspiration whether it be in the field of education, jobs, or anything else."

American Negroes and whites have never been as far apart as they are now, in Mr. Wright's opinion, largely because national progress has far outstripped the progress of the Negro. When America was primarily agricultural, the contrast between the two groups was less marked, he said. But, with the development of the United States as an industrial nation, and increasingly urban during the past seventy years, the "psychological differences between Negroes and whites have widened," and the rate of progress of Negroes "has lagged far behind national progress."

Mr. Wright said that the problem of the 15,000,000 American Negroes is "symbolic," pointing out that more than two-thirds of the world's two billion human beings "are in the same position."

Two Hours with a Great American

Michel Gordey/1946

Abridged verson published in *Les Etoiles*, 22 October 1946. Translated by Michel Fabre. The complete interview is printed here in translation by permission of Mrs. Gordey. All rights reserved.

Richard Wright, the black American writer whose works are outcries of pain and suffering; Richard Wright, whose ruthless and forceful accusations already risen and flooded twice over America in the shape of best-selling books; Richard Wright, whom one imagines as a man with clenched fists and set jaws, locked in bitterness—Richard Wright opens to me the door of his apartment in Greenwich Village, the Montparnasse of New York City. At once I can feel the calm, the kindness, the reason radiate from this middle-sized, dark-complexioned man with soft, intelligent eyes behind rimless glasses, the glasses of an American college professor.

We spoke for a long time, more than two hours. After a few minutes, I no longer knew who is being interviewed, Wright or me. Questions are bandied about. Wright wishes to leave for France in a few weeks and asks me about Paris, about French writers, daily life and problems, about political struggles and intellectual debates on the Left Bank. I realize he knows French literature and is even cognizant of Existentialist squabbles. He is bursting with impatience.

It is the dream of my life, *he says,* this trip to France. My wife and I were about to leave in the summer of 1939. About to leave for Paris. But Hitler decided otherwise. I have been waiting for six years. Now I am counting weeks and days. In May, I hope to be in Paris with my family, my wife and four-year-old daughter. I also want to go to the South of France. I want to meet those French writers whom I admire so much because, it seems to me, the literature of your country has always expressed the crises and problems of its time immediately instead of distilling them in a sophisticated way, channeling them very slowly into literary works as we tend to do in the United States.

92

I tell Wright that his books begin to be known and liked in France. He is quite surprised. He knows, indeed, that Native Son *was translated and published in Paris, that* Black Boy *will soon be published by Gallimard—this is his ruthlessly true and painful autobiography, his biggest success and his greatest book—but he is deeply moved at the thought that he already has friends and admirers in France.*

Next we talk about his most recent success in the United States. Black Boy, *which came out six months ago, was a best-seller in American cities for a long time.*

550,000 copies have been bought by readers, many of whom, *Wright notes,* certainly read it with more pain than pleasure. Never before has a book written by a black author met with such commercial success. Even before publication 350,000 copies of *Native Son* had been printed. The stage adaptation of the novel, directed by Orson Welles, has been performed in New York and in major American cities with unbelievable success.

Such sales and success are all the more remarkable because Wright never dressed up the truth, because his books are fiery with indignation and revolt, because he has become a spokesman for Twelve Million Black Voices, *(the title of one of his books), and because most of those who bought his books were undoubtedly white people.*

I tell Wright about the sadness and despair that get hold of a French person confronted by the racial problem in the United States. Wright gets up, looks at me, and says, very slowly:

There are no insoluble problems. I refuse to believe that any exist. The "Negro problem" in America can be solved. It should be investigated, but no one wishes to deal with it. There does not exist in this vast country one single association or group, black or white, that even wants to put in writing a proposal for action. This or that particular aspect of the situation has been addressed. It has been spoken and written about for three-quarters of a century. But no one has had the courage to say: this or that should be done. There are tens of millions of black and white Americans who are, at heart, full of good will and who would like to act and do something. Nobody, listen to me, nobody ever told them what they should do.

Is the situation better or worse now than it was before the war, in your opinion?

It is difficult to answer such a question. With the industrial age, black people (I am speaking of blacks in the North because those in the South live in quite different conditions) have literally been confined to large cities, or rather to a few congested districts in these industrial centers. As unskilled laborers in factories or day laborers hired to do the most strenuous and lowest paid jobs, blacks have no choice. They wanted to become farmers, to live in the country, but every time they attempted this they were driven out of the villages and small towns. They were driven to the large cities where, living among themselves, they could at least survive. In the small rural communities of the North, even in areas where anti-Negro feeling is not violent, life was made impossible for them. As a result of their being concentrated and isolated in the large urban centers, the gap became larger between new generations of whites and blacks. Previously there were still vestiges of paternalism and remnants of the great plantations, residues of former contacts and living in common. Now there are compact blocks of blacks in the midst of the white population and, so to speak, no contact.

But don't labor unions attempt to foster such contacts, at least up to a certain point?

A few unions have tried to do that. In the CIO, there are 750,000 black workers. The total number of unionized blacks in the United States is 750,000. In the American Federation of Labor, known for its reactionary policies, black workers are generally not admitted. This is the reason why there isn't a single black railroad engineer or a black carpenter, and this has been going on for three generations. But one must confess that even within the CIO, mostly composed of left-wing elements, we are still relegated to a lower position. Blacks represent some 15% of the CIO members, yet there is not one black worker on the Executive Committee of this labor union. Also, in matters of defense industry problems of seniority and promotion, the CIO will not support blacks as it will white workers. Yet, *Wright adds,* it is important that these three quarters of a million blacks (which means at least two million people involved if one takes their families into ac-

count) can fight in terms of the class struggle instead of fighting on
the level of race.

*Wright's eyes grow somber. He lights a cigarette, thinks a while, and
speaks slowly as though he were contemplating the destitution of his
racial brothers in his mind's eye.*

We have everything and everyone against us. It is simple. In the field
of economics, we are not allowed to progress. We are cheap labor and
are being treated and kept as such. Besides, this is the basis and the
reason for the "Negro problem" in the United States. Everything has
been woven around this basic truth. If, by some extraordinary miracle,
one black person gets rich and wants to start a business, he is then
refused staple goods and markets. If, after innumerable sacrifices, a
black doctor or lawyer succeeds in proving his abilities, he may struggle
as he wishes, but his patrons will only be black people.

And there is also this. A people can only rise by dint of education.
Well, Negro education in the United States has been entirely in the
hands of so-called philanthropic organizations, financed by the Rocke-
fellers, the Carnegies, and the big businessmen in the South. In every
school, for generations, obedience, submission, and acceptance have
been preached to black students. In this way our elite are corrupted at
the root. For years, in black schools and colleges, our youngsters listen
to bland speeches about racial cooperation and equal opportunities. Each
black student is told he must consider himself privileged. He ends up
believing it. This is the end, for without intellectual weapons what hope
is left to black Americans, who have already been deprived of economic, social, and political weapons?

*I ask Wright whether political action cannot yield results, considering
that there are twelve million blacks in America.*

Yes, *he replies,* but with the two-party system an immense swindle
is repeated at all elections. Democrats and Republicans include in their
platforms fine-sounding declarations in order to attract a maximum
number of black voters. Their machines multiply promises of all kinds.
We vote—in those States where we are allowed to vote; in the South,
with the poll tax, blacks can hardly vote—we vote, and once the results

are in, whoever the winner is, he forgets completely about us until the next elections.

The only party which has made an effort in favor of blacks is the American Communist party. Regrettably, in twenty-five years of struggle, it has achieved strictly nothing. In the South, before the war, there were Communist organizers, white men, whom I admired in the way I would have admired German Communists under Hitler. But the war came and a well-known tactical change took place: the CP completely liquidated its organizations in the South. In May 1945, a French Communist leader, Jacques Duclos, had to raise the American Communists from their slumber. But the absence of any concrete result over twenty five years seems to me a clear condemnation of the CPUSA, at least as far as blacks are concerned.

I ask Wright which are the dynamic elements among black Americans who struggle and are capable of achieving any results. Are blacks war veterans among them? What problems does their coming back home entail, after the freedom and social equality they have enjoyed in France and Italy?

Here are the dynamic elements, *he replies.* There are a few intellectuals but their action is necessarily limited. There is the Brotherhood of Sleeping Car Porters, under the leadership of Philip Randolph, a militant and a truly exceptional man. It managed to force Roosevelt to proclaim, for the duration of the war, the principle of equal pay for equal work, whatever the worker's race. This union, which regroups the more politically conscious workers, is leading a vanguard struggle in the social field for the whole black population in the United States. There is also the black press. Our newspapers address a black readership exclusively and, as a result, they are not influenced and channeled by capitalistic interests comparable to those that shape our education. The black press, which was the first to raise the flag of rebellion, to tell the truth, to protest ever more strongly, is one of our most powerful assets.

Wright then talks about the return of black veterans.

These boys who were torn from their farms and their mills in order to fight for democracy (*a bitter smile appears on Wright's lips*) have seen non-slaveholding civilizations in Paris, London, and Rome. They could see, they could experience freedom in foreign countries. They are now coming back home, and conflict, strife, and hatred are resulting. Every day the newspapers report that in the South our boys discharged from the army have been insulted or beaten up because they would not "stay in their place," as they say in those States. In the North, too, bitterness and cynicism are very high among young people. You see, the worst of all is that all these developments could be predicted. Something more could have been done. The government could have taken care of it. Here again, it did nothing. No proposals, no plans to facilitate the return of veterans.

We end up talking about the dangers of fascism in the United States, a topic related to the return of the veterans. They could, should there be unemployment and an economic crisis, provide the rank-and-file of an American neo-fascist movement.

The greatest danger, *Wright says,* is not due to the reactionaries in the South who have only one obsession: the black peril. With such a slogan, they could, for instance, quench in blood any attempt to organize black Southern workers into trade unions. But they will attract no one in the North with such a program. No, the real danger comes from the Lindberghs, the Vandenbergs, the Northern Republicans who despise and hate the common people and who, with huge amounts of money at their disposal, might be able to exploit the discontent of certain strata of the population. It may happen. Here anything can happen.

My country, *Wright continues,* shows concern for all the world. It is one of the most beautiful traits of our national character. One is concerned about the Chinese and the Armenians, and rightly so. Yet one never thinks of the destitution of blacks who are right here, outside our door, on the sill. One is concerned with free elections in Greece, but Mr. Byrnes, our Secretary of State, who has so much trouble because of the wretched Greeks, is opposed to abolishing the poll tax, which prevents almost all blacks in the Southern states from voting. Mr. Byrnes does not forget that he was formerly a Southern senator.

As to anti-fascist forces, *Wright pursues,* they are desperately disunited in America. Blacks, Jews, labor unions would be the first to be wiped out by fascism, whatever shape it may take in America. Those three elements detest one another. And each group is not even united. As it did after World War I, the left wing shouts obsolete slogans. Just like then, they will be eaten up by the others, those who want to push us

into a war with Soviet Russia, or into a ferocious reaction. If one thinks
seriously about it, I believe that in the final analysis human beings never
learn from experience.

I leave Richard Wright, who in large letters, inscribes Black Boy *for
me: "Freedom belongs to the strong," he writes. Only strong people
are free. May he keep the strength necessary to his struggle, the
struggle for the true liberation of his oppressed brothers.*

Richard Wright Tells Us: The White Problem in the United States

Raphaël Tardon/1946

From *Action* (Paris), 24 October 1946, pp. 10–11. Translated by Keneth Kinnamon.

Several months ago, arriving at the Saint-Lazare Station, Richard Wright responded to a reporter for a morning newspaper who asked him what he thought about the "Negro problem" in the United States. Wright shot back humorously:

"There isn't any Negro problem; there is only a white problem."

Paradox?

The author of *Black Boy, Native Son, Uncle Tom's Children,* etc. was willing to explain himself.

"The problem is white because only whites can resolve it. Whites number 130,000,000 compared to 15,000,000 blacks. They hold the political, industrial, and social power. They are everything. Has anyone ever heard of practical jokes played by blacks on whites? The problem is a white problem because it is the whites who pose it every day."

"How does this problem affect blacks?"

Richard Wright laughed briefly, showing his splendid set of teeth.

"How? Listen closely. It is very important.

"The American Negro is an American. After the passage of the Thirteenth Amendment, he has had all the rights of an American. His racial equality is acknowledged. The right to work. The right to vote. The honor of bearing arms—and he has proven that he is as capable of bearing them as anyone else. The right to live free within a great democracy.

"All of these rights are constitutional.

"But practically—racial equality? It doesn't even exist on the battle-fields of Europe or the atolls of the Pacific.

"The right to vote? Senator Bilbo of Mississippi has just expressed himself publicly on how to prohibit blacks from exercising this right. Jean-Paul Sartre, Paul Beringuier, Michel Gordey, and others have explained to the French how all black participation in voting is eliminated

by poll taxes and Pirandello-like qualifying examinations. There is
another way that your compatriots have not been bold enough to speak
of—direct threats to one's body or one's house. Senator Bilbo has just
acknowledged this method. It is an unbelievable fact that one Negro
dared to vote in the last Mississippi elections. Maybe he was tired of
living."

"Has something happened to him?"

But Richard Wright ignored the question. He mused, motionless,
leaning on his desk close to his typewriter. Papers are stacked on his
table. His fifth novel is being completed. Next month Wright is going
to Switzerland, then to England, and finally to America.

"Mr. Byrnes, Secretary of State in the State Department?"

Wright is coming out of his meditation.

"In Europe Mr. Byrnes plays the part of a champion of the freedom to
vote—voting without constraint, total, general voting—of Yugoslavians
and Bulgarians. Mr. Byrnes knows well that in his own country there
are 15,000,000 men who, in fact, can't vote. Mr. Byrnes should first
occupy himself with what is happening in his own house before setting
himself up as a tutor for foreign peoples. Mr. Byrnes shuts his eyes and
stops up his ears in his own country. In Europe, he opens his mouth. As
you can see, the greatest suffering for an American Negro is psychological in nature."

"Isn't that what you are explaining in your short story 'The Man Who
Killed a Shadow'?"

"That's it. It's very serious. As long as the American Negro has not
managed to locate, define, and rise above the sickness which affects
him, he will always be the victim of an inferiority complex.

"But psychologically it seems impossible to overcome this inferiority
complex. But even if Negroes could know of the existence of this key,
they are not authorized to get hold of it. Individually, perhaps, the thing
is possible up to a certain point. But listen to this! Don't you see that
opposite to this black inferiority complex there is a white superiority
complex? The annihilation of one complex depends on the disappearance of the other. Unfortunately—and here we touch on the notion
of powerlessness—the superiority complex is, in its essence, specifically American. It is a mental formation that doesn't need to be taught.
It is atavisic, geographical, spontaneous. It's a reaction. It's visual. It's
latent. It's olfactory, auditory. It is monumental. This is prejudice!"

"Without failing to recognize the importance of the psychological factor, are there a great many social means of dealing with it?"

The author of *Uncle Tom's Children* shrugged his shoulders with a weary gesture.

"Theoretically. For this purpose we have trade unions, the Labor Party, etc. And then what? There are 750,000 Negroes in the trade unions, almost all of them in the North. But these organizations are Negrophobic.

"In the South, where nine million of my race live, the C.I.O. tried to recruit from this mass of people. No success. You would think that in the nine Southern states, with a large black population, Negroes would be able to get away from their 'high rank' (he laughs) of third-class citizens and quickly reach the status of real citizenship; if they could vote and hold public office, two-thirds of these positions would fall into their hands. And this presents again the economic and political aspects of the problem.

"The churches? Theoretically again they preach the good word to Negroes out of the divine plan. They strive to attract the black masses and to focus on them. They procure modest jobs for them in posts enhancing their obedience. But the churches—and their whole policy is directed to this goal—pretend to consider Negroes as unruly and naive children whom it is important to catechize, to have on a leash and to maintain in a state supposititiously voluntarily puerile. Their Negro policy still seems inspired by resolves of the last century. And the perennial nature of this policy is easy to prove. These resolves? They are orders, rather, edicts, approved and proclaimed in the time of slavery, and they still remain the backdrop of the actors performing on the proscenium.

"It is in the matter of the 'commandments' whose spirit still inspires the descendants of those who enslaved them.

"Presbyterian ministers meeting in Harmony, South Carolina, in that era resolved that the kingdom of our Lord is not of this earth; His church, as such, does not have the right to abolish, to change, or to blame any human institution, political or civil; that, inasmuch as the relative duties of master and slave are taught in the Scriptures, as well as those of parents and children, husband and wife, the existence of slavery is not in itself contrary to the will of God; and that whoever suffers from scruples of conscience about recognizing these relations as lawful is 'righteous beyond what is necessary, wise beyond what is written in Scripture.'

"The memorial of the Baptist Association of Charleston addressed to the legislature of South Carolina begins with these lines: 'The undersigned do not believe that Holy Scripture brings into the least question the morality of slavery. Jesus Christ in particular found this state of things in full strength in the society in which he lived, and he did not undertake any plans to reform it. He left this question entirely to the consideration of human beings.'

"The Methodists in their Southern Conference resolved unanimously that 'the annual conference of Georgia does not look upon slavery as it exists in the United States as a moral evil.'

"All of these resolutions, as I have said, are past, but if the men who made them are dead, their echo blows from the same direction."

Looking out over his glasses, he concentrates again, thinking. We listen, motionless.

"Well. The churches. The good Negro was always a child, laughing and singing. That's the image that is spreading in Europe, even here in France. You turn the dial of your radio, and right away you are listening to jazz in a rowdy dive. And then some merry songs. It's always like that. It's for export. Then you tell yourself, 'The American Negro is happy, as happy as a child.'

"Everyone is mistaken. Inversely, it is imposed on the United States that the most democratic countries in Europe—France, Sweden, or Denmark—are Negrophobic. More anti-Negro than the States. You understand that under these conditions the American Negro cannot even cherish in the bottom of his heart the melancholy certitude that across the ocean there are some countries where a Negro can be considered as important as any other man.

"Nevertheless, tens of thousands of black American soldiers have lived for some time in Europe. They can, they can (Wright repeats) make out the difference between treatment and life. But only in their conscience. That is another source of bitterness. But let the ex-servicemen look out if they let their feelings show! Since their return to the United States, more than forty-five of them have already been lynched."

"Nevertheless, we have it from a good source that the French Antilles battalions that had to take their training in the U.S.A. were very well regarded. Some stayed almost a year and had access to all circles."

Richard Wright nodded his head.

"I know. It was a wartime situation. It was known that these Antilles troops were only going to be there for a more or less brief time and that they were French since they were wearing pinned to their shoulders the insignia 'French West Indies.' Some American Negroes wrangled with the help of dollars to pass for French in order the penetrate some forbidden circles. Listen to me, I just met a Frenchman of color just back from the U.S., where he stayed four months. Well, he told me, 'It's worse than under the German occupation of Paris.' "

After a moment, a question fell from my lips: "Everyone knows that there are some rich and famous blacks in the U.S.: Marian Anderson, Duke Ellington."

A great laugh, broad and free, poured forth.

"Yes, yes. There are some. But, as you say, it's a dog's life. They have 'arrived' at the cost of tireless work and constantly threatening vicissitudes. And then what? To arrive in their case means only that their value as a singer or musician has been recognized. Their existence as blacks has not changed. Their psychological suffering will last until they die. It's like this for all Negroes, from the poorest to the richest, and there are not very many who are rich. As for the material conditions of life in the large cities, they are ghettoized.

"New York, for example, is divided into five boroughs. Most of the Negroes in the city—around 500,000—live in Manhattan in the middle of two million whites. Their living conditions are at this point lamentable, desperate, so that 53% of crime is the work of young blacks, of adolescents. One cries out: 'Negroes are savages, primitive, bloodthirsty; they have only bad instincts.' It is obviously easier to say this than to say that we should put the ghetto in order, provide hygiene, grant funds for the education and training of these blacks. What we have done so far is insufficient. Give them the right to work anywhere. But think about it!

"Harlem occupies an area that is really too restricted. Yet the population density there is the greatest on the globe. They live in a 'black' misery. That's why the mortality rate there is also the highest in the entire world. But each year the black migration from the South to New York of people looking for freedom and illusory high salaries is so considerable that Harlem always remains the geographical place with the highest density at the same time that it is an infernal melting pot for the disintegration of blacks.

"For the most part blacks can be employed only by other blacks; in the same way, they can only trade among themselves. Thus it is impossible to get rich."

Richard Wright offers us a Camel.

"Look, Mr. Wright, speaking hypothetically, what if it turned out that the owner of this brand of cigarettes, Camels, was a Negro?"

"Well, whites would smoke something else."

Somewhere in the Latin Quarter a clock struck out the twelve chimes of noon. We got up.

"One last word. Are there any abundantly rich Negroes in the U.S.A.?"

"There are some. First off, there was one, now dead, named Madame Walker, who invented beauty products capable of bleaching the skin of blacks as well as cosmetics to straighten kinky hair. She made a large fortune. Her trade secrets? She sold them before her death."

But Richard Wright continued. "There are also the organizers of the numbers racket, which earns a lot of money. Finally, the richest black man in America, Mr. Sheppard. Mr. Sheppard made a colossal fortune as an undertaker." He laughed fiercely before going on. "An undertaker for blacks. It's a job that enriches whoever exercises it."

"Goodby, Mr. Wright, and thanks very much. Fortunately, the intellectual domain is left to you."

He was surprised.

"The intellectual domain? Funny! Do you know how many blacks there are in the great American universities? Listen. At Yale, for example, one black is admitted each year, sometimes two. At Harvard, the same thing. As for Princeton, no black has ever been authorized to set his foot there. As for the Southern states, the matter never even comes up. 'Never any Negroes.' Therefore there are universities for blacks, schools for blacks, churches for blacks, neighborhoods for blacks, and cemeteries for blacks.

He reflected a second.

"There is now even a God for whites, who is Jesus, and a black God for blacks, who is Father Divine."

Richard Wright showed us to the door.

"Are you staying in France for a long time yet?"

"I'll go back (he shook his head) to the United States in about three months."

"How's that? After all that you have just told us? We had been thinking that you would have cried out with us: Vive la France!"

He pondered a moment by the stairwell, melancholy.

"My life is back there," he said.

An Interview with Richard Wright

Peter Schmid/1946

From *Pan-Africa,* 1 (August 1947), 37–38; (September 1947), 29–
31. Originally published as "Die Stimme der Entrechten," *Die Welt-
woche* (Zurich), 15 November 1946, p. 5. Reprinted by permission.

The other day, when Richard Wright was making some purchases in a
Zurich shop, the young lady attendant who waited on him asked shyly:
"Are you Don Redman?" He laughed. At the moment the Negro jazz-
band leader was the rage. His picture decorated the walls of all shops,
restaurants, hotels. At the same time the most distinguished Negro
writer of America was dwelling among us without attracting the attention of any but a few devotees of literature.

Richard Wright is known here through the only one of his works
which has been translated into German, *Native Son.* In this novel, he
tells the story of a young Chicago Negro who, because of an inferiority
complex growing out of the race conflict in the United States, is led to
commit an atrocious murder and end his life in the electric chair. It is a
strange and fearful world which is revealed to us in this book, a world
of the despised, depressed, pursued. We are introduced to the psychology of a people which for generations has known nothing but the
immitigable and cruel law of white supremacy.

In Paris, Wright told me, he happened to meet a Negro from the
French Colonies. He was brought to France as a child, grew up there,
went to school and was trained as a psychiatrist. When the Germans
moved in he naturally joined the underground. He fought so bravely in
the guerrilla warfare that after the liberation the French Government
gave him a Distinguished Service Medal and, as further recognition,
awarded him a scholarship for study in the U.S.A. He went there—a
Negro from the free air of France. He could not stand the way the
Negroes were treated over there. After four months his nerves broke.
The terror of the Gestapo, he said to me, was child's play by
comparison.

Is it as bad as all that? I asked. We hear, to be sure, about the violence of the poor-whites in the South and of the mummeries of the Klu-

Kluxers. But, really now, America is a democracy in which the rights of the individual are protected by the Constitution.

Wright laughed, laughed a clear, free laugh without bitterness. Yes, that's just it! he went on in his melodious English. The constitution is ideal and it promised us a paradise on American soil. But the most notable thing about American life—and not only in relation to the Negro—is the breach between preaching and practice. Among the Anglo-Saxon peoples the confession of faith in the sacredness of individual freedom is perfectly sincere, and they are ready to fight for it . . . at least for themselves. For actually this individualism has been developed on the basis of the supression of an entire race into menial service. Equality . . . . Freedom . . . . yes, the Constitution gives us the vote, a right which, in some sections of the South would give the 9,000,000 Negroes the majority. But just for that reason, means have been found to keep our people away from the polls. 15,000,000 Negroes among 140,000,000 Americans are represented in Congress by only two legislators. Human rights are for the whites, not for us.

—But hasn't the war, in which black troops fought beside the whites and which black workers gave such a good account of themselves in the factories, furnished a means of bridging the gulf between the races?

No. On the contrary. The tensions have never been so sharp since the days of the Civil War. The demobilised soldiers come home, look for work, and see Negroes who, as a result of war conditions, have been able to work their way into better positions. And hatred grows. Eight Negroes have been lynched in a single month.

—And how about the demobilised Negroes?

They return as different men. In the army many of them lived a fine life—in some cases as masters of white people. Their inferiority complex is gone. They demand their rights as human beings—and so sharpen the conflict.

—And do you see no escape from this situation? Is it not, for example, possible that Negro culture as demonstrated in the fields of music, the dance, and literature will so permeate American life that it will draw together the two opposite poles? Have not a long list of Negro artists, Paul Robeson, Marian Anderson, etc., brokn through race lines in securing recognition of their artistic achievement?

Yes, they have won recognition as artists but not as human beings. People accept them on the stage, but seldom in their homes. Despite their wealth, they must live in some segregated section. I know this from personal experience. People read my books, but beyond that they want no dealings with me.

As to the infiltration of Negro culture into American life, don't over-look real distinctions. Never forget that suppression has robbed the black man of his character. Often he expresses himself, not as he actu-ally is, but as the white man want him to be.

I once asked a coloured waiter who seemed specially hearty and friendly in his work, why he smiled all the time. "I am not smiling," he answered, "I am just showing my teeth." The sleeping-car porters in the Pullman cars are thought of as the best-trained and most docile Negroes, but precisely these men are the most rebellious and belong to the most militant union. This sort of enforced duplicity extends into the cultural world. Because the white American likes to picture the Negro as happy-go-lucky or lyrically sentimental, the Negro, who is by nature a good actor, plays the part that is expected. But never forget when you hear the jazz or the spirituals that back of them simmers bitter rebellion. Do not overlook the fact that hatred is the element in which the Negroes live, the hatred of the disinherited from which no black man can isolate himself!

—But does not this suppression dictate a positive attitude towards fate? Does not Christianity offer submission and freedom of the spirit within the conditions of material oppression as a way of release for all the weary and heavy laden?

Sadly he shook his head. There is a degree of suppression for which there is no sublimation. It is so immediately and insistently painful that it is impossible to assume an attitude of spiritual contemplation, to regard the situation as an example of human tragedy. The Negro, more-over, is no saint. When he is struck, he does not turn the other cheek. When he can, he will strike back. When he can't, his resentment will stew and grow within him. It is true that the Baptists and Methodists count 9,000,000 members among the American Negroes. But these churches are social organisations rather than bands of faithful believers. The Negro, despite his formal profession of the Christian virtues of meekness and altruism, is by nature not a Christian. His motivation springs, not from religious faith, but from the shared feeling of victimi-sation. Such altruism and benevolence as he may exhibit are the results of need, a part of the imposed technique of survival.

—But is not this consciousness of oppression a universal spiritual situation—in America as in Europe? "The burden of existence," to quote Heidegger, "is one of the fundamentals of Existentialism." It seems to me that we have here, at least for the intellectuals, a bridge from the world of the blacks to that of the whites.

There you are right. During the twenties American literature finally discovered our unhappiness, first in Dreiser, then in Lewis, Faulkner, Caldwell, Dos Passos, etc. The individual discovers that he is a sacrifice to society. Among young American intellectuals the visit of Sartre has not been fruitless. This consciousness of sacrifice is developing about two opposite poles: among the whites the pole of psychological consciousness, among the blacks that of the realistic-social. As you suppose, this parallel development affects on both sides only the narrow circle of those who are alive to the present spiritual situation. In general, Americans, despite their writers, carry their *malaise* as something undefined within their consciousness—like an invalid who conceals his symptoms from his physician. The Europeans have reached a higher stage of awareness.

—Then you have the impression that Europe, despite its apparent exhaustion, still has something to say to the world?

I think so. My journey has been full of surprises. I expected to see a decadent, hungry, dying continent, and I discover that I not only eat well, but that the spiritual life is extraordinarily active—especially in Paris. I am really frightened at the extent to which the French are losing themselves in abstractions, at the way in which they forget the struggle for bread in the struggle for ideologies. The realities of life constantly deteriorate. The more they vote, the less they get. This hectic situation is dangerous. It might lead to a revolutionary explosion.

—So you see similar pictures in Europe and America. On both continents we go in the direction of a catastrophe. Do you see any possibility of escaping this fate?

That we are driving relentlessly toward a decision no one can deny. But I do not foresee a catastrophe. Humanity is now forced towards the point at which it must make a decision to change the basis of its existence. But in this situation there is a source of healing. The suffering which is at the heart of it schools us to recognise the actuality, and the technique of survival which I mentioned as a part of the Negro's reaction to his situation will develop in the broader field of the whole human race. Every ordinary mortal possesses something which is precious, wife and child, a piece of land, a little house. These are positive forces to which we must appeal to find a way out of the ideological crisis. We do not know what the future holds, and the more we plan, the deeper will be our disappointment. All that we can do is to keep alive our faith in the nature of the human animal.

No Film Has Ever Depicted the Life of Blacks in American Cities

Lucienne Escoube/1946

From *L'Ecran français,* 19 November 1946, p. 12. Translated by Keneth Kinnamon.

Outside a small number of initiates, the name of Richard Wright is still little known in France. Nevertheless, this black writer belongs among the most representative figures of the younger generation in American literature. Born in a Southern state, Richard Wright experienced a difficult youth. Before becoming a writer he tried a lot of jobs— including cashier and elevator boy—and he suffered the humiliations common to his brothers of color. It is on the black problem that his three novels published in the U.S.A. turn. Their printings have reached several million copies. Translations of these works will soon appear in France, where Richard Wright has definitely decided to make his home.

An apartment still flooded with sunlight, the pale sunlight of autumn. From nearby Boulevard Saint-Michel rise the familiar morning sounds of the Latin Quarter. That neighborhood which, for all the foreigners settled there, remains the cradle of freedom! Freedom of speech, freedom to adhere to different political beliefs and faiths, freedom to be a man among men. There, despite hard times and the tiring problems of daily life, this spirit of eternal youth still reigns, a refreshing fount for intellectuals and artists from all over the world. Without a doubt this is what keeps Richard Wright here.

We talked about the cinema first of all, the American cinema of Hollywood.

Is the problem of censorship still as important as it was?

Sure. Moreover, for some time censorship has been increasing under the influence of a person nicknamed "Pope Breen," an Irishman by the

name of Joseph I. Breen, an insufferable censor! Just think! He did not
find *Nicholas Nickleby* proper enough to be shown to the American
public! This way of keeping the public on leading-strings, of keeping it
always in an atmosphere of catechism, of perseverance, is harmful to
spiritual health, as are harmful the taboos in all countries, whatever they
may be!

From this point of view, what impression do you have of French film?
French films are the freest I've been able to see. But the French spirit
too, till now, is one of those which have known best how to defend
itself from taboos!

*Why do these limitations exist in the United States, where freedom
still seems very great?*
In fact, in many points freedom is very great. Two domains exist
where freedom of expression is almost total: on the one hand, on the
Broadway stage, and on the other hand, in the novel!

*Does this perhaps explain the important number of novels that appear
each year?*
Without any doubt. Every protest, every criticism, every denunciation
of a social injustice gets to express itself through the medium of the
novel. This is the way that my books have been able to appear, while
the films that can be made remain in the category of American taboos.

Why?
For a number of reasons. First, as I have indicated, because of the
censorship of Hollywood. Censorship is especially strict because there
exists within each state of the United States a local board of censors
always apt to prohibit a film in which the sense or the tendency doesn't
suit them and which seems to them likely to stimulate changes of opinion, to cause trouble. Hollywood does not want to have any difficulty
selling its films to each one of the forty-eight states! In this way cen-
tralized censorship remains rigorous.
    A second reason is that the taboos exert themselves to the detriment
of minority groups. There, like everywhere else, minorities are more or
less bullied, except when they manage to get hold of the control levers
for a while. Occasionally that is true for the Jews, occasionally for the
Catholics. At present, Breen's influence is shifting the balance to the
Catholic side. But this is never true for the blacks! With the exception

of *Hallelujah* and *Green Pastures,* there have never been any great black films! Even those two do not depict the life of blacks in the large cities. No film has ever done so. Americans really love to put blacks in their films on the condition that they are servants or common laborers content with their lot. To present a black in any other way would be impossible. Public opinion would certainly be shocked. It is understood—and this has the force of law—*that a film should not be made that would go against majority opinion!*

What is the result?

The result is that Hollywood makes any number of films that are charming but without any surprises. One knows that they will always have a happy ending. One knows that they will never expose the real problems of married life, and, finally, that the standard rules of morality will always have the upper hand. That deprives most of these works of truth and verisimilitude.

What does the American public think about this?

The masses don't think a lot about it. The intellectual elite have been protesting for years against the general insipidity of cinematic works, but the American public is dumb. It is not in the habit of thinking; it scarcely has a critical sense. From the social point of view, there still hardly exists a sense of class, in spite of the millions that belong to labor unions. This absence of class consciousness is partly related to the fact that the standard of living of the worker is quite considerably higher than that of the worker in the rest of the world, and also to the possibility of moving up offered to all—leaving aside the taboos inflicted on minorities! Every American worker can become not any longer a Ford or a Rockefeller, of course, but a person who can afford a car and whose children and get into the most expensive universities—if Dad is successful.

If there is no class consciousness, is the general mood of the public satisfied? It is optimistic?

I don't think so. I wouldn't want to distort my view by declaring that the American citizen is one of the most unhappy beings that there are. I am fully aware that at present the world is undergoing a profound crisis. In America, the physical life of the worker has become easy. Machines aid him in most of his tasks. The war has been won. But with

all this, with no more to do, the individual is left before a void, a feeling of uneasiness that he cannot gratify. He does not know where to turn
to regain his equilibrium and his spirit. In general Americans are especially remarkable in moments of crisis; they know what is required to
conquer. But they all experience at present this great depression that
arrives unexpectedly after victory.

At this point, Richard Wright smiled a smile that contradicted the pessimism of his pronouncements. Large, strong, his face expressed poise,
health. And when he laughed, one could not imagine that anyone who
laughed in that way was not, at bottom, a firm optimist.

Richard Wright in Paris

Maurice Fleurent/1946

From *Paru*, 25 (December 1946), 7–8. Translated by Keneth Kin-namon

A curious literary career, that of the great black American writer! Before even one of his works had been translated into French he was
known and valued, and a vast audience awaited with interest the publication of the three novels that had found more than a million readers on
the other side of the Atlantic. We owe it to the truth to say that one of
his novellas appeared during the occupation in the excellent review
L'Arbalète and that *Les Temps modernes* a few months ago published a
long story, "Fire and Cloud." Almost unknown but already celebrated,
Richard Wright submitted amiably to this interview, punctuating his
sentences with a big laugh while his looks sparkled with mischief.

"I was born in Natchez, Mississippi, in 1908. My parents were small
sharecroppers, and I spent my childhood in the country. Then, still very
young, I went to work."

"School first, no doubt?"

"Very little."

And his musical laugh burst out.

"Above all, I worked. I suppose I had too much good sense to go
to college! And I worked in all kinds of jobs—dishwasher, insurance
salesman—a hundred others that I no longer remember. Without brag-
ging, I can assure you that I know how to do anything."

"You were already writing?"

"Sure. In 1938 *Uncle Tom's Children* was published."

"And it was a success?"

"Not entirely, since the printing at that time was only twenty thousand copies. But in 1940 three hundred thousand copies of *Native Son*
were printed."

"The black public could not fail to be interested in you, but what kind
of reception did the reviewers have in store for you?"

"*O.K.!*"

And at once Richard Wright translated in his very hesitant French: "Trés bien . . . Trés . . . bon!"

"We know the expression. Thanks! In your opinion, who are the other good black writers?"

"There are quite a few—Langston Hughes, Claude McKay, Countee Cullen, and still others who have unquestionable merit."

It was pointless to ask him about the black problem in the U.S.A. He has expressed himself at length on this subject, which constitutes the essential theme of his work.

"Could you tell me about *Black Boy*?"

"It's an autobiography published late last year. It immediately had great success in America and the world over."

"Except France, where we have just become aware of this work at the end of this year. Right?"

"Exactly. It has already been transplanted into Russian, Spanish, Danish, but I don't know exactly. All that is complicated."

"Which French writers do you prefer?"

"Classic or modern? I love Maupassant, Proust, Gide, and above all the marvelous Malraux. And I have the pleasure of knowing—and appreciating—Sartre and Simone de Beauvoir. Perhaps I will have the pleasure of meeting a lot of other French writers if I stay here long enough."

"One month, two months?"

"Maybe more. More if I can. But I am not here solely for my own pleasure; I also come to France as an agent of the American review *Twice a Year*."

"Are you happy with your reception in Paris?"

Richard Wright's smile brightened still more, and he murmured in French:

"Quelle belle ville! quelle ville aimable!"

We hope that his three works, now being translated or printed, will soon be offered to French readers. The value of the work of Richard Wright will not leave them indifferent.

An Interview with Richard Wright: America Is Not the New World

Michel Gordey/1947

From *Les Lettres françaises*, 10 January 1947, pp. 1, 7. Translated by Michel Fabre with permission of Mrs. Gordey. All rights reserved.

Richard Wright, who belongs among the half dozen major American writers of today, is without any doubt the greatest black prose writer in the United States. He received me in his small apartment on Boulevard Saint-Michel a few days before his return to the United States. Once more, during a two-hour interview, I was struck by the calm, serene lucidity of this man whose outcries of revolt and protest have been resounding for a decade with increasing vigor. These words of revolt have been heard since Wright became a best-seller in the United States. His books are appearing now throughout the world—in France, Italy, England, Denmark, and Sweden.

Richard Wright is now completing his first stay in France and in Europe. He has spent most of 1946 in our country. He has lived here observing, listening, avidly absorbing for the first time in his life the mood of a country exempt from the violent racial and color prejudice that have burdened his black brothers for more than two centuries. Wright likes France, her culture, her mind, her people. He was quite conversant with her literature and admired it before coming to Paris last year.

He says:

I was deeply moved by the welcome given to me by the French literary world. The whole literary milieu in France has welcomed me in Paris with a warmth I did not expect at all. I am deeply grateful to the French government for granting me the advantage of an official mission and invitation. I had been invited to spend one month in France, but I have been here for eight months. It shows how appreciative I am of French hospitality. I'd like to tell French people that their government is the only one that had the courage to tender such an invitation to a black American writer.

What are your impressions after eight months here?

They are necessarily limited to one section of France. I do not presume to claim that I can pass an overall judgment on French culture as a whole. But I can say that its impact on an American writer, especially a black American writer who has just left the "confined" atmosphere of the United States, is absolutely prodigious. Among the sharpest impressions I have had in Paris as well as everywhere in France is the humanistic feeling which so deeply pervades the rituals and customs of everyday life, just as it does literature, architecture and the arts in France. What a surprise for me to discover the regard in which a man of letters is held in France, especially when compared to the rather precarious relationship between American writers, be they white or black, and their home country.

Moreover, I have discovered such a contrast between French and American culture that within these months spent in Paris, I have learned more about America than I could have done in five comfortable years in New York. Here I could see clearly what we have got and what we lack in the United States. I am personally more and more obsessed by the feeling—which has become my conviction—that life in America is full of strangely inhuman elements. It seems clear to me that American civilization is based, in spite of its early traditions, on an utter disregard for human emotions, sensibilities, and personalities. Here in Paris I have been able to gauge how much the civilization of my country was a matter of quantity, as opposed to the qualitative aspects of French civilization.

Richard Wright reflects for a while as though he were looking for a simple and neat formulation. He goes on in a calm voice:

The crude brutality of American life is taken for granted by Americans. We are so much absorbed in the task of accumulating and increasing comfort and material goods that we have no time to stop and think about what ultimately benefits the individual in this state of things. We ask of a person, "How much money does he earn?" We don't wonder whether human needs are satisfied or achieved. For in America the classic question is "How much does he make?" In France one asks, rather, "What opinions does he hold?"

It is generally supposed and admitted, *Richard Wright goes on,* that

America is a very young country, a new world that one contrasts with the old world of Europe. Admittedly, from a historical point of view, America is young. But the social components of America are among the most ancient to be found in the contemporary world. Our social structure has known no notable change for three centuries. It operates and functions as it used to do at the time of the Pilgrim Fathers.

As for Europe, it has forsaken its former structure and is now in the throes of social struggle, striving to forge a new social order. In this sense, France and possibly the whole of Europe should be considered today as the New World. Rather strangely, in 1947, America now stands for the Old World.

I ask Wright which types of French literary expression have struck him most.

I was most interested in Sartre's play *The Respectful Prostitute*. Jean-Paul Sartre's literary expression I find of enormous interest because he seems to perceive deeply the realities of my country. This acute perception is felt in his play to such a point that, in my opinion, many American writers could use it as an example of the treatment of American realities. The play was inspired by one of the protagonists in the famous Scottsboro Case. Better than any writer who dealt with the case, Sartre has been able to pinpoint the crux of the situation. No foreign visitor has felt with comparable accuracy the incredible naivete of American civilization. In particular, the character of the prostitute is fundamentally true from a human point of view as well as in terms of America today.

Outside of literature, what do you think of life in postwar Europe?

I have seen the suffering and destitution of the French who are trying to rebuilt what has been destroyed and sullied by the Germans. But that does not distress me because I believe that the French are a courageous people. What has troubled me is the sort of "kindness" or naivete in the French which leads them to ignore or forget the brutality of industrial civilization. It seems to me that the French do not consider enough that today's world is dominated by boundless industrial powers. I have often had the impression that France did not want to change in spite of all the changes undergone by the civilization which surrounds it.

I believe that France should attempt to preserve the humanistic elements in its culture, but should at the same time attempt to adapt itself to the needs of modern industrial civilization. For instance, *Wright says with a burst of laughter,*—and this is a rather unimportant instance—I find it unthinkable that a telephone exchange should close from noon to 2 P.M. so that you can't get your telephone repaired or get a bit of information. I understand and appreciate this two-hour lunch break, which, in France, is precisely part of a "human" existence. But couldn't efficiency go hand in hand with culture? During lunchtime, the personnel could probably enjoy their lunch at staggered hours. This is only a trifling example, but you certainly understand what I mean. This is no criticism but concern on my part.

I say I understand and Richard Wright bursts out with laughter, this deep, throaty laughter of his, childlike and clear-ringing. But he becomes very earnest again when I ask another question, as though he felt he was bearing the suffering of his racial brothers anywhere in the world. What I ask him is what he thinks of the French colonial system and its problems.

I have been able to meet, *he replies,* many blacks from the French colonies. To my utter surprise, I have found they were more French than black. I say, to my *surprise,* for everyone knows that France controls vast colonial territories whose population is subjugated, after all, under conditions similar to those in other colonial empires. When speaking with French blacks I have not been able to get acquainted with conditions in the French colonial empire—or what is now being called the "French Union" itself. I was constantly facing students, or civil servants, or intellectuals, but I felt, in some way, that they had graduated to being French, had been promoted suddenly from slavery to French citizenship. As a result, they no longer identified with the lives of their people or with the brutal realities of colonial life. And this is the reason why I would very much like to visit black Africa and see for myself.

Did you work well during your stay here? Which book are you working on now? On his table his typewriter stood ready, with a thick typescript to the right of it.

First, I have met lots of people and have spent a lot of time absorbing the atmosphere of Paris. But I have never stopped writing. I completed a collection of short stories; the French translation should come out before American publication. Besides, I am so happy with the French publication of three books of mine here in Paris: *Native Son, Uncle Tom's Children,* and *Black Boy.* My book *Twelve Million Black Voices* will also come out next year in France and Switzerland.

As you are leaving, these books will come out while you are away.

No. I am leaving for a few months only. I'll be back next summer. I feel that when you have been in France once, you always return. I have not finished getting acquainted with Paris yet. And there are so many things and people I want to see in your country.

While I am saying goodbye to Richard Wright, his four-year-old daughter tells us a fascinating story. I shall not disclose it to the general reader here. Suffice it to say that the story was told in French. Little Julia will return to Paris and the Luxembourg Gardens. And her mother will also revisit the bookstalls on the embankments and the antiquarian shops on the Left Bank. Indeed, the Wright family is on its way to becoming "naturalized" Parisian.

Why Richard Wright Came Back from France

PM's Sunday Picture News/1947

From *PM's Sunday Picture News*, 16 February 1947, pp. m-5-m6.

Last week we went down to a house on Charles Street in Greenwich Village to visit Richard Wright, the novelist, who had come back two weeks before from an eight-month stay in France.

Wright had bought the three-story and basement brick building shortly after his return and was still getting settled when we arrived. The gray-walled, freshly painted living room had pictures stacked in the mauve fireplace, a suitcase in one corner and a linen press full of towels at one side, but otherwise the chairs, desk and sofa were neatly arranged.

"Right now I'm not engaged in any artistic endeavors," Wright told us good-naturedly, "just unpacking barrels and cartons."

A scholarly looking man in his late 30s, Wright was well but casually dressed in putty-gray slacks, brown shirt, tan jacket and apricot-colored tie. His voice was clear and light and his laugh was almost childlike.

"I came from the tranquillity of the Paris boulevards to this," he said, waving his arm to include the state of his apartment. "I bought this house not because I wanted to be a property owner, but because I wanted to be sure of a place to work and live. If I could have my way I'd shear off the two upper floors which I rent out at present and keep the rest of it for my family."

He had not intended to stay abroad so long, he said, but two months grew into eight. His visit to France had been a unique experience in freedom: there he was not a Negro but a human being, accepted and even welcomed.

"As a matter of fact," he laughed gaily, "the French government itself invited me."

The government made it possible for Wright and his wife to meet and talk with writers, including Gertrude Stein, Simone de Beauvoir (now visiting New York), René Maran, a French Negro writer, and Jean-Paul Sartre, the existentialist playwright, whom he regards most highly among French writers.

Wright spoke "a sort of functional French," enough to ask directions, order food or ask the price of things.

"Life is very simplified when you don't know a language," he mused. "I think we all talk too much anyway. We talk ourselves into trouble, too often."

Paris was the most democratic and civilized city he'd ever known, he said. "But I never heard anyone talk about freedom and how free they were. Everybody talks about it here because there's so little of it around."

Wright laughed, then he added slowly and with great conviction, "I did not encounter one iota of racial feeling in France. Not a bit of it. As an American Negro I was naturally sensitive to their attitude. But a Negro isn't a Negro in Paris. He's just another Frenchman. Their definition of a Frenchman is cultural, not biological.

"The French just have no attitude toward Negroes because they don't seem to be aware of any necessity to treat them any differently from anyone else. After about a month there, you stop noticing anything about Negroes as Negroes. They have no complex about Negroes, no emotional psychology built around the whole thing. Our Negro problem is simply inconceivable to them, even though the Nazis had just left their country and had tried to poison them with racist propaganda. They were full of questions about our attitude."

He was interviewed all the time, he said, and from among the papers on his desk he picked out some small square envelopes containing French and German newspaper clippings. As he opened them, we caught his name in the headlines.

Trying to understand America's Negro problem, French reporters had asked if the success of a Marian Anderson or a Paul Robeson or a Richard Wright didn't bring about a better relationship between blacks and whites, if the wide acceptance of Negro jazz and the Negro spirituals didn't bring about a greater friendliness?

Wright's manner was detached as he glanced through his clippings. Then his voice rose passionately.

"Don't let anyone tell you that any Negro in America, no matter what success he attains, has gotten over the difficulties and disabilities of being a Negro. The lives of all of them flow through banks and channels built for them by white Americans.

"Artists are accepted as artists, but not as human beings. They are accepted on the stage and in the concert halls, but not in the same apartment house. In spite of their wealth, they must live in Negro ghettos.

"It shows itself in a dozen different ways. You're refused hotel accommodations on the flimiest pretext—it's too full when you know it's half empty. Or you're shunted to the balcony of a restaurant because suddenly there are only reserved tables on the main floor."

When we mentioned the case of a Negro policeman, recently promoted to the rank of captain, who had said that he had encountered no color prejudice in his career, Wright snorted.

"Well, there were people under the Nazis who collaborated and said what was expected of them.

"The Negro problem of America is not an American problem. It is a world problem of colonials all over the world.

"For instance, while we were in Paris, we met a brilliant boy, Peter Abrahams, a 28-year-old Negro writer from South Africa. They've got a lulu of a situation down there, comparable only to the situation of the Negro on the plantation in the deepest South.

"This fellow was the second Negro ever to have been graduated from the University of Johannesburg. You know how they screen off part of a Jim Crow restaurant? Well, this fellow had a curtain around him in classes to screen him off from the white students. A native in Johannesburg has got to carry around something like 12 passports—one that testifies to his right to live in the city, one to show that he can read, one that he may stay out in the street until a certain time at night, and so on.

"The voice of the American Negro is no longer a lone voice. You hear echoing voices in the people of Burma, China, South Africa. Three-quarters of the world's population is colored. The attitude toward the Negro problem is entering a new phase. I met members of the Colored Writers Association while I was in England. It's composed of young writers, Hindu, African, British West Indian and Asiatic. They're all thinking and talking about this thing.

From one of the envelopes he was holding he pulled a photostat of a letter he had written for *Les Nouvelles Epitres,* a French literary magazine, and handed it to us.

"By social definition I am an American Negro," it read, "and what I'll have to say will deal with Negro life in the U. S. A., not because I think that life or its problems are of supreme importance, but because

Negro life in the U. S. A. dramatically symbolizes the struggle of a people whose forefathers lived in a warm, simple culture and who are now trying to live the new way of life that dominates our time: machine civilization and all the consequences flowing from it . . .

". . . the Negro was snatched from his continent, transported across the Atlantic, made to raise cotton on the vast American plantations. Hence, the Negro is intrinsically a colonial subject, but one who lives not in China, India or Africa but next door to his conquerors, attending their schools, fighting their wars, and laboring in their factories. The American Negro problem, therefore, is but a facet of the global problem that splits the world in two: Handicraft vs. Mass Production; Family vs. the Individual; Tradition vs. Progress; Personality vs. Collectivity; the East (the colonial peoples) vs. the West (exploiters of the world).

"Nowhere on earth have the extremes met and clashed with such prolonged violence as in America between Negro and white and this fact alone endows the American Negro problem with such vital importance, for what happens between whites and blacks in America foreshadows what will happen between the colored billions of Asia and the industrial whites of the West. Indeed, the world's fate is symbolically prefigured today in the race relations of America . . ."

As we finished reading, Wright said, "There's color prejudice in England, too, but it's not as intense or as organized as ours. The whole thing is a blind spot in some British and American minds. America sabotages her own foreign propaganda by her treatment of the Negro population. That's why Byrnes had such a hard time convincing some of these people."

But in Paris, Wright added smiling, in Paris they had a tremendous instinct for minding their own business and leaving other people alone.

Feeling that way about Paris, why had he returned to New York, we asked.

He looked at us with surprise, "I live *here*," he said with soft-voiced emphasis. "The French are in France and the Americans are in America. My work is here. My main job is in this country. I'd like to visit there often, but I belong here. No, I was fashioned in this peculiar kind of a hell," he said, and he laughed.

I Feel More at Home in France
Than Where I Was Born

Nuit et Jour/1947

From *Nuit et Jour*, 21 August 1947, p. 6. Translated by Michel Fabre.

The black American writer Richard Wright has just returned to Paris. Eight months ago he left for the United States, where his books enjoy a tremendous success. First, 30,000 copies of Uncle Tom's Children, *published in 1938, were printed. Then 600,000 copies of* Native Son, *published in 1940, were sold. Finally,* Black Boy, *his latest book, reached a printing of 600,000 copies. Richard Wright declares:*

The United States is the most powerful country in the world today. Its productive potential is enormous. It has not become fascist, nor anything similar. But after sixteen years of glorious "Rooseveltian adventure"—the liberalism of the Roosevelt era—the country seems to be returning to pre-Roosevelt times. This is certainly a step backwards. The United States is both unsure of itself and convinced that it must play a role. Yet this is more an annoying necessity than a deep desire to lead the world. The average American is increasingly certain that he is self-sufficient, and he is quite satisfied with that.

But deep down, his heart shrinks from a lack of certainty which nothing in his comfortable material life would lead us to suspect. The atom bomb does not reassure him in any way; it frightens him even more. So much so that he is spiritually deprived in a world overflowing with food. The civilization that prevails there does not satisfy human sensibilities. And the irritation of the American masses is turning against the Negroes, the Jews, the labor unions, the Soviets, the Communists, the Japanese, and the Chinese.

To be American in the United States means to be white, protestant, and very rich. This excludes almost entirely black people and anyone else who can be easily identified. As a result, the United States is hardly influenced by immigrants, many of whom are poor and find it impossible to go on living as they did in their homeland and still act like Americans. They become quickly assimilated because resisting would

126

entail too many difficulties. Many Europeans go as far as changing their names to make people think they are Americans. Indeed, Americanism is a kind of religion.

Richard Wright is convinced that he must flee from all of this if he is to succeed as a writer.

I like the French way of life. The existence they have been shaping for two thousand years ensures the primacy of aesthetic values and endows their days with a slow, peaceful rhythm.

In France, one instinctively grants importance to human values. As a writer, I feel this profoundly and I am happy to be back. I feel more at home here than where I was born.

An Interview in Paris with—Richard Wright: On U.S. Politics

Michel Salomon/1949

From *Labor Action*, 30 May 1949, pp. 1, 3.

Richard Wright, author of *Native Son, Black Boy* and many short stories, probably the best-known Negro writer in the United States, attended the "International Day Against War and Dictatorship" on April 30 in Paris, organized by the RDR (Rassemblement Démocratique Révolutionaire—Revolutionary Democratic Assembly). As was reported in LABOR ACTION last week, Wright took a forthright stand at this conference (together with Jean-Paul Sartre and Merleau-Ponty) against both American imperialism and Russian imperialism, distinguishing himself sharply from the pro-Washington flag-waving of Sidney Hook and James T. Farrell, the American delegates.

The following interview with Wright was transmitted to LABOR ACTION from Paris by Michel Salomon and we publish it for our readers' interest. It is translated from the French.—Ed.

"I agreed to participate personally in the RDR meeting," Wright told me, "in order to make clear my disagreement with the American left."

He smiled at me and carefully tapped the ash off his cigarette. Sitting there sunk down in his armchair, looking massive and slender at the same time, the author of *Native Son* is the prototype of those writers for whom social problems are not merely cold abstractions but questions of "human destiny."

I asked him if there was any truth to the rumors of a coming split in the RDR between supporters and opponents of the Atlantic Pact. Wright immediately reassured me.

"There are no split-differences, properly so called, in the French political movement known as the RDR—at least not to my knowledge. One likewise finds a rather substantial unity of viewpoint everywhere in Europe among the parties and movements which, like the RDR, are based on revolutionary socialism. It is, rather, a question of a fundamental difference between the European Left and what may be called the American Left.

"When the American delegates arrived in Paris, they expected that, like themselves, I would take a position resolutely in favor of the Marshall Plan and the Atlantic Pact. I immediately told them that my position on these questions—and on many others—was not the same as theirs.

"In fact, I maintain that the American Left, to a certain extent, is not completely free from anti-Semitism, from a discriminatory policy against Negroes, and from active collaboration with capitalism in many fields. The American trade unions are very different from the European unions. As far as social policy is concerned, they are at least a half century behind. The Europeans and the Americans may use the same words, but these words rarely have the same meaning here and there.

"The American Left is very little concerned with the class struggle. Its social demands are never political but simply aim, within the framework of the capitalist state, to ensure the well-being of the unionists through a compromise with the capitalist state.

"Moreover, the American Left is above all doctrinaire, wearing itself out in sterile ideological discussions, without understanding the deeplying interests of the working masses. Thus it is that Sartre, for example, who is not a Marxist, is politically and concretely much more to the left than Sidney Hook, who proclaims to high heaven that he is an orthodox Marxist. . . ."

"Is that the only reason why you did not take the floor at the meeting?"

"Yes! I spoke to Sartre and Merleau-Ponty, and they decided to abstain together with me, to support me. Sartre, who was recently in America, is also acquainted with this curious Left in that country. Since, however, we wanted to present our point of view to the conference, we sent a joint message."

I tried to recall how this message read. It had followed the pro-Atlantic Pact declarations of James T. Farrell and of De Kadt; the latter was a Dutch delegate and one of the rare Europeans who took the side of the American wing:

"We condemn, for the same reasons, both the more or less disguised annexations in Eastern and Central Europe by the USSR, and the Atlantic Pact. It is by no means certain that this pact will slow up the coming of war. It may on the contrary hasten it. What is certain, on the other hand, is that, a little sooner or a little later, it will contribute to make it inevitable."

"Your declaration sounded a bit like the one which Paul Robeson made to the Communist Peace Partisans' Conference. . . ."

Wright vehemently shook his head in denial.

"Robeson claimed that if a war broke out between America and the Soviet Union, no American Negro would fight against the Soviets. Such assertions are not only dangerous but totally false. The American Negroes will fight for their country under any circumstances. That is my deep conviction, but I do not want to do what Robeson did—talk in the name of 13 million American Negroes when he was actually representing only the little circle around Wallace."

Wright's voice grew softer.

"I like Robeson very much—as a singer. He is a wonderful artist; he knows how to convey the humiliation and burning hope of the American Negro in his songs. There is also a kernel of truth in what he says.

"In the United States the Negroes represent a terrible reservoir of despair and bitterness. They have been disillusioned time and again; and Truman's promises—which, personally, have never convinced me—will, like those of the other politicians before him, go into the cemetery of lost illusions. But the American Negroes will fight for the conquest of their civil rights within the traditional framework of the American parties and by their own means."

"But don't the Communist Party and Wallace's crypto-Communists have a certain amount of attractive appeal for the Negroes?"

"You saw proof to the contrary in the last election. The American Negroes do not have a short memory. They know the Communists, their methods and their promises—in which no more reliance can be placed than on those of the bourgeois parties.

"During the war the American Communists did not oppose racial discrimination in the armed forces. They told the Negroes to tolerate everything, to have patience till the war ends. Meanwhile the Negroes were supposed to bend the neck before the stupidest of stupid Jim Crow practices. The Red Cross itself kept the blood of Negroes separate from the blood of whites.

"There were better aspects. The war drew a large number of Negroes into the industrial occupations. The Federal Employment War Service was created with the stipulation that there was to be no racial discrimination against any worker. Negroes began to participate actively in the trade-union life of the AFL and CIO, and did so in spite of the Communists, who prefer to see them disorganized and therefore more easily subject to CP control. In many of these cases, for example, when the Negroes got ready to make demands or go on strike, it was the Communists who denounced them to the FBI."

"What are the political perspectives before the American Negroes today, after Truman's re-election?"

"If Truman does not repudiate his pre-election promises tomorrow or the day after, that is only because of the cold war now raging. If there is a settlement, if everything is arranged in Berlin and elsewhere, Truman will forget all about his statements.

"That does not mean that he will no longer be able to count on the loyalty of the Negro population, who do not expect American politicians to be consistent in fighting for their rights. The Negroes in the United States stand alone. They certainly do not reject alliances, and from all sides allies—and disinterested ones—are coming forward. They are beginning a long and hard struggle under the guidance of their political leaders and their intellectual elite. The Communists have ridiculed, for example, an organization as timid as the National Association for the Advancement of Colored People, but this organization has done more for the colored people than all the virulent and flamboyant maneuvers of the Communists."

"Let's talk about you for a moment. All French progressives are happy to have you among us, and we are happy to see that you are at the side of Sartre and his friends in the struggle which counterposes freedom through socialism to various forms of concealed fascism. Have you any definite plans?"

"I am a foreigner here and my collaboration with Sartre is limited to certain special fields. I cannot be a member of the RDR since it is not fitting for me to take part in questions of internal French politics. But I am in complete agreement with the RDR as far as its views on international questions are concerned.

"I am especially happy to be able to live in France, in a climate of liberty and tolerance where I can carry on my work. The question of liberty is posed much more in the United States than in Europe. To be sure, the individual has fewer obligations to the state; he is apparently freer; but a permanent pressure of coercion is brought to bear on him.

"Over there men are at the mercy of a public opinion which is manufactured by second-rate publicists, speakers on the radio, and leagues of righteousness. The influence of the intellectuals, which is so important here, is almost nil in the United States; there a wall of complete silence is erected around works which do not correspond with the 'American way of life.'

"America demands the abdication of the personality in favor of its conventions. Besides, all the political parties stand for a discipline which also sacrifices the man to ideological coercion. I agree with Sartre, who thinks that the individual can do something by himself.

"I have no ready-made solution, but unless we are persuaded that there is one, we will never find any. I am against the pessimists; I have confidence in man. We need an ideology which proposes a new definition of the values which have made man what he is, and these values imply in the first place the idea of liberty.

"I have heard politicians, churchmen and party leaders say: 'Follow me—I have a plan to solve your problems, but it will not give you liberty right away. Have patience, you must struggle, you must be organized, you must be disciplined; later you will also have liberty, but the struggle will be long and hard.'

"In my opinion, liberty is indivisible; it is acquired gradually, like something which one buys on the installment plan. At each stage, one enjoys a little more liberty, and this permits you to carry the struggle on more effectively. But it is not with methods which abolish liberty that we will struggle for liberty."

Richard Wright, the Black Dostoevski

Ramuncho Gomez/1949

From *El Hogar,* 28 October 1949, pp. 22–23, 75. Translated by
Keneth Kinnamon.

Visiting our country is Richard Wright, "the black Dostoevski" according to the sonorous definition of his racial brothers. His is not just one
more "literary visit." He comes with am ambitious plan: to film in our
city [Buenos Aires] the cinematographic version of his popular novel
Native Son, known here under the title *Black Blood.* Orson Welles, "the
boy genius," staged on Broadway with great success the dramatization
of this intense book. Wright himself wrote the play in collaboration with
Paul Green. Four years later, Narciso Ibañez Menta brought to us a
theatrical version in Spanish, running in 1945. Now Buenos Aires gets
the privilege of the shooting of the first film version of the famous work
with the direct participation of the robust writer in the important three-
part work of writer, actor, and producer of the film.

Native Son is a book widely published throughout the world. It has
been characterized as a book of "racial resentment." Bigger Thomas, the
protagonist of its crowded action, is a criminal. An obscure impulse
springing from his black blood drives him to the tragedy. He cannot live
relegated to his ghetto, bounded by the high barriers of white prejudice.
"They have things," he says, "we don't." His black color makes his
cheeks burn with resentment, and with fatal determination he moves to
crime and then to expiation. All of Wright's work is an exposure of
wrongs and a demand for rights. His autobiographical novel *Black Boy*
also describes the progress of his frustration, impelled by social injustice, and presents a protagonist attracted by communism, even though
later disillusioned because that system resolves none of his problems.
He also exposes rawly the problem that afflicts him in *12 Million Black
Voices.* His passionate, unadorned language bursting forth like whip-
lashes finds an echo in thousands of readers. He has a hard style, typically American. His works have a stylistic similarity to those of Sinclair
Lewis, Erskine Caldwell, and Ernest Hemingway. Nevertheless, it is
characterized by a very personal vibration of intense emotion, by a cer-

133

tain violence that is not literary and psychological like that of William
Faulkner, but of environment, of character, as if an entire people influenced him.

Richard Wright is forty-one years old and began his literary work at
fifteen. A black editor in Jackson published his first work. It carried a
strange title: "The Voodoo of Hell's Half-Acre." It is the melodramatic
story of a villain who tries to rob a poor black widow. His literary pre-
cocity demonstrated, at the same time, his racial sensibility. Now he is
here with us, trying to animate with images—one of which will be his
own image—one of the many sordid dreams of his racial brothers.

"Atchoo . . . atchoo . . . atchoo . . ."

While he was shaking hands jovially, the strong writer of color
Richard Wright explained that it was not the liturgical greeting of some
black ritual, but the triple sneeze of a cold that was bothering him.

"The best way for a tourist in Buenos Aires to identify with the city is
to catch a good port dweller's cold," he added smiling while he invited
us to sink, comfortable and easy, into a deep armchair.

"Novelist of racial resentment" is what literary critics have baptized
Richard (Dick to his friends). On the other hand, the impression we got
from his very cordial reception was that of a jovial young fellow with
an almost explosive friendliness.

Dick (we could no less than call him that from the beginning) is one
of those persons of rare personal charm who seem to be old acquaintances at the very instant of first meeting them. Through his literary
work, deep, expressive, and at times with a hopeless accent, we had
dreamed up the image of a large black man, sad, rebellious, and aggressive. The man who smiled at us, with one hand placed on one of our
knees and with a cheerful expression, was exactly the opposite of what
we had imagined. We revealed our not very diplomatic perplexity in this
trivial question (a faithful copy of our confusion):

"How old are you, Richard? Oh, pardon me, Mister Wright."

"Please, not Mister Wright; just Richard, or still better Dick, like old
friends," he urged us with sweeping simplicity.

"Thanks, Dick," we replied recklessly, "but—how old are you?"

"Oh, just forty-one. What did you think?"

"Nothing, nothing. Only I find you made into a 'black and young boy.'"

"Sure. That's the way it should be. I've lost quite a few pounds and

twenty years of age. I have to put myself in shape for my role of Bigger
Thomas, the protagonist of *Native Son*—or *Black Blood* as you people
have rebaptized it—that we will film in Buenos Aires with all these
good friends." With a full gesture and affectionate smile he pointed at
Pierre Chenal, the French director; Jaime Prades, one of the coproduc-
ers; and Atilio Mentasti of Argentina Sono Film, which will provide the
studios. All three were present in another corner of the vast living room
where we were talking.

"Life has odd designs," he added. "Here you have me about to become a movie actor in the leading role of a novel I wrote in Brooklyn
ten years ago."

"Do you like Buenos Aires, Dick?"

"A lot. When I open the shutters in my room in the north quarter,
I don't feel homesick for Paris, and when I walk around downtown,
with its urban traffic, I don't miss Chicago. Besides, I don't believe that
anyone can feel like a stranger here. The city has such a cordial physi-
ognomy that it smiles on all foreigners equally. Its friendliness doesn't
make distinctions; it's a city without prejudice, that is to say an ideal
place to produce free from pressure the film I dream of based on my
book."

"It's very pleasing to hear you say that, Dick. But how is it possible
that you have not carried out your project in Hollywood? There the
racial problem would have as a market part of the public that lived it
and observed it."

"The answer to your question is not difficult. There they inevitably
set up some reservations with respect to the black problem. There I fear
the 'machine,' that is to say, the marvelous technical perfection and the
great many conventional lies that leave books 'without a soul and without an argument.' Hollywood will continue being as it is now, 'the industry of pure fiction.' For example, my book *Native Son* should have
been turned into a film there. I sold the rights, but I withdrew the script
because they wanted to turn Bigger Thomas, a black boy marked by
fatalistic destiny, into a white character. That is to say, they were only
interested in the political plot of the affair, causing the social meaning
of the drama and the racial problem to disappear. But these are the basic
matters that serve as the distressed background of the plot."

"Does racial prejudice exist, then, in U.S. movie production?"

"Not in such absolute and exact terms. Many films about blacks have been made in Hollywood. But blacks have never felt themselves to be faithfully portrayed in these films. Neither *Green Pastures* nor any other film has gone inside 'black reality.' Perhaps these films were well intentioned, with excellent black actors and even faithful descriptions of the environment, but they lacked the real meaning of the spirit that drives the men of my race."

"And what is the present dimension of the black problem in the United States?"

"In general, the situation of blacks is not better, and in many aspects it turns out to be worse. When we began to film the exterior scenes of *Native Son* in Chicago, I verified that things had gotten worse. The black population has doubled in the last thirteen years, but the excess had to be absorbed into the same old neighborhoods. Those who had enough money to strive for better houses in other neighborhoods heard violence pounding at their doors. Rocks always broke the windows of those who dared to live far from the black ghettos. Police protection is always doubtful, because the police are also prejudiced."

"So that the attenuated symptoms of the problem are not very visible."

"The lower classes have made some gains, mostly through the work of the unions. The black problem, like anti-semitism, is based on a deep prejudice. The people of the United States are still not psychologically prepared to attenuate the terrible effects of the differentiation of races. Furthermore, the black citizen demands the place that belongs to him in American society and democracy. As the first settlers of the land after the Indians, blacks have abundant rights with their white brothers to equality in the free and honorable exercise of citizenship, both political and social. When it resolves the problem of prejudice against blacks, my country can demonstrate completely that it is democratic and the cradle of the four freedoms that are proclaimed in the land for all the inhabitants of the nation."

This reporter heard break forth the deep tone that Richard gave to his opinions about the black problem in his country. His jovial speech now touched a grave register; the strong convictions and hopes had changed a little his jovial face. A broad smile returned to light it up when we spoke of Paris (a city that evokes in the reporter a recent nostalgia). Dick (our new and at the same time old friend) is a familiar figure in Parisian literary centers. His graceful silhouette and his casual clothes are familiar to those who frequent Saint-Germain-des-Prés, the new center of the "existentialism" that is changing this Paris neighborhood like a nonconforming neighbor. He has lived there for three years with his wife and two young daughters, and there he works with singular dedication. He has just published, in French, his latest book, a series of short stories entitled *Five Men,* and he interrupted another work in progress to make the trip to our country.

"Why have you lived in Paris for some time, Dick?" we asked with our impenitent indiscretion.

"Because it is a city where one breathes in the warm aroma of liberty without restrictions and without prejudices; one works in very free intellectual company, and the very soil is fertilized with centuries of culture and dense with thought."

"Do you notice the influence of American writers and novelists on French letters?"

"Sartre and Camus show that. French writers realized that action was lacking in their novels, at least in the raw, rapid, sure form that charac- terizes the good American writers (Hemingway, Caldwell, Lewis, and others). We should make clear that this only concerns the focus of some chapters in which the fiction is presented in vivid terms, without appar- ent style, to lay out a very intense impression. Now, in philosophical and conceptual matters, the influence is null. France has an illustrious literary history and a cultural domain hard to surpass."

"You are a friend of Sartre, aren't you, Dick?"

"Yes, I am. Moreover, I collaborate on his journal *Les Temps Mo- dernes,* but I am not an 'existentialist,' and not even Sartre is in an absolute sense. I have stopped practicing the '-isms.' I just share with this illustrious French thinker his 'militant humanism.' As far as politics is concerned, I explained in my book *Black Boy,* written in 1945, my disenchantment with communism, which I have just recently con- demned in the magazine of Sartre I mentioned." (This reporter recalls, as a matter of fact, his writings in the *Daily Worker* and *New Masses,* the newspaper and magazine of the Communist Party, as sins that can be called youthful).

The reporter had let himself be subjugated by the charming talk of this very pleasing friend of color, but he woke up to the tyrannical reality that he now had four pages left to say everything. He inserted Richard Wright into the center of his journalistic objective—the film— and he quickly stepped on the gas to do the note.

"When does the filming of *Native Son* begin?"

"We began to shoot some exterior scenes with Chenal in Chicago in the black neighborhoods. There we were on site (in accord with the geographical reality of the book), together with Gloria Madison, who will accompany me in the leading female role. Here we will work in the studios to do the interior action of the film."

"Did you do the adaptation from the book?"

"Yes. With my good friend from Paris, Pierre Chenal, I discussed different aspects of the film version, which will follow faithfully the spirit of the book. He has now chosen the local actors here, who for the most part are effective interpreters and connected to the American colony here, among them some magnificent black Americans, all of whom speak English."

"You yourself have described a strange and lucky parabola, Dick, from ticket taker in a movie theater to writer and actor."

"A sign of the times in which we live. We are in a century of opportunity, provided that we work to take advantage of it. I was a ticket taker in Memphis and in Mississippi, afterwards a writer lucky with *Native Son*. By virtue of providential circumstances [he smiles again at his friends in the enterprise that are listening to him], I have now become the producer, the screenwriter, and finally the actor (this the least expected) of my film."

"Well, Dick, good luck. We would like to see the finished film this very afternoon and appreciate this honest effort by all of you."

"And I," he said to us while he vigorously shook hands, "would like to be by your side in the first row."

We will wait until the moment arrives of the fruit of this joint effort, that will appear under the name of "independent production," financed by dollars, francs, and Argentinian pesos. One should add a word about the participation of a twenty-year-old black girl, Gloria Madison, who comes from Chicago to play the female lead. She doesn't have many film credits, just one in a university film. She is enrolled at the University of Chicago, where her father is a professor of advanced studies in sociology. When she finishes the film she will return to Chicago to study medicine and, in passing, get married.

Interview with Richard Wright

Revista Branca/1950

From *Revista Branca*, 1950. Translated by Michel Fabre and Keneth Kinnamon.

PARIS. Rue Monsieur-le-Prince is the boundary between the Latin Quarter and St. Germain des Près. Every afternoon in the Romance Bar on this street Richard Wright gets together with a group of friends to discuss the great issues of the day. There is a pianist as well as pretty admirers of Wright. Sometimes Sartre or Camus drops by. The last time I was there Wright invited me to come the following day to his apartment, a little way up the same street. I arrived punctually at two o'clock to keep the appointment. On Wright's table—typical of an American writer—were typewriters, flashbulbs, an ultramodern radio, gadgets whose use I did not know, and, naturally, books and manuscripts. Richard Wright, who had just come back from Buenos Aires, told me confidentially: "I stopped at Rio and Sao Paulo, both going and coming. One night in Rio I went into a hot night club, a fantastic place where the samba was danced."

"Did you run into some Brazilians there, some friends of yours?"

"To tell you the truth, my stay was very short. But I got an excellent impression of Rio. I noticed that there was no racial prejudice and that is an immense step, really, in comparison to the United States. It is always necessary to transform racial problems into class problems and then to find a quick solution."

"What were you doing in Buenos Aires?"

"Shooting a film derived from my novel *Native Son*. That book, by the way, has been translated into Portuguese by Monteiro Lobato. They have praised his translation highly. In the film, I myself played a role." (Wright rummaged through his table, found a portfolio, and showed me one by one photographs taken during the filming.)

"But why did you make this film in Buenos Aires?"

"It was the only place where shooting such a film was acceptable."

"You are closely tied to Sartre and have been writing frequently in his

review *Table Ronde* [sic]. Do you share completely Sartre's position
taking into consideration today's political tendencies?"

"I agree with him on several points. Our mission as writers is to tell
the truth at all costs. We should not be afraid of reprisals, Russian or
American. Russian communism and Americanism, as they now appear,
are not two forces one of which is good and the other evil. They are two
evils confronting each other, and in my opinion the errors of both
should be exposed. Meanwhile, maybe I have feeling about life, a respect for life, greater than Sartre, who is too much the philosopher. Undoubtedly, the danger of war arises from the fact that each day millions
of people listen to Russian propaganda and American propaganda.
Surely our duty is to demonstrate, to prove, the bad faith of both lines
of propaganda. But if war broke out tomorrow, neutrality would no
longer be permitted. My position is this: in the capitalist world, the hope
of change exists. There is a flexibility not to be found in the Soviet
world. They talk about revolution. But the liberty most important to a
citizen is his political freedom. In the U.S.S.R. individual political
freedom does not exist. That's why I say that the U.S.S.R. is a counter-
revolutionary country. In this respect one cannot say absolutely that the
United States is a revolutionary country, but it is less reactionary than
the U.S.S.R. Above all the point is to safeguard peace. Because if there
were a war all humanity would be the loser. There would not be a real
victor in case of a world conflict. Distress would be universal. Moreover, in the case of war my position would be on the American side. In
time of peace, though, I believe that we writers should not take a position for or against Russia. We should side with and commit ourselves in
the direction of a progressive struggle for democracy, for improvement
in the living standards of workers, against racial prejudice, etc. To
struggle for concrete things, for human situations, not for or against
abstract, totalitarian systems. In this struggle, I am in the company of
Sartre, Camus, Claude Bourdet, André Breton, and several other lucid
men of good faith. I will go farther and tell you this: the Russian leaders
and the American leaders are men of bad faith, and they know it up to a
certain point. We must convince the masses, the millions, of our purity
and good faith. We must convince them, give them proof that we are
not in the service of one imperialism or the other, but in service to the
cause of humanity, concrete and immediate. We must show that there
are Americans who have something to give to the world of the disinher-

ited. The United States, in the Caribbean and elsewhere, has followed a
frightful colonial policy, and is losing the trust of Asians. It is difficult
for us to go up to Asians and tell them that although we have oppressed and scorned them, we are the defenders of their liberty. The
Russians have at least brought to the Chinese something they did not
have before: a modern, well-equipped army. We must regain the sympathy of the entire world, and there is only one way to do that—
change. We have to change. England survived and is adapting itself
to the postwar world because it gave proof that it had a great deal of
flexibility, because it accepted change. If we resist change in order to
retain the status quo, perhaps we will lose what is really essential. For
the last four years the United States has been bestowing billions of
dollars all over the world with extraordinary prodigality, but all the
while it has not been able to sell its concept of life. Why? Our Republicans would take exception. It's just that something exists in our system that others don't want. It is easier for us than for the communists
to change and earn the friendship of the whole world. Therefore it's
up to us to change."

Wright spoke without stopping, as if he were giving a speech. He
spoke with the accent of sincerity itself. Then, suddenly tired out, he
put his feet on the table. We lit a cigarette. I explained to Wright that,
not being American myself, I was more captivated than he was by the
American way of life because it has more good things and because the
bad things could always be improved in the United States. In short in a
country where freedom of speech reigns, protest could succeed in cor-
recting wrongs and injustices. But Wright is a black, he was brought up
in the South, he suffered from racism, and he retains a certain bitterness. That's why years ago he took up residence in Paris, from which he
is always going off on trips in Europe and Africa.

"What are your affinities to other American writers?"

"I admire Faulkner, but I do not know him personally. We have
corresponded. I served a term as president of an association of American writers, and I am still in contact with James T. Farrell, whom I
know well. As to the people I admire, there is Dreiser, whom I knew;
there is Hemingway. But the decisive authors during my youth were
European. European realism influenced me more than that kind of
American impressionism. I owe a lot to Dostoevsky, Turgenev, Flaubert. I also like the works of Gertrude Stein a lot."

"And that which relates to you—*Black Boy, Native Son,* and *12 Million Black Voices*—are they autobiographical?"

"*Black Boy* is entirely autobiographical, the story of my struggles while growing up. The other works are fiction. Not in the sense of being purely novelistic, because they contain some of my memories and my actual experiences. As much in *Uncle Tom's Children* as in *Native Son.*"

"Do you have a book under way now?"

"I am now writing the scenario for a film on Toussaint l'Ouverture, the liberator of Santo Domingo. I am writing a film script and at the same time I am playing a role in it!" (This is an entirely new fashion, and Wright is not the only writer to work this way in the cinema. Some famous names figure on the lists of people doing the same thing.)

There is a new pause. The photographer passes near us buzzing like a fly. During this time Wright speaks to me about an organization that he has just founded of which he expects a great deal. It is a cultural group called the Franco-American Fellowship, in which Sartre and Simone de Beauvoir are playing a part. The object of the association is to work to clarify the great problems of the day, to study ways to safeguard human freedom in the presence of modern industrialization, to struggle against racism, to stimulate education in all countries, to arouse interest in supporting modern art, to defend the dignity and freedom of the individual. The group will not be neutral because neutrality is a passive attitude. On the contrary, it will be engaged on the side of good faith and truth. We then spoke of James Burnham. Wright acknowledged that his thesis on the subject of the managerial class and the technocrats is quite reasonable, but he adds:

"The power of the managers can become real only if it becomes a political power. But at present managers have no political power at all. The dominant class in Russia is a class of political organizers; in America the dominant class is the capitalists. Before Burnham's thesis can be verified, I believe that it will be necessary to wait half a century."

I left Richard Wright with an excellent impression of a great man, lucid and of good faith. And also one of the best American writers.

An Interview with Native Son

Jeanine Delpech/1950

From *The Crisis,* 57 (November 1950), 625–626, 678. Originally published as "Avec l'enfant du pays," *Les Nouvelles Litteraires,* 14 September 1950, p. 1. Reprinted by permission.

Richard Wright is beyond doubt the most significant post-war American writer. Moreover, his talent appears even more robust when it is contrasted with so much of today's gossamery work. What we get in Wright is the image of a man sculptured out of a solid block of wood swamping the iridescent curios of Carson McCullers and Truman Capote, which remind you of nothing so much as *The Glass Menagerie* of Tennessee Williams. Richard Wright does not make his Negroes, his brothers, mouthpieces of outrageous demands, but the heroes of rewarding dramatic tales which have opened the eyes of Europeans to some of our present many insoluble problems.

When I listened to the author of *Uncle Tom's Children* relate the adventures of "The Man Who Lived Underground," and saw him give reality to the agony of this unfortunate cellar-wretch by a look or a shrug of the shoulders, my first thought was

"What a marvelous actor he would make!"

That was two years ago. New York audiences will soon have the opportunity to applaud Richard Wright playing the main role in his own screen version of *Native Son.*

"To make the screen version of a novel into which I had put so much of myself," explained Wright, "was a dream which I had long hugged to my heart, and it was quite painful until it happened. Orson Welles staged the play in New York City. Then it was played in London, and almost everywhere, even in Prague, where I was invited to attend, but where I didn't care to go for reasons you can easily understand.

"In Argentina the great actor Mente cropped his hair, blackened his face, and with a blackface troupe, played *Native Son* with astonishing success. Pierre Chenal, who happened to be over there at the time, saw the play and wanted to transfer it to the screen. Back in France he plunged into the job and we were almost successful, with our contracts

143

drawn up, when some mysterious power said no. Freedom seems to be vanishing everywhere in the world, but I had thought France one of its last refuges. However, I must confess I was mistaken."

"And production would have earned you dollars, which you need, would it not?"

Richard Wright broke into his soft, infectious smile and went on:

"We then tried to reach an agreement with Italy, but no luck. Then the Italian producer who had pleaded my cause at Rome left for the last country in the world which I thought would permit production of a film on the Negro question—Argentina. Over there everything was miraculously settled, and I must admit that we were given every possible facility during our stay."

"So your movie is Argentinean?"

"Oh, no! That would be too simple an explanation. It's really an American production with American white and Negro actors [Gene Michael, Jean Wallace, Nicholas Joy, Willa Pearl Curtiss, and Gloria Madison], a French director, Pierre Chenal; Argentinean capital; and an Italian producer."

Then I asked Wright:

"What about studio equipment over there?"

"As good as in France," added Wright.

"And would you say, as so many novelists do, that the screen adaptation betrays your book?"

"Certainly not. I offer no alibis for this picture. Good or bad, it's what I wanted. We stuck pretty close to the novel, but we did make a few changes in the trial scene, which we thought too static. We had to put in some action there."

"Do you enjoy acting?" I asked.

"Very much, but only on the screen. I went to great trouble to do the best by my role with the knowledge that I had just one chance to fix my features on the film. That's why it seemed to me so meaningless to be doing the same thing all over the next day. How do actors ever get used to it?"

"What do you think's the difference," I asked, "between the art of the writer and movie expression?"

"The work of the writer is essentially individual, solitary, and concentrated. Movie work, on the other hand, requires cooperation. It is public and impersonal. And what's more important, you can write a book for a minority, but you can't produce a film for a minority."

"I'd like to do a second picture," added Wright. "However, when I consider my books, I hesitate among several subjects. The translation [French] of a collection of my novellas which have appeared in American magazines is now ready. The book should be out soon."

Since Richard Wright lives in Paris with his wife and two children, we naturally began to talk about his fellow American writers and artists resident in France.

"I'd say," commented Wright, "that generally they don't make a go of it. The American is a social animal. In order to preserve his integrity and not drink too much or covet his neighbor's wife he has to be restrained by fear of what his neighbors will say. Missing such restraints in France, he soon sinks into moral decay. But then one mustn't generalize."

Our Main Problem Today Consists in Enlightening Man about Himself

Geneviève Heuzé/1950

From *France-Etats-Unis,* November 1950, p. 2. Translated by Michel Fabre.

Mr. Richard Wright is back from South America, but he is a U.S. citizen. For some five years he has been residing mainly in Paris but has traveled over Europe, in Italy, Belgium, Switzerland, and Germany. The author of *Black Boy* has an extraordinary sense of humanity. He is interested in individuals first, before nations and continents. Yet, worried by the intense propaganda which tends to standardize peoples who have their own values, he wanted to provide a general estimate for our benefit.

Do you think of any precise example?

I think of the "Negro problem," which I have experienced and studied in all its aspects. I would be sad, for example, if France should cease to be for blacks a broad-minded country ready to welcome any citizen of mankind. To tell people about the United States does not necessarily mean to impose one's views or customs of the other side of the Atlantic on the Old World.

Would it not be a way of bringing back to the old continent an updated version of what left it once?

I don't think so. Deliberately or not the pioneers in the New World cast aside cultural preoccupations. For a long time their only problem consisted in overcoming daily difficulties, in clearing the new land and tilling the soil. This is still a characteristic of our new, strong, and brutal civilization, which considers the production of goods before anything else. What France should go and search out in the United States is industrial organization.

Were not U.S. missions for technical aid created precisely for this?

Yes, but even here some reservations should be expressed. The point

146

is not for you to do what is being done back home, but to adapt it to your needs. The problem is that of Man and Industry. Man must imprint his mark, not receive that of the machine age. Machines should be no more than an instrument of power in his hands.

Do you mean that the main problem consists in forming the spirit of man?

Man must first learn about himself. Everything depends on him, and one must make him aware of his own resources. And the meaning of the word "education" must be searched for in Europe, particularly in France.

Yet the American school system, with your open air programs, seems to be the highlight today.

Oh, our practical achievements are fine. What is wrong, in my opinion, is the spirit. In the United States, we have a romantic conception of education: the human subject is considered a priori as a genius with many applications. With you, the child is an evil little animal who must be civilized.

Don't you believe that this old civilization may be encumbered with useless traditions?

I'm afraid that you may have too many of them, while we don't have enough.

It is evident, however, that the United States of America would not have become united so quickly if their background had been as cluttered as that of old Europe.

You are right, but I trust those old nations, as you call them, to make allowances in favor of European unity.

Should luck grant you the opportunity of an interview with Mr. Richard Wright, the extreme intelligence in his eyes, the conviction his hands express, and his big resounding laughter will certainly have filled you with confidence by the time you leave.

A Black Writer Becomes a Movie Actor

Johannes Skancke Martens/1950

From the Oslo *Aftenposten,* 9 November 1950, p. 3. Translated by
Michel Fabre and Keneth Kinnamon.

Richard Wright, one of the most remarkable and interesting phenomena
of American literature, has returned to Paris after having spent ten
months in North and South America. His novel *Native Son* has been
filmed in Chicago and Buenos Aires. "Why Buenos Aires?" I asked the
forty-year old black writer in the course of an interview in his elegant,
clean house located near the Odeon Theater. "All the events take place
in the north of America."

"When my book appeared in 1940, it immediately proved itself suitable to be made the subject of a film. I had several propositions, but the
film producers wanted several changes—one of them even proposed to
make the hero white instead of black. I did not want this under any
circumstances, and I was hoping that one day public opinion in the
United States would become liberal enough to permit seeing a film
presenting in a realistic and true way the situation of blacks in American
society. Thanks to Orson Welles I took the initiative of writing a play
based on my book, and it was a big success on Broadway. But a Hollywood film is directed toward a larger public. And that would yield
nothing for the film. After the war, America was subject to reaction,
and I lost hope of making the film there. I had propositions in France
and Italy, but like the others negotiations with Rossellini over three
years yielded nothing. Last year I accepted the proposition from Argentina, and in January I flew across the Atlantic with the director Pierre
Chenal. He had seen the play *Native Son* in Buenos Aires when he was
a war refugee there, and he hoped to make the film. The exterior scenes
have been filmed in Chicago. We also went to South America, where
we shot all summer."

"You played the leading role of the film. Had you acted before?"

"When Chenal proposed the role to me, I thought he was kidding.
When I understood that he was serious, I thought that I should first

learn to act. 'Not at all,' said Chenal. 'You just need to lose twelve kilos.'"

"Are you satisfied with the result?"

"Yes, and I can say that I have complete responsibility for the film. I wrote the dialogue. The producers and the director gave me carte blanche in whatever concerned my role as actor. If the film is bad, it's all my fault. The premiere will take place in New York, probably at the beginning of November. The film is certainly American and will be shown first to the North American public, who will serve as a test. In Europe the film will be shown at the end of the month."

"You referred to the American reaction. Is the situation of blacks getting progressively better?"

"I don't think so. Segregation—difference between whites and blacks—is basically unchanged. From Maryland south blacks have their separate tracks, separate cars, their separate entries and exits in stations. They can't go into hotels reserved for whites, they can't have an orchestra seat in the theater, etc.

"We constantly hear talk of new liberalization—black students in white universities, black functionaries, black officers. Against their will, out of shame, under world pressure—and because racial hatred and pressure against blacks are of use to the Russians in their propaganda—there have been some small changes. But what would it matter if a couple of blacks had the possibility of studying at a university where there are several thousand white students? The black is seated at the back of the class behind a screen! At the West Point Military Academy some black students from three northern states have been accepted, but in the army blacks are grouped into their own detachments. When the Red Cross asks for blood, black blood is reserved for blacks. In fact, very few black Americans fall for communist propaganda, but in spite of that the dogma of racial superiority and inferiority, which can't be proven or defended, is very deeply anchored in the mentality of the masses."

"Does Paris still please you?"

"I am at home in Paris and I'm staying here. After visiting New York, Chicago, Montevideo, and Buenos Aires, I love Paris all the more."

"What are your current plans?"

"I would like to make a film on Toussaint l'Ouverture, who organized the revolt of the natives of Haiti at the end of the eighteenth century. I am putting together the elements, but nothing is settled yet on a deal."

One hopes that Richard Wright does not become so busy with the cinema that he does not have time to write more novels, novellas, or articles such as the one in *The God That Failed,* a book just translated into Norwegian.

An Interview with Expatriate
Richard Wright in Paris

Allan Temko/1951

From the *San Francisco Chronicle,* 30 December 1951, This World
Sec., p. 19. © San Francisco Chronicle. Reprinted by permission.

The unofficial leader of the re-established American expatriate literary community here, where Edith Wharton and the genteel tradition and later, Scott Fitzgerald and other romantics of the Twenties, once reigned in a graceful political vacuum, is now Richard Wright, the 43-year-old Negro novelist who has made his reputation as a fierce critic of racial and social injustice in the United States.

But, in post-World War II Paris, the term "expatriate," which literary Americans in Europe once considered almost a badge of honor, has lost some of its attraction. Even Wright, who with his wife and two young daughters has lived on the Left Bank since 1946, doesn't like the word when applied to himself.

"Put it this way," Wright says, "I don't think of France in terms of staying or leaving. I don't have any conscious feeling of leaving home. I just feel at home in Paris right now."

Why does he feel more at "home" here for the moment, instead of New York or Chicago?

Richard Wright's answer is complex: "I am an American, and will live and die an American, but personally I lean to the European world-feeling. This is not a matter of intellectual processes, but of feeling."

"I think I know why," he continued. "In my case there is a racial aspect. My life in the United States, which engendered in me a certain anxiety and watchfulness of society, has led me to feel deep sympathy with the anxiety of Europeans for their own historical plight."

In France, Wright asserts, he discovered an especially sympathetic relationship between his own personal attitudes as an American Negro and those of Europeans who had suffered under Hitler, although he would not try to "equate" Nazi oppression and the position of the Negro in the United States.

"When I came to France in 1946," he explains, "I met many French who had become acquainted with my books during the occupation. My work, which may seem too tense, too hard-driven to some Americans, did not seem so at all to the French, who felt a kinship in the two things."

Wright claims that this feeling of kinship is becoming worldwide. "When I meet a man from India, for example, who has suffered under the British, or a Negro from South Africa, or a Frenchman from the Resistance, there is an immediate understanding."

This common ground, he feels, has prepared the "third way"—more commonly referred to by left-wing British Laborites and other European Socialist intellectuals as the Third Force, or a middle way between American and Russian policies.

But at this point Wright said he didn't want to talk politics: "I'm not selling any political medicine."

He is, however, selling a great deal of nonpolitical medicine in the Franco-American Fellowship, a "cultural exchange" organization which he recently helped to found.

This group, not yet widely known in Paris, has already held several open meetings with leading French and American intellectuals as guest speakers, including Jean-Paul Sartre and Louis Fischer, the biographer of Ghandi, and Irwin Edman, essayist and philosopher, who is here as a Fulbright professor at the Sorbonne.

The fellowship occupies most of Wright's time when he is not writing and he hopes to establish it as a permanent "cultural exchange of ideas, especially for artists and intellectuals who find themselves far apart because of international tension." Too often, he declares, Europe and America are "incomprehensible" to one another. A typical case, he says, is the recent issue of an American magazine completely devoted to the "next" war. "Political illiteracy," says Wright flatly, who is convinced that most Europeans were shocked and horrified by the special issue.

Nevertheless, he is still "preoccupied with American problems and the American scene" and he has recently begun to present his ideas in motion pictures as well as on the stage and in fiction. In 1950 he went to Argentina to film "Native Son," in which he played the leading role of Bigger Thomas. The film has been distributed throughout the United States, except in the South, and according to Wright it has generally received harsh reviews, perhaps because the American version has been severely cut.

At present he is working on his first full-length book since *Black Boy*, a collection of short stories to be entitled *Ten Men*, parts of which have already appeared in the United States and Europe. The major characters, as in all of his work, are Negroes, and although the emphasis in these new stories "is not race consciousness," Wright, after five years abroad, does not feel that his writing has turned from primarily American considerations. "I am not," he declares, "going in the Henry James direction."

An Interview with Richard Wright

Hans de Vaal/1953

From *Litterair Paspoort*, 8 (July-August 1953), 161–163. Translated by Edward Lemon.

Richard Wright is a friendly, personable man, with an open character and an unpretentious manner. He speaks plainly, his voice has a musical sound, and in his manner of speaking is the inclination to feel responsible for whatever he says. He gives the impression of being a healthy person with a good memory, an intelligent view of the things around him; he has an intellectual manner of reacting. He answered my questions with spontaneity and interest, and during the two hours I spent in the salon of his apartment, it seemed clear to me that this American author was conscious of what he could attain by his writing; his creative occupation—that of the social artist—is appropriate. Richard Wright is—I say this for safety's sake, although I realize that it is not actually necessary—the author of *Uncle Tom's Children, 12 Million Black Voices, Native Son,* and *Black Boy,* along with a great number of articles, reviews, etc. and other short stories than those collected in the first-named book, which are published here and there in periodicals and anthologies. In March of this year, his new novel *The Outsider* appeared in America.

Richard Wright lives, with his wife and children, in a quiet apartment in the Rue Monsieur-le-Prince in Paris, and there the following interview took place.

Mr. Wright, how do you consider the literature of the American Negro: as "American Negro Literature" and thus an isolated literature, or as belonging to American Literature in general?

The literature of the American Negro takes on a certain validity in connection with the attitude of the whites (in America) with respect to the Negroes. While and as long as the American Negroes are oppressed, their means of artistic expression gain in intensity. Around a half century ago, the historian and essayist Booker T. Washington doubted whether Negroes could express themselves intellectually. Booker T.

Washington was of the opinion that the American Negro was fit only for handiwork, and he foresaw a great future for Negroes as farmers, merchants, servants, and technical craftsmen. Alain Locke (professor of philosophy at Howard University) revolted against Booker T. Washington's ideas, and resisted the entire context of ideas about the situation of the Negroes in America. From Locke comes the concept of "The New Negro." His train of thought inaugurated a new era, as it were, an era of reform, enlightenment, and a radical change from antiquated theories.

Seen against this historical background, I regard, for the present, the literature of American Negroes as a distinct means of expression, which is true for the attitude of the Negroes with regard to the attitude of the whites toward the Negroes. Moreover, or rather, as a result of this, it is evident that the so-called American Negro Literature is bound with unbreakable bonds to what is usually understood as social literature, literature which has thus arisen from, or been caused by the situation to which it has been directed. Since he has for a long time been hindered from expressing himself in artistic or intellectual areas, the Negro has always had a kind of fear, or reserve, from expressing his bitterness. Now the fear or reserve has disappeared, and the modern American Negro literature fits completely into the mood of the literature of the Twentieth Century.

How do you see the future of the American Negro Literature?

It won't change as long as the attitude of the whites toward the Negroes remains unchanged. On the other hand, it's possible that the American Negro Literature in the long run will become a literature in which the problems of the world are summarized.

What is your opinion of the so-called "racial type?" Are you of the opinion that it consists of certain psychic characteristics, perhaps or perhaps not hereditary, or do you think the whole racial type idea a farce, in the sense that Toynbee expressed it in his A Study of History: *"The so-called racial explanation of differences in human performance and achievement is either an ineptitude or a fraud"?*

Indeed, that is correct. We don't know anything about race. Whenever we speak of race, or use the term racial type, we speak, in fact, of a void which cannot be filled. I believe that it must be the task of the American Negro artist to liquidate this nonsense about race. The word

"race" should—as long as it is current in our speech—actually always
be obliged to be placed between quotation marks. Race is a social myth,
not a biological fact.

You perhaps know what John Stuart Mill wrote in Principles of Political Economy *almost a century ago: "of all vulgar modes of escaping
from the consideration of the effect of social and moral influences on
the human mind, the most vulgar is that of attributing the diversities of
conduct and character to inherent natural differences." Do you agree
with this classical observation?*
Yes, of course. It is evident in other respects that not enough stress
can be laid on this. When the Western World began racial discrimination in the colonies there was little or no protest from the side of the
races that were discriminated against. In America, this protest began at
the beginning of the Twentieth Century. William E. B. DuBois was one
of the predecessors of the "New Negro" movement. The pressure to
avoid this Western discrimination arose from him, and can be explained
by the ideas of Marx, whose philosophy was the seed from which the
"New Negro" was born.

Do you think a political Negro population possible in America?
Theoretically yes, but practically, no. If all Negroes should unite
themselves as a close group to fight discrimination, they would not get
much farther than to get themselves eradicated, one and all. This is not
the way to liquidate discrimination. Do not forget that there is, in fact,
no Negro problem; *there is a white problem.* However militant the
Negroes may be in their fight for civil rights, they must always compromise and take heed of and work together with the whites of good will
and progressive attitudes towards unsocial conditions.

*Do you believe that in the future the Negro problem—which is in-
deed, as you have said, a white problem—will disappear?*
That's possible. The so-called Negro problem is America's problem
and it will be dependent on the social changes that are to develop in the
American society, whether the discrimination against Negroes is to
disappear or not. Of course, much has already been attained, and more
is yet to be done. The Negro problem in America is very different from
the one in South Africa. The American Negroes are Americans; in other
words, they are just as original inhabitants of America as all other

Americans, with the exception of the Indian, who is the only 100%
American. The Negroes want what all Americans want and legally are:
nothing other than to be regarded as American citizens, in other words,
to have all normal civil rights which belong to every American citizen.
The American Negroes can and want to live nowhere else but in the
United States of North America. The national countenance of the United
States makes a miserable impression on the rest of the world, as long as
the Negro problem remains a problem. Progressive influence from outside can make the American people deeply conscious of the impossible
social aspects of American society. For example, I am convinced that
the admission of Negro students to various universities in the Northern
states has been a success as a result of international suggestions. The
situation of the Negroes in America, their position in American society,
can not otherwise be observed and approached than from a sociological
standpoint.

The Negro problem is, in fact, a social-economic problem, including
all the psychological facets of such a problem.

*What does the church in America do towards the Negro problem; or,
in other words, what influence does religious activity have on discrimination?*

The church, fundamentally, does little and stimulates not at all. Religious activities do not occupy themselves with the oppression of the
Negroes. There exists a definite fundamental idea, an observable interpretation of the Christian faith, but its influence on the relation between
Negroes and whites is very little. The activities of the church—if they
ever were important with regard to the Negro problem—have never
brought about a favorable change. I believe that in the future, too, we
can expect little from the side of the church. Also, the Negroes themselves have never been made aware of their social position by the
church. This is remarkable, considering the fact that after the civil war
the church had played a rather important role in the education of the
Negro population; already many Negroes do not acknowledge this fact.

*Are you of the opinion that—seen in the light of the attitude of the
Southern states (of the United States) toward the Negroes—the South is
fascistic?*

Fascistic is not the correct word. The South is feudalistic. Moreover,
it is too disorganized to develop into a fascistic power. The difficulty in

the Southern states is, that as soon as the Negro starts to develop himself in a upward direction, in intellectual and other areas, discrimination
increases.

*Then you agree with what Walter White once said: "lynching is much
more an expression of southern fear of Negro progress than of Negro
crime."?*
Yes, that is correct.

Do you attach any value to the American Creed *as regards discrimination?*
The *American Creed* has, in principle, great value; I attach, however,
no single value to the attitude of countless white Americans with regard
to the *American Creed.* If you as a Negro, above all in the South, show
yourself with the ideas of the *American Creed,* they'll immediately
throw you into an insane asylum.

*What is your opinion of organizations like the NAACP (National
Association for the Advancement of Colored People—founded in 1909;
Walter White is director—H.d.V.)?*
Such organizations work, it is true, on the principles of the *American
Creed,* but they form no political movement and are only active in a
humane sense. Their significance is of importance, but they are not
opposed to social abuses. They perform social work, and help when and
where they can.

*Do you see in a favorable sense a stimulating influence on the masses
from films like* No Way Out *and* Home of the Brave*?*
To tell the truth, I distrust their influence. I believe that such films
produce little good. They correspond rather to a search for sensation
than a cause of a healthy reaction by the public.

What is the theme of your new novel?
Man without a home, without rest, without peace, in an industrial
culture. The main character is a Negro, but he, in contrast to Bigger
Thomas in *Native Son,* does not react as a colored person in a domi-
nating white world, but as a human victim of social circumstances. The
background is Chicago and New York.

For what reason do you live in Paris?
I like Paris, and I like France. I like the life here—the "live-and-let-
live" idea. Paris has a good climate for working.

Where else have you lived or travelled, excluding France?
I have lived in South America, and I've travelled in Italy, Switzerland, and England.

Have you any plans for returning to America?
During the six years I have spent in France, I've returned to America
twice, but for the present, I have no plans for returning.

What do you think of Europe?
Europe is in many aspects a sad part of the world. It has a dilemma.
It stands before the choice of defending itself against military powers, or
deciding to provide complete social security for its population.

Do you have any definite plans for the future?
To write, just to write.

To which authors do you find yourself attracted?
In the first place, to the pre-revolutionary Russians. Also Flaubert,
De Maupassant, Kafka, Gide, Proust, Sartre, Camus, Thomas Mann,
Joseph Conrad, Thomas Hardy, Thomas [sic] Moore, Sherwood Ander-
son, and Theodore Dreiser.

*Are you interested in American novels written by whites that have the
Negro problem as subject?*
The novels I have read have not especially impressed me. But I must
add that I find it difficult, with the exception of French literature, to
read novels. I keep myself busier with literature about psychology,
anthropology, and sociology.

Are you interested in music or painting?
I like Jazz, Beethoven and Schubert. Abstract art appeals to me.

*Have you ever come across a false interpretation of your literary
work, in a criticism or something similar?*
I can remember a critic who dealt with the "typical Negro soul" in my
work. That is, of course, ridiculous. There is not, nor has there ever
been, anything like a "Negro soul." There is only a human soul.

Conversation with Richard Wright

Johannes Skancke Martens/1954

From the Oslo *Aftenposten*, 12 August 1965, p. 3. Translated by
Toby Pedersen.

The American author Richard Wright, known among other things for his
novels *Native Son* and *Black Boy,* recently took an interesting journey,
which at the same time was quite an experiment. Being an ancestor of
Negro slaves who had been brought by force to the United States from
Africa, he went to the Gold Coast—the wealthiest and most highly
developed Negro colony—in order to see with his own eyes the land
from which his ancestors came. In other words, a journey to "the old
country"—in the fifth or sixth generation!

"How do you know that you are a descendant of inhabitants of this
particular part of Africa?" I ask the forty-five-year-old, cultivated,
friendly, and cheerful author during a visit to his home in the Latin
Quarter in Paris. He has now lived in France for six years with his wife
and two young daughters.

"An American Negro can never be quite certain where his ancestors
came from, although certain physical features can give a hint as to
which part of Africa they were abducted from. But we know that the
largest and most numerous shipments of slaves occurred from the stretch
of land that has been named 'The Gold Coast.' The tribal chiefs took
their slaves here from the interior and sold them to white buyers. The
blacks had slaves, too, mostly prisoners of war, and they could see no
wrong in this institution; having slaves was a natural part of the country's political, social, and religious structure. The black chiefs saw
nothing immoral in selling their own slaves, although they probably had
no suspicion of the terrible fate many of them met during the horrible
passages to 'the new world,' and the inhuman treatment they so often
were subject to. Slaves were a commodity being bought and paid for in
cash. That white, Christian societies imported slavery and regarded
colored heathens as being little elevated above the animal stage, is an
entirely different matter that we will not deal with here."

"Did they not also conduct regular roundups of blacks?"

"Oh yes, some kidnappings did occur, but most Negroes were sold by other Negroes, then to be sold again—with good profit—by the white buyers."

"I assume that you, being fully imprinted by Western civilization, did not feel much kinship with the population of the Gold Coast?"

"The strange thing was that I almost felt something like that," Richard Wright says, and smiles with white teeth in his distinguished, oval, golden-brown face. "But I must admit that the fact that my skin is dark did not help; I had to study anthropology and familiarize myself with many customs and ways of thinking that to me naturally were entirely foreign. A race being governed by another race, a people whose existence is being dictated from above by strangers, develop their own mentality. What is interesting is that in Africa western ideas mix with the older, heathen ideas. They do not constitute two separate, different worlds; they blend together, and there is no doubt that the original deep-rooted tribal culture is most prominent. The heathen ideas gain more acceptance as the Negroes gain more self-government. In spite of 500 years of colony rule, the people are fundamentally untouched by Christianity!"

"Being a Christian, how do you feel about this development?"

"To that I would just answer that we have to realize that rarely do things work out the way we would like them to, or the way the white man had hoped and thought they would, in the countries he colonized. As colored nations again become free and self-governed, they will follow their own ideas across the perceptions of the west. When the Europeans tried to convert the heathens, they only drove them further into their own world. Missionaries I have talked to did not seem as convinced as they often were before. Now they are mostly trying to help the population, and they put less emphasis on categoric regulations about what they feel is best for the blacks to believe. The national movements are very strong everywhere in Africa, they are deep and intense, and maybe most of all in the Gold Coast, which is a highly developed country."

"No, I can't say I was very well received," Richard Wright answers one question and smiles again. "A colony will always remain a kind of geographic prison where one is afraid that strangers can bring unrest, and where one maintains a coolly waiting attitude. But the governor and the English senior officials have retreated more and more, and all the internal matters of the country are now being governed by the natives. For five months I was the guest of the prime minister, the Negro Nkrumah. Over three-fourths of the land is owned by the inhabitants of the country. Earlier, the English ruled through the chiefs, but these receive less and less power. The Europeans are now more interested in doing business; the Gold Coast is enormously rich, and is earning lots of dollars. Here is gold, naturally, and manganese and bauxite, and timber and two-thirds of the world's cocoa plantations. The country has a population of 4.5 million people."

"As a colored man, how do you view the condition in Kenya?"

"The conditions there are different, as the whites there forced the inhabitants away from their land and took it away from them. The blacks were pushed into the primeval forest, away from the areas where they had lived for ages. Mau-Mau's task is to take back the land of their ancestors. This problem does not exist in the Gold Coast. I see the Mau-Mau movement as 'frustration turned into violence'—disappointment and despair finding an outlet in violence. It is regretful, but one must not forget that the African people have a keen sense of what is unfairness toward them. Unfortunately, I fear that the future of South Africa will be bloody. The black population does not want the country to be either white or black; they want their rights, and they know that whites and blacks need each other. The whites in South Africa behave in an incredibly stupid and short-sighted way; the oppression of the many million colored people can only result in a terrible explosion."

"But do you think Mau-Mau can achieve anything through their terroristic murders?"

"They have already achieved something," Wright says. "No white man wants to go to Kenya and take land there today! No British now want to settle as farmers in the country."

Through the huge door opening from the author's library I see Mrs. Wright entering the dining room with a tablecloth and plates to set the table for lunch. After receiving some photos that Richard Wright himself has taken in Africa and hearing the assurance that they both are happy to live in Paris, I wish good luck to the book *Black Power,* which will be out this fall, and I conclude the conversation with an important man who is intensely concerned with the racial problems and racial conflicts that seem to characterize the middle of the twentieth century.

Richard Wright: I Curse the Day When
for the First Time I Heard the Word "Politics"
L'Express/1955

From *L'Express*, 18 October 1955, p. 8. Introductory paragraph and
questions translated by Keneth Kinnamon.

The great black writer Richard Wright, author of *Black Boy, Native
Son,* and *Uncle Tom's Children,* has just published, with Correa, *Black
Power,* his impressions of a stay in Africa. He was willing to reply here
to a questionnaire that we had submitted to him:

Why do you write?

Writing is my way of being a free man, of expressing my relationship
to the world and to the society in which I live. My relation to the society
of the Western world is dubious because of my color and race. My
writing therefore is charged with the burden of my concern about my
relation to that society. The accident of race and color has placed me on
both sides: the Western World and its enemies. If my writing has any
aim, it is to try to reveal that which is human on both sides, to affirm
the essential unity of man on earth.

Which books have influenced you most?

The books that have influenced me would make a long list. I'll be
selective. Foremost among all the writers who have influenced me in
my attitude toward the psychological state of modern man is Dostoevsky. Proust's work has painted for me what I feel to be the end of
the bourgeois class of Western Europe. Gorky represents to me a writer
and artist whose courage and humanity towered above politics. Of
American writers, Theodore Dreiser first revealed to me the nature
of American life, and for that service, I place him at the pinnacle of
American literature.

Who are your favorite contemporary writers?

I don't do much reading in contemporary novels. I find myself drawn
more toward historians, sociologists, and anthropologists. For the past

few years most of my reading has been the works of Freud, Malinow-
ski, Theodor Reik, Nietzsche, etc. Most contemporary novels are too
"cute" for me.

Is the writer an intellectual?

The writer is an intellectual in spite of himself. He may pretend that
he simply creates, but, in writing, he handles the basic assumptions of
men, and, in doing so, he feelingly selects facts and experiences for
presentation. One might say, then, that the writer's intellectualism is
indirect, but it is there all the same.

Do you write for a fixed audience?

No, I do not write for a special audience. I write and trust what I've
said may strike a responsive chord in some one else. During my career
as a writer, my so-called public has changed several times. I've found
that my audience changes with my own changing outlook. I do not seek
for an audience; I let the audience follow me, if it is interested.

Do you think that a writer should subsist from his writings?

A writer either lives in his works or he is no writer. Of all the arts
in the world, literature is the most exacting and the most revealing.
Writing is a way of living. Hence, if he can put himself totally in his
writings, he will find that he can live from them, perhaps.

Do you believe in defending ideas in your writing?

Yes, I defend ideas in my writing to the degree that I defend man's
right to live. Those ideas which I feel are harmful to man, I fight and
seek to destroy. Those ideas which I find life-furthering, I seek to
defend and extoll. From the position where I stand as a Negro writer,
such questions are not abstract. Those ideas in people's minds that are
against granting a fuller life to people of color, I fight. Those ideas I
find in the world which urge toward a richer sharing of life, I defend.

To what degree are you interested in politics?

In spite of myself, I'm passionately interested in politics. But I curse
the day when I first heard the word "politics." My racial identity places
me at the focal point of world politics. Merely to read my morning's
newspaper is to encounter political ideas debating the destiny of the
colored majority of mankind. Politics are policies, devised by the leadership for vast masses of people; these policies are for defense, attack,

or the subjugation of others. Hence though I'd like to forget politics,
I can't, for I find too many hostile policies subtly directed toward the
subjugation of peoples and races and nations.

To you, what is the historical date most charged with significance?
The 1905 victory of the Japanese over Russia. That date marked the
beginning of the termination of the Godlike role which the Western
white man had been playing to mankind. That date marked the beginning of the de-Occidentalization of the world.

Are your favorite heroes in real life in literature?
I have no political heroes in life; all politicians, to me, are misfor-
tunes. My heroes are medical and scientific ones: Einstein, Pasteur, etc.
In literature some of my heroes are: Raskolnikov in Dostoevsky's
"Crime and Punishment"; the *I* of Proust's "A Remembrance of Things
Past"; *K* of Kafka's "The Trial"; Melanctha of Gertrude Stein's "Three
Lives"; and Nietzsche in his own "Thus Spake Zarathustra".

Do you believe in the future of man?
I don't feel that the future is as black as some think and surely not as
bright as others paint it. Man, I fear, will continue to stumble along in
the future more or less as he did in the past, paying terribly for each step
forward he makes. The future for me holds neither Hell nor Heaven,
just the same struggling and fumbling that man has always done. Man is
the most stubborn and habit-forming of all the animals; once an idea
gets into his head, only death can take it out. Hence, man will make
progress in the future just as painfully and slowly as he made progress
in the past.

Interview

Raymond Barthes/1956

Transcript of a radio broadcast on ORTF, Paris. Translated by
Michel Fabre.

*You have recently been traveling a good deal, visiting Africa, the Gold
Coast last year, and then spending some time exploring the customs and
beliefs in Spain, and finally reporting on Asian and Oriental nations in
your volume about the Bandung Conference. . . . I suppose you travel
in order to keep in touch with what is happening in the world?*

Yes, I make many voyages to keep in as close contact with contemporary man as possible. It is my way of avoiding the barrage of propaganda from all quarters and of exposing myself to reality at first hand.
This is what I think the artist should do as much as possible in order that
his sensibilities can carry a rich burden of concrete reference.

*This is your definition of your ambition as an artist. What is your
ambition as a writer?*

Writing is for me a means of being free, a means of defining my
relationship with the world and with the society in which I live or which
I am observing. I do not write for a special audience, but I always hope
that what I am writing will arouse some echo in somebody else. My
audience has changed insofar as I was myself changing. A writer lives
through his work; otherwise he is no real writer. Of all artistic attempts,
writing is the most exacting one; also the most revealing. Writing is a
way of living.

*By those changes in your career, do you mean that your former books
and autobiographical narratives and that you later wanted to bear witness on the major problems of our times through* The Color Curtain,
through Black Power? *Does your reverting to the pure novel form with*
Savage Holiday *represent yet another change?*

Well, I don't know what you mean by "pure novel." In my opinion
all novels, of necessity, possess an autobiographical basis. The work of
Marcel Proust was surely anchored firmly in the autobiographical material. The same is true of the novels of James Joyce. I could say the same

thing of the tremendous novels of American life written by Theodore
Dreiser.

It is true that in my early work I was almost wholly concerned with
the reactions of Negroes to the white environment that pressed in upon
them. Having left America and having been living for some time in
France, I have become concerned about the historical roots and the
emotional problems of Western whites which make them aggressive
toward colored peoples. You can see from this that my travels into the
Argentine, into Africa and Asia even have an autobiographical inspiration. I was looking for explanations of the psychological reactions of
whites. In my novel *The Outsider*, the hero of which was a Negro, I had
already abandoned the black hero proper. That novel is anchored mainly
in reflection and is concerned with problems that would beset anyone,
black or white.

In your last novel, Savage Holiday, *there is no longer any question of
racial problems, nor does one encounter a single black man.*

The protagonist is called Erskine Fowler. He is a rather wealthy New
York insurance agent in his forties. He is white. But, as his name indi-
cates, his problem is mostly moral, or it has been defined in terms of
social morality. Fowler brings to one's mind the notion of being "foul,"
of defiling, of not behaving according to social rules.

*This Erskine Fowler is at the beginning of a very long holiday. By the
way, the title of the novel stresses that notion of being on holiday.*

Indeed. In this novel, I have attempted to deal with what I consider as
the most important problem white people have to face: their moral dilemma. This is why I have chosen this white New Yorker as a protagonist. Now, after some thirty years of service in an insurance company,
he has just been retired although he is barely forty-three.

*Thus finding himself unemployed—or more exactly, on vacation—
very unexpectedly. Is this why you chose* Savage Holiday *as a title?*

The reason is that my character, Erskine Fowler, discovers that being
free and wealthy (for he has enough money) at his age does not at all
represent the kind of wonderful opportunity most people would wish.
The very fact that he feels he is free, free from any compelling obligation, is for him the most terrifying thing that ever befell him. He proves
unable to take advantage of his freedom, to even simply bear it, because

he is inhabited by a sense of guilt which makes him unhappy and pushes him to the final catastrophe. Until then he had been capable of forgetting, we can even say repressing, his feeling of guilt through his acquisition of material wealth. And now he finds himself suddenly deprived of his job and work.

If the sudden freedom Fowler is plunged into drives him to despair, is it not because he had been unable to establish relationships with other people? Was he not living in a kind of vacuum?

This inability, and mostly his conflicting feelings, appear most clearly in Fowler's relationship with the mother of a young boy in the apartment next to his. This woman's behavior would be labeled as immoral. And from the beginning the protagonist is tortured by two contradictory impulses. Should he love and redeem Mabel Blake or should he hate and destroy her?

The moral dilemma becomes an acute one after a rather funny incident—a fait divers *of the sort one finds in the newspapers.*

Yes indeed. On a Sunday morning Fowler leaves his apartment stark naked in order to pick up the newspaper in front of his door. The door slams shut before he has time to step back and he finds himself trapped outside of his place with nothing on. Such a condition brings to the surface, to his consciousness, acute feelings of anguish and utter panic which had always been latent within him and had conditioned his life although he had tried to fend them off.

I was struck by the fact that when he retired Erskine Fowler was a rich man. Working at the insurance company where he had started as an errand boy had enabled him to save some fifty million francs.

Several French friends of mine shared your reaction. This, however, is a rather common thing in the United States, where it is relatively easy to climb the social ladder and to make money. It is provided you consider work as a kind of religion, as your *raison d'être*. But I would say it does not really matter in *Savage Holiday* whether the protagonist is a rich man or a poor one. What matters is his fear of assuming the responsibilities entailed by his new kind of life, a holiday, i.e., a life deprived of the props and supports of a daily task to perform. His dilemma brings him to be responsible for two deaths—he is accidentally responsible for the death of his female neighbor's son, and he deliberately murders her some time later.

Richard Wright

Fernanda Pivano/1957

From *Il giorno*, 19 January 1957. Translated by John C. Stubbs.

Shortly after the end of the war, the French government invited the American novelist Richard Wright to Paris in the capacity of an "honored guest." The invitation had been solicited for him by Jean Paul Sartre, then the uncontested hero of the French literary scene. Wright accepted the invitation with enthusiasm and brought with him to Paris his wife, his daughter, his Siamese cat Nabi, two typewriters, and a good supply of lined, yellow paper. It was a little after that period when he came to Rome for the first time. In Rome, he underwent with polite amazement the slightly provincial assault of our photographers and interviewers. These people lost no opportunity to emphasize the color of Wright's skin, as opposed to the significance of his books. In his presence, they went so far as to improvise a kind of referendum to find out from the ladies present how many of them had no objection to "sleeping" with him.

For the writer who was by then accustomed to be known as the major exponent of American "protest literature," this kind of curiosity must have seemed strange, to say the least. Especially puzzling must have been the fact that very few of these people know what he had written and what he was trying to do. In Paris, his fame was, on the other hand, a very solid thing. For some time, he directed the journal *Twice a Year* there and became later on one of the promoters of *Présence Africaine*, which introduced in France so many Negro writers and poets from America.

During this period in France, Wright lived in one of the most luxurious and "bourgeois" quarters of Paris. If you walked through his two-story apartment, among easy chairs and divans, flowers and lace objects, lampshades, and chinaware, you would come to balconies which overlooked Paris and the Seine. Wright would do the honors of the house with the smile of a man happy to be kind to superficial acquaintances. But real friends he conducted upstairs to his "studio." It was not a true studio, but a small room, a kind of garret, which con-

tained with difficulty a small folding bed, a bookcase jammed with
books, a phonograph console with a spare typewriter on it, and a table
with the number one typewriter, reams of yellow paper, a telescope to
see into the houses of other people, a row of pieces of colored marble,
some boxes full of little white stars, records on "the way to learn
French," a stapler, a large pair of scissors to cut away mistakes, and,
in short, a deluge of objects indispensable to his work and life.

Sitting on the bed, chatting in a relaxed manner, but not smiling,
Wright told his story. He told it without rhetoric and, at bottom, without rancor. Dishwasher, streetcar, ditchdigger. At twelve, a paralytic
mother to watch over. Then the migration from Memphis to the North,
to Chicago, and the attempts to become a postal clerk. Then an agent
for an insurance company. Then without work, at the point of despera-
tion, at the point of going to the welfare office, he was given a job at
a hospital, washing the stairs and cleaning up the cages of the experi-
mental animals. While he talked, Wright stared at the letter from the
French government which had invited him to France. The letter was
affixed to the head of the bed. It was framed. Perhaps, the writer didn't
actually see it, absorbed as he was in his past. His real life began with
the New Deal of Roosevelt, when the Federal Writers' Project allowed
him to begin his literary activity. His first story in '35 and his first
collection of stories in '37. His stories opened up for him a series of
literary prizes and fellowships. With his collection of stories, called
appropriately *Uncle Tom's Children,* Wright had clearly delineated his
position as a protest writer. When *Native Son* came out in '40, the
book's success grew to the point where, the following year, it invaded
Broadway. Orson Welles became the producer of a theatrical version
which Wright himself made from his book (but together with Paul
Green, because Broadway "could not" present works of Negro writers
which weren't co-signed with a white signature).

Then we began to speak about the "life structure" of Wright. For
those of us who were interested in American fiction despite the advice
and judgement of the authorities and the academies, news about Wright
arrived stealthily. But in America, the leading intellectuals were already
in the process of systematizing his guilt complex, producer of hate and
fear, and consequently of violence, in a true and proper psychological
"structure" which consisted essentially of the clash of feelings that agitate man in his everyday life. This "structure" explains how Wright, in

his autobiography, can define himself as both cowardly and rash, thief
and gentleman, and so on. The only way out, the only refuge, it seemed
then to Wright, was violence, all the violence possible, in all directions.

In the tiny room in Paris, while speaking of such violence, Wright
stroked his cat Nabi with his beautiful, aristocratic hands. He was a very
clear image of the contrast which is the keystone of his poetic world.
There was no doubt that the first one to hate such violence was he, there
in Paris to forget that racial and protest literature existed and to become
solely a writer, at base psychological and moral if you will, but outside
polemics of races and sides.

In this direction, the years have led him. Since then Wright has
travelled much and has written books on his impressions of his travels.
He went to Argentina where he enlarged his range of activities to include playing the protagonist in a film version of his *Native Son*. He
now lives in the St. Germain quarter of Paris, on an elegant street and in
a tasteful, sober apartment. His wife, who is also his literary agent, has
assimilated the fashions and dress of Paris to perfection, and the daughters of Wright (now there are two) take turns appearing in the living
room to greet guests according to the dictates of a rigid European education. No longer are there records for learning French around. The
French in Wright's household keeps, to the ear of a foreigner, only a
light accent that is exotic and charming. The mother often takes the two
daughters back to the United States, and the father departs often on long
journeys. When the family is reunited, guests are received with great
courtesy and great frequency. Not always, but when his work is going
satisfactorily, it may happen that Wright will come out of his studio and
join the conversation for a moment.

Wright does still maintain a "studio." However, it is no longer located in a tiny room. In this house, there is no need to give up any mid-
dleclass comfort. His table is still the same, and it is still covered with
objects of all kinds. But there is also a reading desk, since the work of
Wright now often has scientific bases that require large research volumes. The bookshelves are jammed with books, but Jaspers and Heidegger are no longer in sight (I believe that Wright was one of the very
few who read these authors at a time when it was enough to glance
through a novel by Sartre to consider yourself an existentialist.) In sight
now are books by scientists and psychologists and volumes of French
literary journals.

Wright has almost no need anymore to smile in order to show himself a happy man. He continues to detest crowds or mobs, especially carnival crowds ("You never know what kind of a thing can break out in a crowd.") He continues to love cats ("Cats treat well those who are loyal to them and do them no harm.") He continues to love spirituals ("I like them, but I don't like to talk about them or read what people write about them.") He continues to be a person of a very fickle humor and to be subject to a sensitiveness that stretches as far as divination. He continues to write books, and he continues to be, in spite of his present work, the leader of a whole generation of writers who look back to his past work, the literature of protest of the depression generation. This is the case even if Wright has now changed his protest from the sphere of the social world to the more insidious, untrustworthy one of the psychological world.

Are the United States One Nation, One Law, One People?

La Nef/1957

From *La Nef*, 14 (November 1957), 57–60. Introduction and questions translated by Keneth Kinnamon.

Since 1947 the black writer Richard Wright has been an "American in Paris." His first trip to France goes back to 1946, but as soon as he went home to the United States he decided to return to France and settle with his family (two daughters fifteen and eight years old). In fact, he values Paris as one of the only cities where he can work freely: "The racial problem," he says, "does not play as prominent a role here as elsewhere." It is this question, in fact, that is at the bottom of Wright's entire life.

Born in Mississippi in 1908 of a schoolteacher mother and a peasant father, he did his first studies in a school attended only by blacks. At sixteen he left Mississippi and began to work in Tennessee as an office boy. Two years later he went up to Chicago, where he spent several years as a postal worker. Meanwhile he was reading a lot and beginning to write.

In 1932 he joined the Communist Party, where he was to remain for ten years. At that time he contributed to the *Daily Worker* and to various communist magazines.

In 1938 he published *Uncle Tom's Children* and in 1940 *Native Son*. In 1942 he left the Communist Party and brought out *12 Million Black Voices*, which is still unpublished in France. In a long article entitled "I Tried to Be a Communist" he explained the reasons for his changing sides. This article has appeared in France in a work assembling several testimonials entitled *The God of Darkness* [English title: *The God That Failed*].

Today Richard Wright devotes himself to the essential task of struggle against racist feelings. In 1945 he published *Black Boy,* in 1955 *Black Power, The Outsider,* and *The Color Curtain.* On 19 October of this year he brought out *White Man, Listen!* in New York.

Because of his knowledge of the issue and because of his

personal situation, Richard Wright can understand better
than anyone else the recent events in Little Rock which he
comments on below.

Q. *During the last few years a movement against segregation has begun
in the United States. How do you explain the renewal of racism that we
ascertain today?*

A. It is impossible to understand the racial question in the United
States without first putting that question in its proper historical setting.
The first black slaves were brought to America in 1619, and, upon the
landing of these slaves and upon their being sold for labor, a racial
problem arose. That problem has assumed many forms: moral, cultural,
political, economic, social, etc. The first conflict was moral, for the introduction of slavery in America violated the ethical convictions of the
men who did it. Economic motives overruled these ethical doubts when
the cultivation of cotton became the dominant economic activity of the
South.

The rapid rise of the industrial North, presaging another and different
type of civilization, changed the racial problem from an economic one
into a political one; the issue was: what kind of labor would America
have: slave or free. Because there were millions of poor whites doomed
to eventual slavery if slavery had remained in America, and because
machines were more efficient than slaves, the industrial North won its
fight against the South, thereby "freeing" American labor, but allowing
the South to continue to maintain a kind of semislavery over millions of
"freed" Negroes who were deprived of the vote and all right to access to
the basic riches of the nation and of all right to participate in the social
life of the nation.

This state of affairs continued roughly until World War II, when, in
its conflict with Russian Communism, America's racial problem left its
domestic orbit and became an international issue by reason of America's
assumption of world leadership. During the so-called Cold War period,
the racial problem assumed acute importance because of America's attempt to influence Asians and Africans. The Supreme Court decision of
1954 was an attempt to bring American practices in line with American
preachments, though this attempt inflamed many Americans who have
been taught in church, school, and the press that they were biologically
superior to Negroes.

The present rise of racial feeling in the United States can be said to be a continuation of the Civil War passions, for it was directly after the Civil War that the victoriously industrial North abandoned the political fruits of their military victory and allowed the South to have its way. The present occupation of Little Rock by federal troops is a direct resumption of federal activity which left off in the South directly after the Civil War. Had those federal troops remained in the South and made sure that the Negro had his constitutional rights, the racial conflict in the nation today would have been resolved. In short, by compromising with the South, the North collected "moral" taxes one hundred years ahead. Today is the time for the historical presentation of the "moral" bill.

In a strict sense, there has been no resurgence of racial feeling in the United States; racial feeling has always been there. During the past ten years, due to the Cold War, America declared that she officially had no Negro or racial problem. Any Negro who said the contrary was dubbed "insane" or a Red. Today, after the Supreme Court decision, such a claim is no longer possible. The Negro, having been terriorized for a century into silence, is now pressing for the fullfulment of constitutional rights which have always been his.

Q. *Can one explain exactly why these recent events happened to take place in Little Rock?*

A. The centering of the present racial tensions in Little Rock is sheer historical accident. The Negroes anticipated that the South would elect to make a stand or a test somewhere. The test came from that segment of the South where "poor whites" found irresponsible, demagogic leadership in the person of Faubus, the governor of Arkansas. Yet the present conflict in Arkansas cannot be said to be wholly racial. The implementation of the laws against school segregation is being done through decisions of federal courts; Faubus decided to challenge the federal courts and see how far a state could go in nullifying federal law. If federal law could be successfully nullified in one state, then each American state could be free to have the types of racially segregated schools it wanted; but, also, it could declare itself free from the federal union, for such would be the meaning of the nullifying of federal law in the several states. Hence President Eisenhower's reactions to Faubus's challenge was to reassert the authority of the theory of one nation, one law, one people, as the American Constitution so clearly provides.

Q. *Do events such as those of Little Rock impel blacks to pursue the struggle or to resign themselves?*

A. The Negroes in the United States have *never* been resigned to racial segregation. They have been terrorized into accepting it. And those instruments of terror have been so elaborate and so widely accepted and practiced by whites both North and South that many white people have come to feel that such an arrangement was natural. This system of terror was practiced daily, intimately; any Negro who voted or tried to vote in the South did so at the risk of his life; he had to live in a separate area; he went to separate schools; all of his institutions, shops, hospitals, newspapers, etc., were run by black people. The Negro never asked to erect these racially separate institutions; he had either to build them or he would have perished. In short, there exists in the United States a black nation within the white nation, a form of sub-life rejected by the nation.

Yet the Negro in his schools, churches, neighborhoods, reacted to and lived by the same ideals, mores, and incentives that the whites lived by. Black children studied the same text books that the white children studied, but under vastly inferior educational conditions. For example, in the state of Mississippi, until very recently, white and black were taxed equally, but for every dollar that was spent to educate a black child, *five* dollars were spent to educate a white child. Naturally, the black child's educational status reflected this disparity of unequal treatment and inflicted upon that black child a handicap for life in its attempt to earn a living or to adjust to the American scene. Psychologically, the Negro suffered from his handicap. The militancy with which the Negro is pushing to obtain equality in education reflects his desire to overcome this handicap.

Q. *During the Rosenberg affair most American writers were struck dumb. Will the same reasons impel them to be silent in the presence of Little Rock?*

A. Question No. 4 is a "European" question. The American writer does not occupy the same moral position in America that the European writer enjoys in Europe. Hence it is wrong to look toward American writers for comment upon current questions; it is, rather, to the press that one must look for comment. The American press was filled with comment in both the Rosenberg and the Little Rock events. You will find in the Negro press much comment about the plight of the Jew in the United States, and you will find many Jewish organizations concerned with the Negro problem in the United States. But there has never existed in the United States, except under direct Communist leadership, groups of creative writers taking stands upon political issues. The American form of political action is less ideological and more pragmatical and direct. Therefore a European will look in vain in America for certain forms of political action among artists which are common in Europe. But this does not indicate any broad lack of interest among the Americans on any given subject.

Q. *Do you conceive of conditions under which racism in the United States would disappear?*
A. It is easy to *conceive* of the conditions under which racism in America will vanish, but the *establishment* of those conditions is quite another and different thing.

The abolition of manifestations of racism in the United States could have been rather easily achieved if, after the Civil War, the federal government had not compromised with the racist dictates of the South. Had the North clung to the political fruits of its military victory, the racial problem in the United States today would have been of manageable proportions. The North, however, compromised, left the white South to its own methods and that white South created the racial problem which the nation today is trying belatedly to solve.

There is no hard and fast guarantee that the problem will be solved. The Negro in the United States might well meet the fate that the Jew met in Germany. Manifestly, the problem of race relations in the United States today is more difficult than it was directly after the Civil War. Today racism has sunk deep roots in the United States, both in the North and in the South. It is difficult today to conceive of the several states actually fighting a civil war about the question of the Negro. Yet the Negro is there, pushing for what he had been taught to be his birthright.

It has been conveniently forgotten that some two million American Negroes, directly after World War I, organized themselves under the abortive leadership of Marcus Garvey and sought to leave the United States and return to Africa. The movement was romantic and impractical; but today, if the Negro feels that his position is hopeless, he cer-

tainly will repeat that effort. The Little Rock events, displaying as
they do violent white racist attitudes, are not reassuring. The Supreme
Court's 1954-integration decision has heartened the Negro fight, but the
violence in Little Rock has caused a tide of "nationalist" feeling among
Negroes, a tide which has reached its highest level since the time of
Marcus Garvey.

The Negro problem in the United States has been and is a *white*
problem. Whites created that problem and maintain it. The price of
America's leadership of the "free world" might well hinge upon the
manner in which white America meets her racial problem. If America
feels that she will not accord the Negro, who lives intimately in the
nation, his democratic rights, then the Asian and African will know
Americans hold toward them the same attitude of racial scorn that she
holds toward the American Negro. Hence the American Negro problem
is compounded of tremendous domestic and international tensions.
There is one statement that I can make with certainty: the Negro in the
United States will not accept, after his rights have been spelled out by
the Supreme Court, returning to his old status. Whether that means a
mass emigration from the United States on the part of the American
Negro or his adjustment to America depends upon the Negro, but upon
the moral feelings of white Americans. The maintenance of the present
status quo of present race relations, with their resulting psychological
crucifixion for some 18 million Negroes, is too high a price to pay for
Negroes who live in and support a nation that demeans them. The world
will watch with passionate interest to see what the white American answer will be. And when the white American answers the questions of
the Negro, he will be demonstrating his racial attitude toward one and
one-half billion colored people on earth today.

Q. *How do antiracist whites manifest their solidarity to blacks?*

A. Fear, timidity, emotional tension, evasion, hysteria, violence, and
an attempt to "talk" the problem of the Negro out of existence are common characteristics of the normal white American attitude toward the
Negro today.

Militating against these negative white racial attitudes are some impersonal and striking gains for the Negro. America's industrial civilization is filled with machines who do not care who runs them; trade
unionists know that they can maintain high wages only by incorporating

the Negro worker into their unions; the nation needs the manpower of
the Negro in times of war; the profit motive overrides the racial feelings
of many spheres of business life; and recently the church has sought to
create a "conscience" in the American white about racial relations . . .
Beyond these vague and impersonal tides of American feeling and action, there has been no real honest national effort at the betterment of
racial relations in the United States until the Supreme Court, in 1954,
ordered educational integration; and, of course, the recent Civil Rights
Bill is an indication that the heads of the nation realize their racial
stance before the world and are belatedly trying to present the American
ideal to the masses of Asia and Africa free of racial taint. This process
will be long and drawnout, for it has to overcome three hundred years of
racial indoctrination which white Americans instilled into their children.
Will racism vanish from the American scene? Only the hearts of white
Americans contain the answer to that question.

Black Culture

Jean José Marchand/1958

From *Preuves*, 86 (April 1958), 32; 87 (May 1958), 40–41. Translated by Keneth Kinnamon.

We asked a certain number of personalities to respond to the following questionnaire:

1. What does the term "black culture" mean to you *today?*

2. In your opinion, before the arrival of Europeans did a single black culure exist, or were blacks divided among diverse cultures, as whites, for example, can be white Judeo-Christians or white Brahmans?

3. What is the share of the colonial situation and that of modern industrial evolution in the spiritual crisis of blacks today? Does industrial progress (capitalist or socialist) compromise the future of an original black culture?

4. Does the birth of multiple religions in black societies of the present day represent progress or regression for the culture?

5. Several black poets of Africa state that they write in French or English because the ancient languages are no longer suited to their inspiration. What do you think?

6. What so you think about the present level of black sculpture? What future do you see for it?

7. According to you, what is the future of "Negro music?"

8. How do you judge the effort of numerous blacks in Brazil and the United States to adopt "white values"? Is the attempt illusory or fruitful?

Richard Wright: *The Black Is a Creation of the White*
Born in 1908, the great American writer, author of Black Boy *and* Black Power, *supports the traditional thesis of humanism. Black culture, even in its most admirable productions, is a culture of oppression. The disappearance of oppression will effect the disappearance of what is mistakenly called the "black soul." There is only one human species.*

1. For me, a Westernized black American, the term "black culture" represents the external aspects of the emotional and psychological expression of American, English, Dutch, and French people of African

ancestry reacting against their relation with the dominant white society
that has governed and conditioned their lives for the last four hundred
years or more. Although such an expression of culture may be called
"black," it is in fact the kind of expression any minority group makes
when it is placed in a situation where racial domination exists. In short,
blacks express themselves as "blacks" because they are treated that way.

2. In my opinion, before the Europeans invaded the African continent, there existed, in the largest and most general sense of the term, *a
single* culture among blacks in Africa. I am aware that such a response
provokes reflection and presents a number of difficulties. Whether they
prevail among African blacks or any other peoples, all the old religious
cults seem to me manifestations of a way of life and a culture. In observing the culture of black Africa, I would emphasize the principal
salient traits of that culture more than the customs or the local and
geographical differences. Now the culture that brought to blacks in
Africa a sense of life before the arrival of whites was that which *all*
shared before becoming "the evil ones," that is to say, learning to
reason and to be objective.

3. With the exception of South Africa, blacks in the United States,
and those who live in the British Commonwealth, today "black culture"
has no direct relation to industrial life. The relation that exists in Africa
is more indirect and negative than positive. Industrial civilization has
already influenced the attitude of the elite of the black world. *Blacks
have made themselves aware and they understand that the future of their
people depends upon the way in which they go about breaking with their
past and evolving in the future a rational society.* A large part of this
comes from the miraculous and tragic success of the Soviet Union.
Admiration for the implementation by the Soviet Union of its plan for
the industrialization of an underdeveloped country is *not ideological* in
origin. The acclamations received by the leaders of the Soviet Union on
their trips to Asia are an example. Because in everything having to do
with the spreading of ideas, the Western world is not very advanced in
relation to the Soviet Union. Thus one can say that though they live
under the domination of the West, blacks have been more influenced by
Soviet ideas than by Western ideas. The great mistake of the Western
world is that it has not taken pains or even tried to create an ideology or
a vocabulary designed for those who live under its domination. Except

for the infantile sermons of the missionaries, there is a void in this aspect of Western thought.

4. In my opinion the present diversity of religious feelings and religious ideas in Africa represents neither progress nor regression. For a population that has neither leaders nor guides, it is a necessary phase of the search for a way to blend the disparate elements into one whole and to meet pressing needs. The psychological imperatives that drive black Africans to meld incongruous elements arise from the void and the lack of a feeling for life into which Western domination has plunged them. Here the problem is not economic, but fundamentally psychological; yet no one wishes to see the issue in this way. Here the responsibility rests on the communists or the naive black rationalists.

5. The concrete problem of artistic creation is a very personal problem—and psychologically it is built on sand. Even a psychologist like Freud categorically refused to answer when such questions were put to him. The black artist, uprooted from his traditional, natural culture and transplanted in another culture, finds himself confronting problems that he often doesn't even understand. Whites themselves, responsible for the original transplantation of these blacks, do not understand the emotional and psychological complexities that will result in the life of blacks. Here we ascertain incomprehension on both sides.

It seems to me that numerous factors, mostly personal, intervene in this problem. For example, the notion of *time* plays an important role in artistic creation. For the artist who develops in his own culture this is not a problem. But for the uprooted, this problem can prove crucial. The problem of time is also complicated by the fact that the black artist who has to take this into account often does not know what broke his moral equilibrum. Brought up in France, in England, in America, or in Holland, he finds it more convenient to use French, English, or Dutch to express himself, *but in doing so he finds himself especially confined to Western themes and to a Western way of seeing things, even though he is describing the life of his people—a life that is on a plane and a level of existence that is completely different.* At last the black artist clasps the language that will gain him the largest audience, whether it is African or European.

6. and 7. I cannot reply to questions of this kind; they are beyond my competence. But what I have said above on the subject of literature applies, in a way, to painting and sculpture.

8. In my opinion, the adoption of "white values" by the blacks of Brazil and the United States is not done consciously, in terms of a racial choice. For everyone, the most natural tendency is to adapt oneself to one's environment. Thus a black American will write like the whites of his native land; it is not a matter of choice. He begins to do it before he is fully aware of the value of the stake on the racial plane. A black American writes more or less like a white American, and for more or less the same reasons. If a different tone exists, it is explained by the way in which the black is allowed to integrate himself into the country in which he was born and to the culture of which he is an organic part. In my view, the problem of fecundity is a personal problem. Here, it depends on the degree to which artist, white or black, calls up the hidden or unconscious powers of creation. Race is unrelated to this. Race only becomes a factor when an artist, for external or artificial reasons, becomes aware of it. Persons who are racially conscious are generally those who *have been led* to an awareness of racial differences—by the hostility of which they are the object, hostility that can go as far as practical jokes and penalties of every kind.

U.S. Lets Negro Explain Race Ills, Wright Declares

Barry Learned/1959

From *American Weekend*, 24 January 1959.

PARIS—"The United States leaves the burden of the racial problem to the Negro to explain. Some of the finest people I've known are whites who fought for the Negro. The many whites who stand up for the Negro should be encouraged to tell about it. It's a white problem, a moral problem. We didn't cause it."

American author Richard Wright, a Negro whose *Native Son, Black Boy,* and other novels have made him one of his nation's best-known writers, finds this his main criticism of the difficult handling of changing U. S. race relations.

"Improvement can only come about when the United States understands its role of leadership," Wright said in an exclusive *Weekend* interview here, where the author has lived for more than eight years.

"The free world should be made up of the majority of the people in the world, and Negroes make up a large part of the majority," he continued. "The United States must find strong tangible evidence of this on its own soil. If the racial problem is handled badly, America's reputation in Europe will deteriorate. If it is handled well, it will be a splendid, shining opportunity and demonstration to the world."

As for such troubles as the Little Rock incident, Wright said he considers the incident as part of the over-all problem, which he appraises in historical terms. "First," he said, "there was the injection of the Negro slave along with convicts and undesirable immigrants into the colonies, then the uneasy compromise after the Civil War which really didn't solve anything. These were the steps leading up to the Sureme Court decision (on school integration) which picked up all the loose threads."

On the subject of the Negro in literature, Wright declared that most Negro writers write mainly about the Negro question because it's the only experience they're allowed to get.

"If they had more chances to have wider experiences, they would

write about different subjects, but they're most at ease in this field,
therefore it's more natural.

"Negro literature," he continued, "is a good barometer of Negro reaction. As fields open up to Negroes, it will be reflected in Negro literature. There is a large group of Negro writers in Europe—Demby and
Ellison in Rome, for instance. All of them are broadening their experiences in a European context."

Wright himself has already published such non-racial books as *Pagan
Spain* and *Savage Holiday*.

"*Pagan Spain* is about a journey—or rather it's a descriptive account
of three automobile trips I made in Spain, the Spanish people I met, the
fiestas, flamencos, bullfights, the feeling of the country, the warmth
of the people and the incredible poverty. It has been published in Germany, Holland, Sweden and Italy, but not in Spain.

"I have an offer to go to French Equatorial Africa. I would travel
around with my notebooks and take copious notes. When you travel
you can exercise your total personality, observing things around you.
If you're in one place all the time, you tend to have a narrower personality," he declared.

"I'd like to get into Africa. I've been trying to advise French government officials about how to handle the Africans. The Africans want a
redefinition of their relationship. The French wouldn't sit down and talk
business with Sekou Toure. It's amazing that personal feelings enter
into the question so much, in spite of bauxite and other valuable min-
erals in Guinea.

"You have to try to explain the mentality of people under coloniza-
tion. It's pretty important, since there are over 200 million people in
Africa. The plantation owners are people who need psychological
luxury."

Now in his ninth year of living in Paris, Wright described the advantages of living and working there.

"It's a kind of brainwashing," said Wright, explaining why he chose
Paris' Latin Quarter as a neighborhood. "Americans make a beeline for
the Latin Quarter, and it's certainly lived up to its reputation.

"As for my being here, for a writer to come to Paris is nothing new.
Strindberg, Dostoevski, Gertrude Stein, Hemingway and the whole
World War I group came here. It's a natural place to come and work.

There's something about the French. Traditionally, they have made a place for the artist."

Wright himself spent his first 18 years as a sensitive Negro boy growing up in Natchez and Jackson, Miss., and Memphis, Tenn., and his experiences are the subject of his latest novel *The Long Dream.*

A Small Portrait of Richard Wright

Kenneth Faris/1959

From *The Negro History Bulletin*, 25 (April 1962), 155–56. ©
Association for the Study of Afro-American Life and History.
Reprinted by permission.

Early in April of 1959, not two years before his death, I phoned Richard
Wright at his home in Paris to request an appointment for an interview.
I stated my reasons, mentioned the names of some mutual acquaintances, and he invited me to come over, giving me an early date when
he would be free for an hour.

Shortly before nine o'clock on the following Saturday morning, I
walked the few blocks from my hotel to Mr. Wright's apartment in an
unpretentious building at 14 rue Monsieur le Prince in the sixth arron-
dissement. I reached the fourth floor and at my ring was let in by a
French maid in white cap and apron who took my hat and showed me
into what must he called a parlor. Wright was sitting with his back to
me in a wing-backed chair, reading a book in French, but he rose and
came to greet me with great civility, shaking my hand firmly and remembering my name, before he showed me to a chair near him.

He looked older than I had expected but this was because I retained
the image of him gained from the photograph usually used on the dust-
jackets of his books. It must have been taken in his early thirties and he
was now past fifty. He was of no more than average height and inclin-
ing to stoutness, although the features of his face were fine and his
hands and feet were small.

The first things one noticed about his face were his eyes, which were
large and round and very dark, but, surprisingly, I thought, reflecting
none of the pain and rage that was so much a part of his work. His face
was relatively unlined, the nose broad, but fine, the lips full with an
almost feminine curve. His ears lay close, and indeed his entire head
seemed compact and well-fashioned, set firmly on his nek. His skin was
smooth and tobacco-brown with a curious pleasing inner luminosity
such as I have occasionally seen in healthy brown skin which is neither
very dark nor very light, such as I have seen, for example, in the face
of Marian Anderson.

Wright was dressed in a single-breasted blue suit with a vest, white shirt, dark tie, small, polished black shoes. I thought he looked at first glance like a prosperous banker in a small Mid-western city.

When he spoke, his voice was high, brisk and youthful. Though he spoke with animation, he used few gestures and looked directly into my eyes. I noticed no Southern accent at all.

That morning Wright was excited about the rehearsals of a play he had translated from the French and adapted to an American theme. He was directing the all-Negro cast for the American Theatre in Paris, of which society he had been made an honorary officer along with Irwin Shaw, also resident in Paris.

Presently I heard a door behind me open slightly and Wright said, "Excuse me for a moment, my wife wants to see me." I never did see his wife, though, nor his two daughters, who I think were away from Paris in school at the time.

I looked about the narrow comfortable room, appreciating the charmingly self-conscious elegance that old French rooms and furniture impart. The rooms beyond seemed large, quiet, and well-appointed.

When he returned and had set down, I offered him a Gauloise but he declined. I got the impression that he neither smoked nor drank, though he indicated that I should smoke if I wanted to.

"When did you come to Paris, Mr. Wright?"

"In 1946. I've been here ever since."

"Do you contemplate ever returning, as so many writers eventually do, to what one might refer to as your roots?"

"No, never. And I wouldn't want to expose my daughters to the conditions I object to in America. There's nothing there for me. I have what I want in Paris."

"I think that your removal from your own people and country is part of the reason why you've largely stopped creating characters and chosen instead to make your statements in non-fiction forms."

"No. I don't think the two things have any relation, but your point is interesting."

"Would you care to say why you seem to have become increasingly concerned in your writing with political themes?"

"Not political per se so much as sociological. Politics, yes, but only to the extent that they affect black people in a given country. I always have been concerned with these problems. It's nothing new."

"Perhaps, I mean to say that your emphasis seems to have shifted from telling stories about individual Negroes to describing the situations of mass groups, if I can put it this way, to have shifted from the poetical to the polemical."

"There's some truth in that, though I wouldn't have phrased it in that way. I've just used the forms that seemed to me most suitable for what I had to say, for what I felt had to be said. In my book *Black Power,* for which I traveled thousands of miles in Africa and talked to innumerable people, Mr. Nkrumah among them, I was trying among other things to show people the force of black nationalism, the unsuspected force, a sweeping, powerful thing."

"Yes," I said, "and in an earlier book, *The Color Curtain,* where you were pointing out the significance of the exclusively non-white character of the Bandung Conference. I thought it was astute of you to have caught and evaluated the religious nature of the motivations of many of the delegates."

"The first time in history that such a thing had happened, an enormous event."

"In view of your political sophistication now, Mr. Wright, I was all the more interested to read your account in *The God That Failed,* where along with some others like Silone, Spender, and Koestler, you discussed your disenchantment with Communism. It seemed to me that the others were members out of conviction and you through accident, simply because the party organ gave you a chance to publish what you wrote. It seemed on your part a naive entanglement while the others knew what was going on and why they were there."

"I think that your distinction is for the most part a fair one. I don't think I really quite knew what was going on. And I was very young at the time."

"Could you envision yourself ever going back to Communism, to embrace it the way, say Paul Robeson does?"

He smiled as though he had anticipated the question. "No, its ideologies are bankrupt. I don't have any use for them."

"Something like Balzac said in the *Psysiologie* [sic] *du Mariage* that when one started with disgust he might come around to love, but when he started with love and it turned to disgust, he could never come around to love again."

"Yes, you could say that. Robeson is a sincere enough man, but he goes at things the wrong way."

"Besides your play, Mr. Wright, what are you working on at present?"

"I'd rather not talk about particulars. I'm doing some translations and some other things. I do work pretty hard. I'm always at something."

He stood up to indicate that our interview was over, then said, "Wait a minute," and walked into a study.

He reappeared a moment later with a mimeographed announcement of his play, and jokingly told me that if I could act, they'd put some brown greasepaint on me and use me in the play since they were short of males. He shook my hand and cordially invited me to come again when we could spend more time. He was, he said, interested in young writers and would be glad to help one along if he could.

I never did get another chance to see him because later when I was again in Paris, he was away. Then in December of 1960 shortly after my wife and I had returned to New York, I learned that Richard Wright was dead, this gifted, friendly man who unquestionably had done more than anyone else to try to insure that a Negro be evaluated as a writer and not as a trained ape.

A Great Writer Speaks Out: Richard Wright Interviewed for the *Morgenbladet*

Johannes Skancke Martens/1959

From *Morgenbladet* (Oslo), 30 June 1959, p. 3. Translated by Keneth Kinnamon and Lasse Dahl.

White people and black people arrived in North America at about the same time, and both have built up the big, empty continent, where only Indians without history were roaming around. But the whites were masters and the colored were slaves, and the freedom and equality guaranteed to Negroes after the bloody Civil War in the eighteen sixties got sabotaged by the palefaces. In his autobiographical *Black Boy,* the famous author Richard Wright tells of the disgraceful situation forced on the blacks with help from the Ku Klux Klan, lynching, injustice before the law, daily threats and humiliation. In race hatred there is a striking expression of what the Nazis became spokesmen for—the idea of a superior and inferior race. As a youth Richard Wright fled the terror and cruelty of the South, but discovered in the large cities of the North that Negroes were restricted to ghettos and that the white masters did everything they could to maintain the status quo with a permanent lower class representing cheap labor.

Much has gotten better, thanks to the Negroes' own struggle, aided by foresighted whites. Obviously it does not work any longer to place twenty million people down at the end of the table. In his realistic novels, especially *Native Son,* which came out in Danish during the war, Richard Wright has made himself a spokesman for his race in a talented and experienced manner. After the war he came with his wife and little daughter to Paris, where in 1946 I met him in his home in the Latin Quarter. "Paris is glorious," he said on that occasion, "but I am an American, my home is in the United States, and I am going back there." He gave up his apartment, sold his furniture, and crossed the ocean again. But three-quarters of a year later he was back in Europe again, and since 1950 he has not visited America.

Richard Wright has attained a respectable position among the French intellectual elite, he has been translated into French, he converses with

Sartre and Camus, and today he is the spokesman of all the colored people of the West. His interests encompass not only his racial kindred in America. He spent time in Ghana before the country achieved its independence and wrote a book about what he saw and heard. He participated in the great colored congress in Java a few years ago, he has written monographs, he has delivered lectures, and he has had radio plays performed.

"The French have given me approval to organize a six-month journey to their black possessions in Africa," Mr. Wright tells us one afternoon as we were sitting in his apartment near the Sorbonne. The living room is an odd mixture of turn-of-the-century furniture and extremely modern art. Beyond the living room lie a large library and study. Some gray is sprinkled in his dark, curly hair, but Richard Wright seems young and vigorous, he gets excited quickly, and he laughs often.

"I will now have an opportunity to find out if the experiment in Ghana has been successful, in other words, if patient Africa is ready to give birth to a child. The Africans you meet in Paris always brag about the great progress made in the former colonies; they will never admit that some of them are not yet ready for self-government. Economic and military forces, together with the missionaries, have ruined the old Africa by breaking up tribal groups. I now want to see what ideas and traditions have survived foreign control and what these new countries can unite around, in what direction their political development moves. The French know my point of view extremely well. I was flattered when the people in the ministry said 'Go!' Let me add that I am not going to visit Algeria.

"The English have been more farsighted than the French. Britain was prepared to have to move out of great parts of its empire. The French have just recently agreed upon self-government by those former colonies. They are improvising. They did not have any plans ready. Therefore the complications are so great and unexpected."

As before, you are probably visited by black American writers and artists?

"Much fewer are coming to Europe at present than earlier. Those who travel are looked upon with suspicion. By staying at home they can prove that they are not communists! It is not popular with the rulers of the U.S.A. for the young people to travel abroad. If they do it, they go as anonymous tourists. We have a new slogan in Uncle Sam's country—Togetherness. We are now going to become just one big family, and those who are not in favor of this idea are suspect. To me this 'togetherness' is a new sign of intolerance. It's a part of the Cold War that is being waged on all fronts.

"It's not a good idea. The panic fear of communism is behind us, but what do people expect to gain from such an artificial, childlike 'life together' that does not exist and cannot exist in the U.S. for a long time to come? You know, we are not yet a nation despite the fact that Americans use this word for themselves more than any other people do. Growth toward 'togetherness' has to come naturally, not as a result of talk and propaganda. But I have to say that the situation is slowly getting better in my native land.

"Previously all the scandals about unjust treatment of black citizens were not mentioned, but now they get extensive press coverage. There is no doubt that well-meaning Americans are trying to find a solution to the race problem. It is discussed everywhere. Nevertheless, school integration is coming eighty years too late. For the time being, tension and uncertainty are greater than ever before in the United States. Neither Eisenhower nor the Republicans have done anything to improve the situation. The honor for progress goes to the Supreme Court, the finest in one hundred years."

You were present at the congress of colored artists in Rome this spring.

"I'm glad you brought that subject up. The newspaper *Le Monde* could quote my opinions, but the fact is that I was not there, either physically nor spiritually. The congress was set up by the Catholic church. I am not enthusiastic about this church because of its view of black pagans through hundreds of years. It was a mistake for both Africans and Americans to go to Rome, and most of them were disappointed too. They were under pressure from both the Catholic and the communist sides. Colored representatives of art, literature, and cultural and intellectual life have to find their own ideals since they were robbed of their own original culture. Africans have received enough prefabricated imported religions. Attempts at 'conversion' have failed completely and will do so again.

"My plans? Aside from the trip to sub-Saharan Africa in October, I have a novel completed, *The Long Dream*, which in French will be called *La longue nuit*. Rights have been sold in Australia, Argentina, Italy, Holland, Germany, and surely in other countries. It treats a

black's childhood in the South. We leave him when he steps out of the
plane in Bourget and drives a car to the Latin Quarter. I have planned
several volumes about this man's development, but these novels are not
necessarily autobiographical. Has expatriation had an effect on my
language? The fact that I have not been in America in nine years has rid
my language of jargon and the latest slang. It is getting cleaner, more
Anglo-Saxon. Distance provides new perspectives, and you will see
unexpected sides of problems. I am in close contact with black cultural
and intellectual life in the U.S. Since I have two French daughters
seventeen and eleven years old, who study, think, and dream in French,
I will also always be able to understand French people. Such things
broaden your outlook.

"In *The Long Dream*," Wright continues, "I want to show how a
Negro becomes American. He cannot become that in the same way as
white immigrants because blacks are always told to stay on the fringes.
They have special difficulties in being accepted in American society as
normal human beings. I got sad news recently. The young black writer
James Baldwin travelled to New York after he had lived in Europe for
ten years. Meanwhile his novels had been published by major publishing houses, and he had received fellowships and grants from the Ford
Foundation. Well, one evening he went into a bar where white women
were allowed. In France he had become used to going wherever he
wanted. In his own country the acclaimed author was beaten half to
death because he dared to go into the domain of white people. Baldwin
was so shocked that he decided not to leave his hotel room, and now he
will soon be on his way back to the more civilized old Europe."

We start to talk about the latest riots in Durban, South Africa.

"This is only a foretaste," Mr. Wright said decisively. "A bloodbath
is unavoidable because of white oppression. South Africa is not con-
trolled by the English but by the Dutch, who dislike British ideals. They
must be filled with self-hatred to conduct themselves this way.

"Yes, I believe that De Gaulle's system of government represents
how the French majority feels. It is a step to the Right again? France has
never been a country sympathetic to the Left. The people are bourgeois.
If France had not been at war, there would not be any censorship. War
certainly brings disagreeable restrictions. But you will find no political
repression here. Besides, who was more reactionary than Guy Mollet
and his Socialist Party? They were responsible for much of the political

stupidity that was committed in Africa—and think of Suez! Don't mention the French Socialists as a progressive, freedom-loving party!"

Richard Wright has the courage of his convictions. He has a rare independence and an unfettered personality, one that gets respect and esteem.

Richard Wright Explains His Work and *The Long Dream*

Maurice Nadeau/1960

From *Les Lettres Nouvelles*, 8 (April 1960), 9–15. Translated by Michel Fabre.

Richard Wright has long resided in Paris, where he is living with his wife and daughter in spite of numerous trips to Africa, Spain, and the Far East. His many works have been published in France as well as in the United States. Some of them, like *Black Boy* and *Native Son*, have enjoyed considerable success. Almost all of them deal with the "Negro problem," which, Wright observes, is not a problem for the blacks but for the whites. . . . One well knows Richard Wright's welcoming warmth, his great ease in conversing now in English, now in a halting but pure French, his gaiety, the congenial aura his personality exudes. Yet he is just recovering from a disease caught during his recent travels in Africa.

I start with a question about the reception of his works in the United States.

I am still published in the United States, but, with each new book, I tell myself this may well be the last time. You see, until the Cold War, black literature was rather well received in the United States. In a few Northern universities, students were even advised to read it. Then the rivalry between the United States, the Soviet Union, and China as they vied to lead the world changed all this.

How come?

Well, United States foreign policy is geared to convince the peoples of Asia and Africa that they had better ride with America than with Russia or China. I am not opposed to such a policy. But white Americans would like black literature to go along with them, to convince black, brown, and yellow people that white Americans are better friends to them than the Russians or the Chinese.

Such a line has generally not been followed, far from it.

In fact, black literature is a testimony about our daily existence. As you could realize while reading it, *The Long Dream* paints a rather frightening picture of white attitudes toward colored people. As a result, white Americans are attempting to suppress such books as *The Long Dream* as well as the play derived from it.

Is this attempt official?

No, and this is the strange side of the case. In their words, Americans favor freedom, but whatever does not follow the line they wish, or whatever they think does not follow that line, they attempt to kill. They are willing to admit the existence of a black literature provided it does not deal with the "Negro problem" in the United States, provided that problem remains taboo. Naturally, I am opposed to this. I am willing to die for my country, but I refuse to be forced to lie for it.

Do you really believe that black literature can hinder American foreign policy?

Of course not. Only American racists can entertain such silly notions in their heads. Look at the Germans; they really went a long way in terms of racism. Hitler burned millions of Jews. This in no way prevents the Germans from getting the biggest share of business deals in Asia and Africa.

There is no need to ask you whether you believe that any literature whatsoever should be free.

Of course, each and every literature—white, black, brown or yellow. When America practices suppression in an underhanded way while proclaiming in broad daylight the benefits of freedom, it places itself on the same level as the Communists. It acts even more brutally than the Communists, who have a longer experience in this matter. To the Communists as well as to the capitalists, I say: keep your heavy hands off whatever concerns the human spirit. I am willing to help my country, but not at the cost of the destruction of black culture in the United States.

Our conversation moves on to The Long Dream. *Wright says:*

The book came out in the United States a few months ago. Naturally, the whites are not pleased with it, but the blacks themselves have been somewhat reticent. I do not flatter anyone. I am really fond of that book, you know. I have been told that it is the best that I have written.

Indeed, you tapped again the same vein as in Native Son *and* Black Boy. *I was fascinated when I read it. Besides the novelistic interest of the story, I think that you are exploring a brand new topic: the description of what could be called the black American bourgeoisie. A few sociologists have researched it, but it remains largely unknown to us.*

That is true. I attempted to show its everyday life through the adventures of a youngster—a *boy*, yes?—growing up in small Mississippi town I know quite well.

Is not that boy yourself to some extent?

Yes, but he could be any white, black, brown, or yellow boy who becomes what society expects him to become through the values it imposes upon him. In the case of Fishbelly, I have shown how the absorption of these values by a colored child can assume fantastic forms.

Indeed, it does. One has the impression he lives within a dream, which is itself nourished by his own dreams.

Remember that he is an American, that he speaks English, and that he is, in spite of everything, forced to look at life from a unique angle. This is what is terrifying: a black human plant forced to grow and live under completely abnormal conditions.

You do not consider social environment solely under its economic and cultural angles. Fishbelly is haunted by terrors which are specifically his, which spring from himself. The attraction he feels for white women can be ascribed to a more general behavior, but he lives it with manic intensity, although he fully knows that all kinds of catastrophes can ensue, that he may be lynched.

Naturally. But this complex was impressed upon him by his environment: the school, the talks with his schoolmates, the streets, his family, the business run by his father (whom he catches with a white-looking woman). He reads newspapers which display sexy white women. He looks at movie posters on which the enormous bosoms of the film stars are flaunted provocatively. In all-black bars white pin-ups are displayed on the wall next to the bewitching Coca-Cola blonde. Fish is forced to dream of white women and to repress the dream into the depths of his innermost being. A somewhat older friend of his was lynched for sleeping with a white woman, however promiscuous she was. The white woman is valued, overvalued by a civilization which builds her up as eminently desirable, sexually desirable, an object which Fishbelly can never approach except under penalty of death.

Still you do not make a saint of him (Wright laughs). *First, he passes a severe judgment upon his father, whose subservient and wily behavior with the whites he does not understand. Or, better, he sees two men in his father: the rich undertaker who behaves like an astute businessman and authoritative boss, who is ruthless with those fellow blacks who are his tenants; then, the man who becomes crawling and stupid in front of the whites. I thought that Fishbelly's judgment about his father would lead him to adopt a more dignified conduct and, since he often thinks of his race, a more dignified awareness of his own responsibility to his race. Yet he resembles his father more and more. Attracted by money and sex, he too, like his daddy, gets a girl whose light skin can delude, and he suggests to his father, whose business he shares, some commercial deals which lack decency.*

There are for him no other possible forms of emancipation. Since money and sex are essential realities in the world to which he is born, becoming a man means making money and satisfying his sexual needs.

Indeed. You show that everything can be bought: the police, the judges, love, and even the right to live. This is a very somber picture.

Just like truth. But it is, at the same time, the novelist's truth. If Fishbelly prefers money to honesty, this is due to his having seen his father build a fortune on the whites' corruption and, though he was black, manage to corrupt them. If he deals with his unsuccessful racial brothers with contempt, this is because he has understood that despising black people leads to success. He is at the same time shy and aggressive, ignorant and kind-hearted. He wants to live but he does not know how, and this is the reason why he is dangerous to others as well as to himself.

Yet he remains a suffering black man who can no longer endure the situation imposed upon him. Is this not the reason why he leaves for France as soon as he gets out of jail? He escapes. Is escape a solution?

Collective flight, by no means; individual escape, possibly. But he has no choice.

What will become of him in Paris?

This I am going to tell in my next novel. After Fishbelly in Mississippi, you'll see Fishbelly in Europe. His adventures will be less frightening but just as singular.

Interview with Richard Wright

L'Express/1960

From *L'Express*, 479 (18 August 1960), 22–23. Reprinted from DICTIONARY OF LITERARY BIOGRAPHY: DOCUMENTARY SERIES AN ILLUSTRATED CHRONICLE, Volume 2, edited by Margaret A. Van Antwerp. Copyright © 1982 by Gale Research Inc. Reproduced by permission of the publisher. Translated by Michel Fabre.

Q: *Your recent book,* Fishbelly, *deals with the position of a colored man within white civilization. Do you consider this a fundamental problem?*

A: The problem of a Negro within white civilization is itself conditioned by a more important problem of color on the world scale. We now find ourselves confronted with what could be called a colored majority in the world; which is the reason why colored communities living in countries with a white majority represent a kind of test.

Q: *Someone once said, "My color is my country." Would you agree?*

A: My color is not my country. I am a human being before being an American; I am a human being before being a Negro; and, if I deal with racial problems, it is because those problems were created without my consent and permission. I am opposed to any racial definition of man. I write about racial problems precisely to bring an end to racial definitions. And I do not wish anybody in the world in which we live to look at it from a racial perspective, whether he is white, black, or yellow.

Q: *What do you have in common with French Negro writers or with other black writers?*

A: I know them. I have read most of their works; I sympathize with the struggle they are waging; I have belonged to their organizations, but I cannot say that I always state problems in the way they do. Most Asian and African writers I have been in contact with are steeped in religious feeling, and their works and political struggle are suffused with their religious conceptions. This seems somewhat strange to an American Negro like me: in the United States, we fight for a real application of the Constitution, which is not the case in African nations. We fight to become part of a civilization which we accept. We do not oppose the West; we want the effective application of Western principles of freedom.

Q: *Where were you born?*

A: In Mississippi. Mississippi is only an immense black ghetto, a vast prison where the whites are the jailers and the Negroes are the prisoners. And the new movement for integration which is taking shape in the United States has not really reached the state yet.

Q: *Have you personally experienced "Jim Crowism" in the United States?*

A: Every Negro has experienced it. Simply because he was born in Mississippi, the first thing a Negro learns is that he was born in a ghetto. Thus begins for him the experience of living Jim Crow: he will attend a Jim Crow school, worship in a Jim Crow church; if he takes a bus it will be a Jim Crow bus, and if he goes to a restaurant it will be a Jim Crow restaurant. In short, he will lead a Jim Crow existence to his grave, when he dies a Jim Crow death. From the cradle to the grave, he will be subject to a kind of racial discrimination which will not even end after his death. Such is the life of the Negroes in the Deep South. This is what the "sit-ins" are attacking, a kind of harsh racial discrimination that does not even stop with death.

Q: *Is this the reason why you have come to live in Europe?*

A: Yes, I wanted to live in a wider and freer world. I still find racial restrictions here, but they cannot be compared to those over there, to that ghetto atmosphere.

Q: *Do you intend to stay here?*

A: I am at home here.

Q: *You do not think you will go back to the United States?*

A: Certainly not. I have no family left there, nobody is expecting me. I feel perfectly at ease here, and I work here. I could even say that, unfortunately, I do not have to return there to write about the United States because the situation changes so slowly: some things are different, but these changes have not, until now at least, been qualitative ones.

Q: *What do you think of the integration of Negro children into American schools?*

A: Well, I have a few facts on this matter. Six years ago, in 1954, the Supreme Court made a decision on that. In six years, less than 6% of black children have been integrated. At that rate, it would take about a century to have all black children completely integrated. I have spoken with reliable authorities, and they have assured me that whatever changes have taken place are not qualitative ones. A black child cannot enter the American school system without being crucified psychologically. This is bound to have a negative influence upon the personality of those children.

Q: *You are recognized and hailed as a great writer in Europe. What kind of audience do you enjoy in the United States?*

A: It has varied according to the books I have written. *Black Power,* which announced the upsurge of black nationalism in Africa, has been remaindered. The United States has a powerful economic system which still entertains very distant relations with the rest of the world. *Black Power* met mostly with skepticism and disdain from black as well as white Americans. In Europe, it met with more understanding because people have a more intelligent awareness of those problems. Europeans have colonies in Africa, and they have an idea of what is going on there. It is rather strange to note that my book on Spain was better reviewed in the United States than *Black Power* or *The Color Curtain,* although some Americans were shocked to see a Negro comment upon white affairs. I was reversing roles: until then, it was whites who would go to Asia or Africa in order to comment on native problems.

Q: *Since you are a novelist first of all, do you consider the novel as a sort of weapon?*

A: I have often been characterized as a committed writer. Personally, I do not consider myself a crusading writer. I imagine perfectly how the things I say may shock people. We Negro writers rarely have to deal with the rosy side of life. If we write directly and brutally about life, this may have an electrifying and, at times, disheartening, effect and may even look like an attack. That is why I always strive to retain some kind of balance in my books. I try to appreciate what the readers are capable of taking in without feeling that I am exaggerating. For instance, I went to Indonesia to report on the Bandung conference, and on that occasion I was sometimes told atrocious things. I checked them and

was able to establish that they were strictly true. For example, during
the Japanese occupation, the Japanese put all the Dutch—men, women,
and children alike—into concentration camps. When the Japanese
started to experience setbacks, they had to withdraw the soldiers who
were guarding those camps and send them to the front. As a consequence, they used natives, i. e. Indonesians, to guard the camps. But
the mentality of the Dutch was such that, while they had accepted to be
guarded by Japanese soldiers, they refused to be guarded by natives.
Someone assured me that the Dutch told the native guards, "If you
touch any Dutch women, if you rape them, we shall kill 1,000 Indonesians for every single white woman." I was told the Indonesians were
so incensed by that insult (at a time when, whatever we may think of it,
they had been entrusted with an honorable mission for the first time)
that they tried to redeem themselves in the eyes of the Dutch in a way
which seems strange at the least. They ordered all the white women out
of the camp, lined them up against a palisade, set up a machine gun and
shot every one of them. Then they asked the Dutch, "Well, now, have
we touched your women? Have we raped them?" Wasn't this a most
horrible incident?

Q: *What did they want, what was their aim?*
A: They were deeply incensed and they wanted to convince the
Dutch: "We are not what you believe; we are not interested in white
women, but in freedom." Now, can you really consider that the cleanest
form of action should be murder? I pondered this and told myself: "No,
I cannot relate such atrocities. The West is not able to listen to such
things without contemplating revenge." It was too horrible. Do you see
what I mean? Now, in Bandung, there were twenty-nine nations linked
together by a common hatred and frustration, by a feeling of degradation. These were profoundly offended people, offended in the deepest
sense of the word: they had been humiliated in their religion, in their
sense of honor and were in the throes of violent exasperation.

Q: *Is there in the United States an important output of Negro literature, and do you number many friends among these writers?*
A: Yes, many. Negro literature in the United States is actually so
important that it even preoccupies our government. American blacks are
testifying against the most modern of Western countries. I am certain
that no one could have foreseen a century ago that Negroes would one

day exert some influence on world events. Yet, this is what is taking place.

In the United States, the tendency is to tell black writers: "Don't be preoccupied with your experience as Negroes. Don't be polarized by it. You are people. Write exactly as any other people would do on any other subject." I would be inclined to tell them, "On the contrary, take your ghetto experience as a theme, for this precisely is a universal topic. And if people criticize you for it, don't worry."

Q: *What does the title of your book* Fishbelly *mean?*

A: This title has some symbolical meaning: the belly of a fish is generally white, but one cannot generally see it when looking at the fish. And I would like the reader to understand that my character is looking at white values with the eyes of a Negro who has entirely absorbed the values of the society around him. This is what one of his companions expresses when he says "The belly of a fish is white."

Q: *The English title,* The Long Dream, *seems less explicit. Could you comment upon it?*

A: This title has an ironical meaning, in the sense that Fishbelly's dream of identification with white values cannot be realized, given the circumstances. When his father tells him, "Don't allow yourself to be carried away too far by your dream," this means, "If you really believe what is written in the Constitution, you will get killed." This is a very special situation. Generally, a citizen is expected to respect and believe in the Constitution of his country, to pattern his life according to it. But if an American Negro pretended or claimed to enjoy all the rights conferred upon him by the Constitution, he'd run the risk of being lynched. This is what "The Long Dream" means.

Q: *What kind of feelings do white Americans really experience towards Negroes?*

A: You are pointing to one of the most serious problems. It is not true that the American hates the Negro. He likes the Negro, but in the way a person likes to have a hot-water bottle in bed at night. It is a sort of greedy, possessive feeling; he likes to possess and use the Negro. During slavery times, intimate contacts existed between whites and blacks: you'd be surprised how close they really were. The whites pretended there was to be no contact, yet, in spite of that, such contacts did exist. White men had Negro women, and they have sired a whole cast of mulattoes, while they used the men as beasts of burden, selling them like cattle. The resulting degradation (as the whites are beginning to realize nowadays) affected the whites more than it did the blacks. The Negroes underwent this degradation without accepting it, without liking it, while the whites debased themselves to the level of their slaves. There lies the horror of it. I believe Abraham Lincoln understood the heart of the matter perfectly when he said, "I would not wish to be a slave, but I would not wish to be a master either."

Q: *Yet, in your latest novel, the white girl who has been in love with a Negro ends up hating him?*

A: In the novel, it is true, the white girl denounces the Negro and has him lynched. I believe it is necessary here to comment upon white civilization as a whole; as you know, in the Western world, in Puritan countries, young girls are submitted to many restrictions. In a Puritan environment the sexual act is followed by reprobation; it is considered something shameful and evil. This is why a girl like the one in the novel finds herself in the ambiguous situation of desiring a pleasure which she thinks is wrong, then redeeming herself through bloody sacrifice, by getting the man lynched to whom she had given herself.

Besides, one must grant that in Paris there is a good deal of naivete on the part of the young Africans who come here straight from their native tribes. In Paris, the attitude toward blacks is different from that in the United States, and many white women find it quite natural to have sexual intercourse with Negroes. Now, these young Africans often believe that they are being preferred for this special task. I have often heard some of them boast of their prowess in this field, which is rather childish. And many people have built up a myth from such boasting, and they believe that Africans are sexually superior to Europeans, which is, of course, simply absurd. Unfortunately, the Africans tend to believe in this so-called superiority. But in the final analysis, what does it mean? They are sort of compensating for what colonial domination has deprived them of. Such people are saying, "They have taken our language, our land, our culture has been destroyed; what is left to us? Maybe a 'genius' special to our race which gives us racial superiority over them."

Q: *How do white Americans and black Americans behave when they are abroad together?*

A: In the United States, there is a whole complex of moral conceptions and ingrained habits which regulate our mutual attitudes. Thus, for instance, if a Negro finds himself in the white residential area of an American city, it is likely that the police will stop him and ask his reason for being there. To that, he will answer that he is working there, or has been called for such or such reason. In other words, there always is a ready-made explanation for the presence of a Negro in a white area.

But as soon as you set foot in Europe, this whole pattern of segregation and discrimination is left behind, and this is why the white American and the black American behave with confusion and perplexity: they no longer know how to behave with each other; ready-made rules no longer exist. They have not become Spanish, French, Italian, or British enough to accept this new situation and behave like human beings. White Americans cling together, forming groups and tiny communities apart, while American Negroes go more deeply into French life, living with French people in almost complete brotherhood. Unlike white Americans, American Negroes are more easily accepted by the French.

Q: *Why this exception in their favor?*

A: Even if the French are anti-American, they instinctively know that the American Negro is not their enemy, after all, because they realize that the black man played no part in the political issues which concern them. If a black man comes into contact with an anti-American group, he'll be told, "Well, you are a Negro," which means, "You are not responsible for what happens." Besides, some Americans should never leave their country; they are psychologically ill at ease because they don't know exactly what kind of relationship American Negroes have with French people, and they are afraid this will "spoil" the Negro and he will no longer be able to fit in when he gets back home. Do you understand? It is truly strange to witness the kind of bewilderment which takes hold of white and black Americans when they no longer feel around them the familiar reassuring framework of American habits and customs, all those stereotyped attitudes which are quite readily assumed. On the other hand, in the American armed forces in France, the old balance of life overseas is retained, because, although there is an effort towards integration in the army, enough American atmosphere still subsists to lend a semblance of "normalcy" to the relations between black and white Americans.

R. Wright: America Is Not Conformist: It Renews Itself Endlessly

Annie Brièrre/1960

From *France-U.S.A.*, September-October 1960, p. 2. Translated by Michel Fabre with permission of Annie Brièrre. All rights reserved.

To be frank, I was a bit peeved because Richard Wright had postponed for several months the interview I had asked him for. My slight irritation has just melted like snow under the sun. His latest novel, *Fishbelly [The Long Dream]*, is such an achievement that it justifies his desire to be undisturbed and his evading me. One finds in it again the great Richard Wright of *Native Son, Black Boy,* and *The Outsider.* As far as its inspiration is concerned, Fishbelly is closer to his first books than to his recent ones. Fish is a black Mississippi youngster born to a well-to-do but not genteel family. His father, Tyree, runs a funeral parlor. As the owner of whorehouses he also performs less honorable activities, and his shady dealings are the indirect cause of his death, inflicted by a white police officer. Fishbelly survives similar dangers and a term in jail.

Reading this novel (it is certainly a long one, but does not seem so), we have not only grown to understand Fishbelly and to find him strangely appealing, but we have familiarized ourselves with the not very estimable and still less enviable mores in the black section of the town; and we have been especially puzzled and fascinated by the relationships between blacks and whites.

Do not imagine that the book deals solely with racial conflict. On the whole the whites are depicted in an even less favorable light than the blacks themselves. But what is captivating all through the 460 pages of the novel is the throbbing, vibrant, loquacious, thrilling, or ardent humanity with which its author has endowed each and every character. Such complex and profound humanity is to be found in the author himself. We all know that he has been living in Paris since the war, and that his many travels always bring him back here.

I began by expressing my admiration for The Outsider *and speak of Dostoevsky. He is not at all shocked by the comparison.*

The notion of crime and punishment is one of my major preoccupations. Furthermore, I return to this theme in *The Long Dream*.

Doesn't The Outsider *contain the notion of implacable fate?*

It is more a rebellion against the social system, more precisely Cross Damon's rebellion against the District Attorney, who restrains this revolt. So much so that the notion of fate assumes a particular form here. I did not want to write an existentialist novel. I believe in the beauty of life, in its infinite richness. One can experience dread and anguish at the idea of being nothing, but then one finds again the multiple potentialities offered by life.

Richard Wright thinks a while, between an egg and a piece of toast, and broaches a wider topic.

There is in philosophy today a return to paganism, to industrial paganism. European philosophy is behind the times. As for America, it must be able to become aware of itself. Few people grasp the meaning of the American experience. It is not over yet. There is in it the capacity for constant change. America is not a conformist country as has been so often been said and written. It renews itself constantly.

One constantly perceives in your novels your preoccupation with philosophical issues, but having achieved such perfection in fiction (whether you write about the lives and adventures of your characters or about their ideas), why did you turn to writing essays which, in my opinion, reach a smaller audience than novels?

Because I am so fascinated by social sciences that I can't help sharing the results of my investigations directly, not indirectly through fiction. Society has become an instrument of coercion, whereas the basic aim of society should be unity, not oppression. The basic social cells are a natural phenomenon. You find them in a primitive state among African tribes. The world cannot do without them. Where wars and revolutions have wiped them out, as in Germany among displaced persons, in Israel, in China, a structure is recreated artificially in order to replace the family. There is constantly an instinctive regrouping of humans into families. As soon as one is destroyed, another form appears, be it only the pimp who manages a whore. Prostitution could be explained in this way.

Do you believe that our era of excessive mechanization is going to destroy the human element and compromise artistic creation?

No, there may be times of lethargy, but human vitality bounces up again and again and always higher than before. For instance, Argentina oppressed by Peron is already freeing itself from his influence. Even during sleep, human vitality manifests itself in dreams and each dream recreates human culture. The religious spirit always endures. Up to now, man has been a religious animal and secular art is a sublimation of the religious feeling.

To go back to your latest book, we can find autobiographical elements in Fishbelly?

I depict white and black relations in some Southern states. Some episodes are authentic; others are imaginary; still others are minimized, as is the case for the Natchez fire in which over 140 people actually died. In my book I brought down the number of victims to forty.

Do you read a lot?

My reading is dictated by outside interests such as sociological studies or travel. I find little enrichment in contemporary novels. As for the novels of the Beat Generation, I have not read them. Among great novelists those I go back to most often are Sherwood Anderson, Mark Twain, James T. Farrell, Nelson Algren, Thomas Hardy, Maupassant, Proust, Dostoevsky. But I'd give them all for a book by Dreiser. He encompasses them all. And I should like to add that I am fond of Freud and Marx, not from a political angle but because they are poets.

Marx, a poet? This is enough food for another interview. One last question. Has Paris, where you came and stayed, ever been a disappointment to you?

Paris has given me everything I hoped for—and even more.

An Unbalanced Relationship

Georges Charbonnier/1960

Transcript of a radio broadcast on ORTF, Paris, October 1960.
Translated by Michel Fabre.

*Richard Wright, the Negro American writer, was born in Natchez,
Mississippi. The French translation of his latest novel,* Fishbelly, *came
out a few months ago. His major works are well-known:* Black Boy,
Native Son, Uncle Tom's Children, The Outsider, Black Power, White
Man, Listen!, Savage Holiday, The Long Dream. *Of course these few
words of introduction and my enumerating some of his numerous works
cannot, by any means, suffice to introduce in satisfactory fashion the
most important among black American writers. This is only a brief
preamble to one of the most important questions that can be asked a
black writer. This question we wanted to pose immediately, before
talking of any literary topic or any other kind of topic. It is the following: "Richard Wright, a lesson comes out of reading your works. A
black man, you say what we, white people, can notice, feel, and know,
i.e., the relationship between whites and blacks is a distorted one. What
is fundamentally lacking in this relationship?"*

There is a lot of distrust between the two races and this creates a
distance. This can be explained somewhat strangely by the fact that, on
both sides, there is a wish to protect one's own personality. Black
people have tried to establish a protected self. With the white man, the
same feeling prevails: he is afraid; he does not understand exactly what
happens in a black person. I have written in my novels several episodes
that deal with crises in the relationships between blacks and whites. For
instance, in *Fishbelly*, I have described a meeting between Fishbelly and
a white police officer. It is not easy to explain this in detail. But the
police officer badly needs information from a Negro—Fishbelly, who is
seventeen—and when he asks questions he well knows that a Negro
cannot answer him truthfully. He well knows the Negro is hiding something. It is a critical moment. They should "put their cards on the table,"
as one says in French, and he finds out that he cannot manage to reach
his aim with a Negro. It is an instance of the distrust between the two

races because the black man too, at this moment, needs the white man's trust and a sense of security. If he could tell the truth in confidence, maybe the situation could be rescued. If the white man manages an honest exchange with the Negro, maybe his own interests will be safe. There is distance between the two and this is a dramatic encounter. On both sides, there are urgent needs, yet nothing happens. There is a distance between the two men and this is a dramatic encounter.

(An excerpt from *The Long Dream*, dealing with the encounter between Cantley and Fishbelly, is read.)

Have you depicted this distrust again in other novels?

I have written many episodes about encounters between Negroes and whites. In my autobiography, *Black Boy*, I have written about simple, human things. During my youth in Memphis, Tennessee, I wanted to read books. It is a Southern city where restrictions against Negroes are very strong, even today as they were yesterday. Today young blacks are fighting to be allowed in the libraries and read the works which contain the achievements of mankind; but this is forbidden, they are against the law.

A long time long ago, I devised a way of borrowing books.

(An extract from *Black Boy* is read, dealing with Wright taking out books from the library with the complicity of a white Catholic.)

You can consider the distrust between the races in another way. An encounter takes place; the whites think something, the Negroes think something else. They face each other, but there is no real communication. In *The Outsider*, one finds an episode which is a little comedy. *The Outsider* deals with the story of a black intellectual who comes to grips with modern life in Chicago. He has no proof of his identity and he thinks: I am black and if I go to town hall to apply for identity papers, I am sure they will make things difficult for me. But I am black and white people like to think that Negroes are stupid. I may be able to derive some benefit from this belief.

(An extract from *The Outsider* is read, dealing with Cross Damon's clowning in order to get a birth certificate.)

The American Novel

Georges Charbonnier/1960

Transcript of a radio broadcast on ORTF, Paris, October 1960.
Translated by Michel Fabre.

If one wishes to compare the American novel and the French novel, one is at once struck by their respective lengths. American novels are generally more bulky than French novels.

Yet one must carefully limit the scope of this statement. Should we consider that *Men of Good Will* by Jules Romains, for instance, is a series of novels or the same novel, untiringly pursued? Did Proust write novels or one novel? Are the works of Alexandre Dumas real novels or mere cloak and dagger stories, hence removed from the category of the real novel, the unadulterated novel? These are only a few remarks. One would have to investigate all cases and, of course, consider Balzac, Hugo, Zola, etc. To say that the French novel is shorter than the Russian or the American novel may be a gratuitous statement. One would have to make measurements. However, we feel intuitively that the French novel is short enough and that its definition is strict, its boundaries clear cut, and that length is not in itself a quality of the French novel. How can we decide bluntly whether this is due to thriftiness or to choice, in order to explain those dimensions which, rightly or wrongly, we believe are rather limited? Must we think, on the contrary, that in France the novel is a genre which obeys imperative rules and that the novel is shorter because it follows rules which are particular to it? For instance, is dialogue a part of the novel or is it excluded from it? Is it one of the components the fiction or is it a characteristic of other genres? Doesn't the American novel give an overly important role to dialogue? We cannot answer such questions precisely. We would first have to define and measure. Of course, we must be content today with initial impressions.

Richard Wright, you are an American novelist. What is a novel, in your opinion?

Usually I think a writer can provide a sufficiently precise answer.

This is rather difficult in my case as I came to literature in a rather strange way. I was a Negro boy in the South. In the city where I lived, there were no big schools where one could study literature. I graduated from the eighth grade and had to start working. I began to read on my own. I started with detective fiction and soon discovered other books. The first great American novelist I came across was Theodore Dreiser. Thanks to him, I discovered a very different world in America and even today I believe that Dreiser is the greatest twentieth-century writer in American literature.

He wrote novels about white people in Chicago who wanted to build an industrial world. *An American Tragedy* provided me with a sense of the life around me. I then wondered whether it would be possible for me to write about black people in the same way. But when I looked for American literature about black people, I found nothing about my environment. Where could I find models or ideas which might shed some light about life in the ghetto? I pursued my investigations in fiction and came across Russian novelists, especially Dostoevsky, Turgenev, Tolstoy. And I realized something at once: here were people who approached life directly. There is something tough, direct, realistic, naturalistic about their fiction. At that time I started writing—not long drawn nor dense efforts but only attempts at writing. I began to try whether I could depict a man who was close by—what could I do with him in words?

What is a novel for me? It is a way of enlarging and increasing our sense of life. It can shed light about other people. The more direct, the more light. The more intense, the more light. The more dramatic, the more intimate the novel. I found in the works of Dostoevsky many ideas towards this end. Some say he is an old-fashioned novelist, a novelist of the past, but he wrote tremendous dramatic works and with direct encounters and passionate exchanges between people. Dostoevsky was my model when I started writing. I was then living in Chicago and there were not around me any such things as Dostoevsky has described, but he provided me with enough self-confidence to try. Other American novelists also gave me some confidence, Sherwood Anderson, who has written short stories and novels. Also Sinclair Lewis, Joseph Conrad, Thomas Hardy, George Moore, D.H. Lawrence—in all of their works I found a light which I could use to look at people. For several years, I lived with them, from 1925 to 1929. For instance, I found a novel by D.H. Lawrence, *Sons and Lovers,* which deals with coal miners in England, so interesting that I read nearly all of his books. I would read

all of a writer's books before passing on to another. I started writing
short stories first because I did not feel capable of attempting novels.
I wrote two or three novels, but I have kept them because I was convinced they were not good enough. I finally gathered enough short
stories to make a volume, and when I left Chicago for New York City,
I took it with me. This is *Uncle Tom's Children*. I had also written
Tarbaby—which was not very well put together—about a Negro youth
in Mississippi. I used the material in another work some time later after
I had dropped the novel.

I am not sure these explanations provide much light about the way
I write. I am mostly concerned with scenes in fiction. I have been told
that I could succeed in writing plays for the stage, but I do not want to.
I mostly work out one scene after the other and try to provide the
meaning of a novel through those scenes, not through descriptions or
narrative passages. I don't like that. I prefer something direct, with
people who speak with each other, with dialogues and movement. Two
years ago, I wrote texts for the German radio and discovered how to
write for a radio broadcast with dialogue, only I did not identify the
characters. It was organic dialogue and you could know who was
speaking and why, and get a description, and all that. I would like to
explain why I attempted to write short stories exclusively in dialogue.
I found that technique in the novels of Henry James, an American
novelist who did many experiments with technique in fiction. Finally, in
Paris, I began this, with dialogue only. It does work and one can say a
great many things with other people's words only. Then dialogue
becomes something more than dialogue. Not only do people speak to
one another but they provide descriptions, they talk about the weather,
whether it is sunny or looks like rain, they can discuss the political
situation or their emotions. Everything is there, in their words, in pure
dialogue.

*I think one can find an excellent example of pure dialogue in your
novel* The Long Dream. *For instance, the psychodrama invented by
three black teenagers. It is at the same time a drama and a game.*

(An excerpt from *The Long Dream* is read, dealing with "If I were
white" fantasies.)

*Richard Wright, what are your intentions when you use the American
language?*

This is a most interesting question. You know that we Negroes live geographically apart from other Americans, in the ghetto, although we speak the same language and use the same words. But in the ghetto words like "justice," "democracy" are used with some irony. There is some distance in the words we use and, in my opinion, this results in some tension in the works of Negro writers. The words are the same, but I think there is some resistance implied when we try to create something. I am not sure I do this consciously or not. We Negroes share the same moral values with whites, we believe in the same Constitution, but when we use words it is with some reservations because we are waiting for the day when words will have the same value for us. This is a psychological matter.

In other words, this does not apply to the writer's words but to the words everyone uses?

Yes. In the United States, you know, we have a language which is called "jive." It is a language particular to blacks and found among jazz musicians. And because Negroes can use language differently and give other meanings to words. This injects some tension into the language. One can speak of a black language in the United States. When integration is completed, this linguistic situation may disappear. But one finds books nowadays, written by people like Daniel Burley, which focus on black speech, that of the sidewalks, the ghettos, the people who use special words. There is a kind of freemasonry, nothing official of course, among blacks in the United States. If a Negro meets another in a section of the city reserved to the whites, they exchange greetings even if they have been complete strangers until then.

Does this tension still exist, or is it different when a Negro speaks to another Negro from when he speaks to a white person?

It exists between blacks and whites, and also between blacks and blacks in varying degrees. They may joke about the racial situation, but generally they will take some distance when they speak in a way which meets existing dangers. They speak in a certain way to ease tensions, but they express their reactions freely between themselves.

A Novel by Richard Wright, *The Long Dream*

Georges Charbonnier/1960

Transcript of a radio broadcast on ORTF, Paris, October 1960.
Translated by Michel Fabre.

Richard Wright, you have said how important dialogue was to you and the place you make for it in your novels. It is, according to you, a dialogue that can express everything, the environment, the mood, the characters. It is a kind of total dialogue which, you remarked, is the natural means of expression on radio. The role you grant to dialogue does not detract from other means of expression to be found in fiction. To render actions you do not hesitate to interrupt the stream of their concatenation in order to depict—in the most classical sense of the word—to render dialogue, characters, idiosyncrasies. In your latest novel, The Long Dream, *which came out recently in France, you have blended intimately all the aspects of fiction.*

Let us recall that Fishbelly's father is a mortician. Fishbelly grows up without enduring the black condition physically and emotionally in his body. One day, for no reason, he is arrested by the police. Now he really becomes a Negro. On his way back home he comes across a wounded dog, dying.

(An excerpt from *The Long Dream* is read, dealing with Fishbelly's putting an end to the dog's suffering, then eviscerating it.)

I wrote this description to show the scope of the moral dilemma among Negroes. Fishbelly comes across a wounded dog. There are two points in the description: he wants to save it but has no means to do so. He is compassionate: better kill the dog than leave it to die slowly in suffering under the glaring sun. I establish in this passage that the boy is humane and also how he keeps thinking about his friend Chris, who has been lynched and castrated by whites. In jail, Fishbelly has endured psychological torture from the white cops, and he wonders about the realities of life. He opens up the dog, cuts off its organs and finds a sort of baptism in this ritual, cutting off all the horror that has come into his life. Immediately after leaving the dog, Fishbelly comes across a white

217

man who has had an accident and who is trapped in his car, suffering and calling out.

(An excerpt from *The Long Dream* is read, dealing with the white man calling for help. But his calling Fish a "nigger boy" prevents the latter from helping him.)

I have written this description in such a way as to balance human emotions in the character of Fishbelly. He wishes to live normally. This is why I described this episode, to tell the reader "This Negro boy wishes to live a normal life, just like you. But look at the things he encounters: what can he do with them? His normal life is blocked and he starts looking for solutions for a life which has become a nightmare for him."

It appears that you have resorted to this process and this attitude in all your works.

More or less. Listen, I found so much misery and horror among Negroes and I devised a way to demonstrate their humaneness. Without any doubt, Fishbelly wants to rescue others. He is totally human. He wants to save the dog and he does what he can do for it. But with the white man, he is confronted with something different: the man can speak, he shouts abuse, and with this Fishbelly's impulse to help is cut short. He is filled with fear and immediately forgets his impulse; he represses it as he would a dream. I attempted through this kind of description to impart to the reader some idea of the pressures imposed upon Negro life. It is not a normal life and it is not possible to perform a compassionate gesture easily. Had it been a normal life, Fishbelly would have been able to help the dog and the white man, but certain things prevented this.

In the novel, Fishbelly's father is a mortician by trade. You did not chose this profession by chance, did you?

No, in real life, undertakers are among the richest Negroes. They are allowed to bury Negroes only. It is a kind of trust, a monopoly. It is the most lucrative Negro job because whites do not want to touch Negro dead. I take it as a symbol of the black bourgeoisie. They make a living out of the sufferings of other Negroes and the whites allow them to do what they wish in the ghetto.

You pushed horror still one step further. This black undertaker is the owner of the Grove, half a dance hall, half a cathouse, which catches fire, resulting in some forty Negroes being burned alive. Young Fishbelly, who is on the scene, asks the police to take away the bodies in order to embalm and bury them. As a result his father, the co-owner of the place who had not obeyed the fire regulations thus being responsible for these deaths, can claim the corpses through the intermediary of his son, and he ends up making on one side the money he had lost on the other.

That's it, and the same thing happens between Fishbelly and Gladys. She works at the Grove as a prostitute. Fishbelly is in love with her and he does not know she is working for his father.

He gives money to Gladys: the money circulates from him to Gladys, from Gladys to his father, from his father to him, from him to the girl again.

Yes, it circulates in a vicious circle in the ghetto.

From one end of the book to the other, one can see this flow of money in a limited circuit. And one feels you have deliberately shown that this circuit can in no way be short-circuited by whites.
I showed this to say, in one word: "Put an end to ghettos, they are a horrible thing."

I believe that in The Long Dream *you deliberately give this impression of a closed world. In your other books, there is more opening onto the wider world.*

This is because they take place in the North where there is more contact between Negroes and whites.

Between Two Worlds

Georges Charbonnier/1960

Transcript of a radio broadcast on ORTF, Paris, October 1960.
Translated by Michel Fabre.

Richard Wright, how can we define the global psychological reactions of a man who presents himself as being part of the black and the white worlds at the same time?

A man between two worlds would be a very complicated thing. He is not *between* two worlds, but really *of* two worlds. He is not apart from the white world and outside of the Negro world but in both of them; and when he speaks in his works, he can speak about two worlds at the same time, and he speaks in a voice which is at the same time black and white.

As for me, after reading your works I can see that you think about the two problems in the way they are thought of from both sides. This seems evident to me, and I never feel the shadow of a psychological constraint, not ever.

Yes, because the writer (i.e., myself) does not feel that he is a Negro writer or a white writer. I am not conscious whether this is a black or a white idea.

Because the writer comes first in your case. You are a writer first and foremost.

Certainly. And I attempt to bring together the reactions on either side. It is a fusion of all this; my aim, my ideal is to blend the elements on either side, to link them organically. I have attempted to solve racial problems not practically but psychologically. To create a fusion.

The fusion is realized because you are a writer; but I think of someone who is not a writer.

Oh, it is far more difficult. And sometimes quite tragic. You are a scientist in your own country, but suppose you live in a country like Africa, England, or the United States. You may be confronted with difficulties. You may be a Negro before being an American, or

220

Englishman, or before being a scientist. You may be a black politician
and aspire to become the President, but it is an unattainable. Until now,
in England, there has not been a single black person elected to the
House of Commons. There are blacks in the French National Assembly,
but I have met Negro technicians who told me that they experienced
some difficulties in France. Not the kind of difficulties found in the
United States, not at all. They can live anywhere, send their children to
any school. But there is an acute job competition in the business world.
I do not know whether this is strictly a racial problem or not. But in
theaters, in places of entertainment, it is much easier. There is room for
Negroes. What is striking is that one is quite willing to laugh with
Negroes but one does not want to work with them.

*I do not agree with you. Take jazz, for instance. Well, in France we
think that white jazz is not worth a cent and every time jazz is good it is
black jazz.*
You are right.

*It is not a matter of entertainment nor a matter of ideas, but a matter
of pure sensation.*
I quite agree with that. I recently wrote a preface for a book called
Blues Fell This Morning, which came out in England a couple of
months ago. It is a volume about the blues, a blues anthology edited by
Paul Oliver. It is a fine book and worth a lot. One does not laugh in the
blues.

*Let us stick to music. Which way is white music heading for in Paris?
It moves towards mathematics. All musicians—whether the very
recently founded algorithmic group or the works of Xenakis—all these
developments have been inspired by mathematics. If I think of a kind
of music which has not been inspired by mathematical works and thus
still reserved to a small number of people, then we have nothing left.
Nothing except songs which themselves recall other songs. But jazz
exists, and strikes everybody and gets hold of everybody. Laughter has
nothing to do with this. Nothing at all.*
It is a real and sincere thing.

*One could say that the music which is good for everyone, the kind of
music that makes people move their shoulders when they hear it, is
black music.*

The roots of jazz are in suffering. Jazz is linked intimately with the blues and the blues with the spirituals. Jazz comes out of a religious place, very long ago, but it begins on the plantations with the spirituals.

This link between jazz and the blues, the spirituals and life on the plantations, finds an equivalent in words in your Uncle Tom's Children. *I would like to sum up very briefly for our listeners the topic of your short story "Fire and Cloud." The action takes place in a small town during a hunger march. The Negroes have gone as a delegation to the mayor to ask for relief while Reverend Taylor, a black pastor, has gone to the relief bureau in the name of his congregation, but the whites have refused to help the Negroes. Reverend Taylor goes back to his congregation at church and starts praying with them.*

(An extract from the story is read, dealing with the behavior of the black congregation expressing helplessness, anger, and hope.)

I mostly believe that in England and the United States the Negroes are allowed to become great Broadway artists but find difficulty in doing something else. The nation can laugh with a Negro, but it cannot live with a Negro. In England, there is a strange situation; people can laugh with a Negro, and there is another field than entertainment where one can find collaboration between blacks and white—medicine. Indeed whites in England prefer Negro doctors, who have much success. A popular superstition leads people to think that Negroes have magical hands when it comes to healing. It is crazy. But this is an exception.

I am thinking only about whites and about the French. We, in France, feel much dryness. We know we are drawn to abstract ideas, to mathematics for example, and we are aware that we are somehow deficient in human depth, in warmth, we lack, how can I put it, a certain kind of lusciousness. All of this we feel and find in the black soul.

You see, I think that the roots of this reality are to be found in the question of Puritanism and the industrial world. I believe that in Japan one can find an organic link between industrialization and organic emotions: there is dance *and* factories. Such things are possible. In England, in Europe, the United States, the world is divided along those lines. I believe that if Asia and Africa have something to bring to our industrial civilization, it is really a different sense of life, an enriching sensibility, and a taste for life. We have discussed political movements and nationalisms in Asia and Africa: we are told we must understand the realities in those countries, and there is something to be derived from such realities, there are deep-rooted instincts. The West has lost track of this reality and can find it again in such places as these. Which means that, at bottom, the world is a house for many people. People need one another. If you cut off a part of others and cast it away, it is a part of yourself that you are casting away.

We need other peoples . . .
That's it.

Richard Wright, For Whom Do You Write?
Georges Charbonnier/1960

Transcript of a radio broadcast on ORTF, Paris, November 1990.
Translated by Michel Fabre.

"Why do you write? Why do you paint? Why do you compose music?"
This is a question one asks creative artists, and this question is often
asked aggressively. It expresses crudely an aspect of the divorce which
seems to separate the creator from those to whom his creation is
destined. Art, being a language, supposes communication; the creative
artist expresses a certain reality and also addresses somebody. The
receptor always remains implied in the work but generally receives it
only after it has been created. Anyway, a work of art exists totally only
in front of an attentive interlocutor. The question "For whom do you
write?" might seem superfluous were it not posed somewhat aggressively. It implies in fact a reproach of esotericism, and some people do
not hesitate to claim that a work of art must touch everyone in order to
be valid. They would not consider a work of art which does not fill this
condition. One knows, for instance, that Tolstoy was one of the most
famous supporters of a thesis which was expressed again by the Prague
Manifesto in 1948. These reflections of mine mostly aim to focus the
question addressed to Richard Wright, "For whom do you write?"
Indeed, this question is too often linked with the notion of experimenta-
tion. One too readily admits that some are destined to undertake labora-
tory research which is, by definition, reserved to a selected few. I do
not consider problems of technique here. My question is about the very
contents of Richard Wright's novels; not about their communicability to
a small or large number of interlocutors, but about the message itself.
This message is, all of it, dedicated to the relationships between blacks
and whites.

Therefore I ask Richard Wright: "For whom do you write?"
Our life is still invisible to whites. It still remains outside the pale of
whites' preoccupations. I'd like to hurl words in my novels in order to
arouse whites to the fact that there is someone here with us, Negroes,
a human presence.

Is this what you attempt to do?
Yes.

You wanted your interlocutor to be a white person first?
Yes, because we are a minority in my country, you know. It is a
white country in the imagination of Negroes. And when I write, I have
a white image of my audience. This is natural because my audience is
white, and I want to make them aware of the fact that there exists a
black life with the same dimensions.

You also have a Negro audience?
I do.

Do you think of them when you are writing?
Yes, I feel that the Negro audience is on my side. When I am writing
a book, if there is one page—should there be a Negro person, he would
say "OK, this is the way it is." To some extent I am working for blacks
and whites but mostly for whites.

Do whites read your works more than Negroes do?
Without any doubt.

*Has it been possible to ascertain that your readers are mostly white
people?*
You know, the publishers are white, the editors are white, the
readership is white.

Are there no Negro publishers in the USA?
There are, but they have little power. The Johnson Corporation,
which publishes *Ebony* and things for the masses, does not really publish books. The publishing world is white. That's the way things are.

*As a result you must apply to a white publisher to reach a white
audience?*
Undoubtedly.

How does this audience receive your books?
It depends. During the Roosevelt administration, there was a lot of
talk about *Black Boy,* my autobiography. But other books are not
welcome. This is the case with *Black Power.* People consider it with
some diffidence because the Cold War is going on, people are agitating
in Africa, people are restless. We have a big problem with the Chinese

community and now the Negroes are beginning too. Not long ago I
received a letter from my New York editor, Cass Canfield, when I sent
him the typescript of *Black Power*. He said, "Richard, this is a fine
book, but I do not believe that the white audience in the US will enter a
bookstore and pay four dollars in order to read a book about something
which does not really interest them." *Black Power* is not selling much—
in a time of liberalism, when people are not anxious, they may take
interest in it. But there are threats everywhere now, and when you write
a book like *Black Power,* they don't want to read it.

Yet Black Power *came out in the United States?*
Yes, it did.

Was it successful?
No, three weeks after it was launched, the book was remaindered for
a few cents.
Nobody wanted it.

*During a preceding talk you spoke of the two worlds to which you are
trying to belong. Does belonging to the black or to the white world
make such a big difference?*
There is no music within you. Belonging to the world helps, in my
opinion, because I feel, perfectly, I feel large enough to be part of both
worlds. They are one, really, the human world.

*You just said when you first talked about Negroes and whites that you
wanted to arouse white people, didn't you?*
I mentioned the distrust which exists between the Negro world on one
side and the white world on the other.

*We all think that the white world is the one who should change most.
You are indeed addressing the whites to tell them that black people
exist. But do you think that they should act alone?*
I believe the burden for the larger part of the responsibility rests with
the whites, because the whites set limits to the existence of Negroes. I
believe that Negroes have a responsibility, too. I believe that the duty of
creative artists is to speak and write ceaselessly about this problem. It is
a sacred duty indeed. To keep the problem visible, always keep the
problem visible.

We all see the argument according to which Negroes can give some-

thing to white people. I believe such an argument rests upon the evident humanity of blacks, and all your works rest upon this evidence. But what must one tell the Negroes? Because the Negroes can make the whole journey, but they may not be able to make the whole journey. I'd go so far as saying that should they go the whole way, the problem would find no solution at all; it would, rather, reestablish the status quo ante.

Yes indeed.

It would amount to moving from one excess to another.

Your solution may be a little too theoretical because Negroes—now in Africa they want to build nations in haste, for reasons of internal policy. Now in Africa they want nations to be formed quickly, in great haste, too quickly for the taste of white people. We are in the midst of a crisis of nationalism among Negroes. Negroes have not explained the way in which they should achieve nationalism because many whites don't understand this process and why there must be nationalism in Africa today. I believe in Africa there is a great lack of books, ideas, cultural movements which might be able to explain why there are so many nationalistic movements in this continent. Among whites, you know, among white people in Russia, in America, in France, the philosophers, musicians, and scientists speak about revolution before revolution takes place but, with Negroes, politicians do things and black poets explain them only later. I think I can criticize Negroes because they let go of a sacred duty—to explain why blacks are so restless in this political manner. Negroes today have not established their level of responsibility in this category. Nothing from Africa explains why this happens. Black people must do something quick to this effect.

Do you believe things will move that way? Can you see changes indicating this orientation?

Frankly, not as far as any cultural movement is concerned. I do not believe that Negroes sufficiently understand the urgency of such work. This is a tragedy because one really needs to understand what is taking place in the Congo and in Nigeria. You see, the white press provides another kind of explanation for it, but it is not the vision of black people. This thing is missing. It is not the responsibility of whites.

Only a black person can say this.

Indeed, it is our own duty.

We can't make the journey.
That's true, it is our job.

Do you contemplate preparing a book about this problem?
Not directly. You know, we Negro artists are in a rather difficult
position: I do not want to criticize Negroes so harshly in public when
I know there are white people around with political power who can do
much harm. They can do harm; they can take my words and use them
against blacks. I'd like to criticize blacks, but I don't want to provide
whites with words to strike at black people. This is a moral trap.

*Which will have to be overcome. Who can build a bridge if this
difficulty is not overcome?*
It is difficult right now.

*Do African Negroes understand, when they read your works, that
your problems as an American Negro are rather different from their
own?*
Yes, I believe they understand this, but I'd like to explain something.
It is American Negroes, from the South of the United States and the
Caribbean, who brought the idea of black nationalism to Africa. I don't
believe many people understand the reason why we, American Negroes,
have done this. We feel we are not really at home in our country. This
is the origin, logical enough, of black nationalism. It begins with
Marcus Garvey in the United States. After Garvey and W.E.B. DuBois,
George Padmore was at the root of this idea. I have worked with
Padmore; he is at the root of this idea and has injected nationalism into
Africa. There are Africans who want to build nations, but they want to
remain somewhat apart in their tribes. American Negroes do not like
tribal people and tribes; they want things in Africa to be a little as they
are in America, in England. And there are whites who want to retain
political power in Africa and who tell tribal chiefs: do not listen to
Richard Wright and George Padmore if you are a tribal chief. No,
things are fine as they are. You are full of wisdom and it is not necessary for your country to become industrialized. Stay as you are.

*To explode the tribal framework in order to make the tribe disappear
in front of the nation—it is possible for you to explain this necessity to
black people?*
There are influences. Americans do not like such an idea. Many

Englishmen do not like it. You know, they want to keep tribes primitive. They cannot grant much publicity to the idea of nations against tribes.

Does the strength of black nationalisms today seem dangerous to you, to any extent?

If one prevents the expression of these nationalisms, things will become dangerous. We have the example of Congo, where there is nationalism and outside forces which prevent its expression, and at once the people think: "Well, we are in a position to lose our freedom. Call the Soviets, call China, call anyone who can help us!" I believe the most important thing in Africa now is the following: to find a way to release the energies of the tribes in order to create nations.

A Negro American in France

Georges Charbonnier/1960

Transcript of a radio broadcast on ORTF, Paris, November 1990.
Translated by Michel Fabre.

The general theme of our talks with Richard Wright is clear: between blacks and whites confidence is greatly lacking because relations have been established on a distorted basis. Our problem is to convert abnormal relations into normal ones. One should not hide that this problem is rather difficult to solve, for it is important to act in such a way that the problem will no longer exist. To change the direction of unbalanced relations would only amount to replacing one evil by another evil. One must thus attempt to establish a balance, and once this position has been reached, to stop there. Not to replace one supremacy by another, one racism by another. Knowledge poses enough challenges to solve, enough difficulties to overcome. It is high time for man to put an end to a behavior which belongs to the stone age and not to the age of science.

Today, Richard Wright, I would like to emphasize some characteristics of badly established relations. It seems to me indeed that if the relations between blacks and whites are established on a wrong basis all the manifestations of those relations will display abnormal features. Everyone's life will be distorted, especially the life of blacks. It seems that relations as different as those in sexual behavior, in sports, or the contacts between whites and blacks outside the United States, for instance, will be distorted. Psychopathology itself and, of course, psychotherapy depend upon those badly established relations. For instance, what can a Negro, or a white, psychoanalyst do for a Negro patient? How can he reinsert into society a black man who cannot find in himself the resources necessary to lead a normal life in a social environment where so many relations are badly established? Richard Wright, how would you characterize the powers of black psychoanalysis today?

Maybe I can try. You know, in New York, in Chicago, there is much talk today about psychoanalysis. I have a little story. One day two patients are in the waiting room of a psychiatrist. A white man and a

Negro. The doctor opens the door and asks: "Who's first?" It is the
white man's turn.

"Come in, sir. Tell me what's wrong with you."

"I am somewhat anxious."

"Tell me how, in which way?"

Well, doctor, when I go for a walk in the streets I have the feeling
that people look at me with some distrust."

"What else?"

"When I enter a shop to buy something the salesgirl looks rather
diffident and annoyed as though she does not want to sell anything to
me."

The doctor says: "Well, in this profession, we have a phrase for your
ailment. It is called 'subjective ideas of reference'." And the doctor
adds: "Well, you just come every Thursday from four to five and close
your eyes and tell me all your thoughts and I can assure you that within
two or three months, you'll be cured. It will cost you twenty thousand
dollars. You understand?"

"Yes doctor, I understand." And the white man leaves.

"Who's next?" the doctor says. It is the black man's turn.

"Good morning, doctor."

"Good morning. What's wrong with you?"

"Well, when I go for a walk in the streets people look at me with
distrust, and when I enter a shop to buy something the salesgirl looks
annoyed and diffident, and I have the distinct feeling that she does not
want to sell anything to me."

"Well, I understand. In our profession, we have a phrase for this; it is
'subjective ideas of reference'."

The black man is upset when he hears this and he says: "Pardon me,
doctor, but you must be raving mad." (Laughter)

*I believe this story perfectly illustrates the evils engendered by
racism, for it presents an extreme case. There is no possible cure but it
is not the patient who ought to be cured, it is the society around him,
which he refuses and which refuses him. Let us examine other types of
relationships. A black American, you are now living in Paris. Have you
established contacts with white Americans in Paris, and what kinds of
contacts?*

My God, you are asking a delicate and complex question. In order to

explain the relations between black and white Americans in Paris one
must first examine relations between Negroes and whites in the United
States. There, in New York, in Chicago, in the entire country, one
encounters traditional relations. When a white man meets a Negro in
New York, there is an etiquette which governs their relations. In
Europe, the Negro is outside of his own country and so is the white
American. There is no structured etiquette to contain their relations.
When a white American comes across a black American in Paris, both
are a little surprised. They don't easily find things to say because the
black man wonders "What kind of white American is he?" while the
white man wonders what kind of Negro he is. One could say that the
problem is worse than in the United States. It is surprising, but you can
easily see the cause of those frictions in their relationship. This creates
rather strange situations among us, American Negroes in Paris. There
are no relations between ordinary whites and ordinary blacks. The
whites want to know what is taking place among Negroes in Paris, in
Europe in general, because no organized structure can be used to help
them know what is happening. And, you see, they ask Negroes to serve
as spies among other Negroes to discover what they are thinking, what
they may be up to. This creates a jungle among blacks in Paris. Because
there are Negro people who watch other Negroes for money, for dollars.
And people who work for organizations in order to watch others. Well,
it creates a lot of distrust among Negroes in Paris. It is a horrible thing,
a nightmare. When a black American comes across another, he has a
question in his mind: "For whom is he working?" And this is brought
about by white Americans who are afraid of blacks. They have no
normal relations with blacks, and no other way of knowing what is
happening among them.

In other words, all relations are deformed outside of your country.
    That's it. All relations between Negroes and whites become a
nightmare outside of our country. In America, one can say they already
are a nightmare, in a moral sense, but a nightmare which is contained
by the structures of everyday life: the black man needs to work for the
white man and the white man needs a black employee. There exist
traditional relations which contain this relationship, but they do not avail
in Europe. And when a white man encounters a black man here, the
problem is worse than you can imagine. And I must say this is the topic

of my next novel. It is no longer suppressed but public now. This is the way things are, a nightmare. This is why, an American Negro, I live among French people. Negroes here associate with French people in order to avoid the American colony. There is no Negro American colony. The Negroes associate with the French to avoid the white American colony. Yet it is not easy to escape those whites. When we are with French people, some of them come with their eyes wide open to watch with whom we are speaking, to know our links with such or such French institution, and the like. Such things do happen. Well, you asked a rather innocent and natural question, and you have an answer full of difficulties.

My question wasn't so innocent. (Both of them laugh). *But I wonder whether the uneasiness of white Americans is not compounded by our French attitude towards blacks. And our attitude can be defined in a very simple way: we do not have any.*

Of course, the French attitude towards blacks—you can share apartment houses, send your children to school, live without any preoccupation about racial questions here. Americans think that maybe if the French could act with blacks the way they themselves do, things might be easier for us. It is easy for Americans to regulate their relationships with Negroes at home, but it is nearly impossible abroad, you see; and there are other questions too, political ones, normal conflicts between one nationalism and another.

Let us consider still other relations, as different as possible from those you were speaking about. What should we think, for instance, about a boxing match when a white man and a black man are confronted?

Yes, this is very interesting because I believe I was the first black writer to deal with this question a long time ago in the United States. I encountered this in a rather natural way as a journalist in Chicago. This was when Joe Louis was young and becoming a world champion. At that time the racial tensions were so acute, you see, that it was not only a match between a Negro boxer and a white boxer, it was a symbolical fight between a black man and a white man, between the black world and the white world. It was a rather strange thing. And when Joe Louis beat Max Baer and another world champion, every time Joe Louis won a victory over the whites there were formidable demonstrations in the

black ghettos. One might have thought this was a political manifesta-
tion. I do not believe it was, now. One can think it was quite natural to
express racial hope in the black ghettos. You see, under the pressure of
the racial burden among Negroes, medical problems become political
problems, the problems of sports become political problems; it is the
natural, normal pressure of racism which twists all the values of life.

*But, you know, one can find similar things elsewhere. A football
encounter between France and Belgium has no political aspects; it is
simply a question of football and sport. But it is not always so and some
international encounters in sport are political confrontations.*
Yes, it is happening now between communist and capitalist countries.
It turns into a struggle of ideologies.

Ideology takes refuge in a ball.
It can be found anywhere and I believe it is the symptom of a disease.
There are normal expressions of sport: it is an entertainment and opportunity to practice gymnastics, something that can give you joy, but in
certain places where political life and racial conditions are abnormal,
sport becomes deformed; it becomes something else today. You see, I
believe that artists can see the metamorphoses of reality under the pressure of events. In the future one can see love tragedies behind political
dramas. One can see this even in the field of art.

*Yes, the pressures upon the individual reflect something else. In the
field of art, this is endless because the pressure brought to bear upon
the artist becomes a topic.*
Yes, that's it.

*And the topic, once it has been treated, itself becomes an object of
pressures and the reason for a struggle. It is an endless process.*
But there are people who think: why does a Negro expressly and
intentionally create a work of this type? They do not understand that
there are pressures. This is the material naturally used by a Negro artist,
this is his life. He considers this every day in the same way as a white
artist considers the problems of whites. In a very natural way. I believe
that in the world today one needs much imagination to know what is
happening to other people. Now more than ever one needs tremendous
imagination to build a bridge between individuals. We can attempt to
build a bridge through art, if possible.

A Negro Novel about White People
Georges Charbonnier/1960

Transcript of a radio broadcast on ORTF, Paris, November 1960.
Translated by Michel Fabre.

Savage Holiday aside, all of Richard Wright's fiction is dedicated to Negro life. This does not mean that all of Richard Wright's characters are black. Of course, in each of his novels there are white characters, but one can say that his vision is different when he is looking at Negroes and when he is looking at whites. It is an objective vision, admittedly, yet a different vision. A vision naturally and intentionally different because the black man and the white man are not seen from inside. I do not mean that Richard Wright is content with looking at the white world from outside. Richard Wright always coincides with his object. I mean that it is from inside the Negro world that Richard Wright observes, determines the area where two worlds, the black and the white one, are brought into contact and face each other. Richard Wright is part of one of these worlds when he describes or judges the other impartially, as I said earlier. This remark made, an important feature is revealed: in all of Richard Wright's works the white world is seen as a natural phenomenon, just like storms and floods are natural phenomena. Well, you cannot take sides against a natural phenomenon. You observe it in order, if not to prevent it, at least to avoid it. To take shelter from the storm, one attempts to forecast it, and in Wright's entire work black psychology, as we, white people, can observe it, pertains to a certain kind of meteorology. Everything happens as though to the list "It is raining," "It is snowing," "It is fine," the Negro soul added the phrase "It is white," which would mean a particularly insistent white presence.

Exceptionally, Richard Wright has written a book about white people, *Savage Holiday*. Nothing reveals that this novel has been written by a Negro who shows an in-depth knowledge of the white world. One detail in this work should attract attention: the book begins on a Saturday and the action starts undoubtedly on a Sunday; it ends forty-eight hours later. It is a Sunday book, a book about the Seventh Day's rest. On Sunday, when man is left alone with himself, when he sheds his social or professional cover and is left naked, vacant, face to face with his nakedness. This man is naked, ashamed, unhappy, dangerous to himself and, as a consequence, dangerous to others. He soon becomes a criminal, unconsciously at first and even in spite of himself, then deliberately out of passion and unfettered savagery. The man whom Richard Wright depicts is a white man and the initial adventure is that of a naked man on a Sunday. The boy who delivers the morning paper has just dropped one behind his door. What is the white man, the naked white man going to do?

(Reading of an excerpt from *Savage Holiday* depicting Erskine Fowler's reactions when the door slams shut behind him as he steps out naked from his apartment to pick up the *Sunday Times*.)

Richard Wright, it seems to me that Savage Holiday *is very different from your other books.*

Yes, this novel is quite different from the others. For the first time in my life, in my professional career as a writer, I tried to tell the story of a white person. I picked a white American businessman to attempt a demonstration about a universal problem. This man has made lots of money; he is rich, retired. Maybe I can explain to you how I came across this idea. I had entered a library and was glancing at books naturally, casually, without any purpose. I came across a passage dealing with the problem of freedom. Not in a philosophical sense but in a practical sense.

It is not a problem of freedom but of leisure. Freedom in leisure.

Exactly.

(Another excerpt from *Savage Holiday* is read, dealing with the desperate feelings of the workaholic without work.)

When you wrote Savage Holiday, *did you depict a Puritan?*

Certainly.

Is Puritanism a typically white feature?

No! You can certainly find Puritans among the black bourgeoisie, but they are not typical.

In other words, a lay society seems to you essential to a humane and superior way of life.

Yes, this is my opinion. I believe that people who can bear unguaranteed existence are those who can bring the greatest gift to mankind.

Are all Negro movements today lay or secular movements?
No, not at all. This is strange, and you asked an interesting question. The Cold War has greatly distorted things with us in America. And in my opinion a society is not very strong when it rests upon a large basis of secret, hidden things, like quicksand. In my opinion, things must be in the open.

It seems to me that in all your works you are strongly in favor of asking all kinds of questions.
All questions indeed. How do you say this in French? "The greatest possible cross-fertilization of ideas."

This is a phrase used in botany—"cross fertilization".
That's it, cross-fertilization among ideas. I believe that a strong society is a society which allows this. One must know what people are thinking.

A weak society is a society which does not air its problems; a strong society airs its problems. This is true in all areas and can be applied to governments and to people.
Yes, I think so.

I asked you whether Negro movements were lay movements and your reply concerned mostly the United States. Is this true in the rest of the world?
Not at all. In Africa they are basically religious. This imposes a psychological distance between me, an American Negro, and African Negroes. It is somewhat upsetting and still bothers me. When I tried to work with African Negroes, I found in their minds something mystical, a metaphysical element. And I wonder what it can be. Because it is absent in me. I think there may be a great strength in the religious spirit of American Negroes, but I wonder whether one can build a strong society upon such consciousness. I really don't know. For me, it is an open question. I wonder.

When you speak in Black Power *of all that took place in the Gold Coast, if I understand you accurately, you imply at the end of the book that the leaders of liberation movements were rather secular-minded but that they exploited religious practices.*

That's it. Outside Africa, especially, people have difficulty understanding this. But black African leaders, especially in areas ruled by the British, have been educated in European schools and they think like white people, they look at their countries from outside. They try to organize this energy into political movements but also to change this energy. They want to make their countries similar to European countries; this is their aim; if I can make a country like France, America, England, it will be modern and strong and able to resist colonial invasion.

Therefore, creating a secular state seems to be the aim.

Yes, in my opinion.

(The continuation of the series, called *Of Time and History,* is missing.)

One of Uncle Tom's Children

Peter Lennon/1960

From *The Guardian*, 8 December 1960, p. 8. Reprinted by permission.

For 14 years Richard Wright, his wife and two children lived in The Quarter—the Latin Quarter of Paris. An energetic, medium-sized, apparently robust man, argumentative, full of restless gestures but smiling readily, he was well known in American ex-patriot [sic] cafes such as *Le Tournon,* near the Senate. When he had the intention of starting out on a tour of French Black Africa we met, and we talked about the subject which was his preoccupation: the Negro problem.

His features were not noticeably negroid and his skin hardly more than a deep nut-brown. His voice, slightly high but clear, had few of the customary Southern slurring and dragging on words, but he had the very Negro habit, when laughing, of laying the tongue on the underlip and laughing from the back of an open throat. He laughed most readily when mentioning some particularly illogical and unjust act of discrimination against the Negro in America.

Since he was born in a State like Mississippi, the area with the highest rate of illiteracy in North America, I was curious about how he managed to educate himself.

I did go to a school, you know, and then I just read anything I could get my hands on, popular pulp magazines, thrillers and things. My taste must have been awful. I just read the books that interested me and they led to others. For example, I read all Conrad because I liked him and then I read all I could about Conrad, and reading critics put me in touch with other books. It developed that way. It was emotionally organised reading if you like.

Do you think you missed anything by leaving school at 15?
I did gain by not being conditioned in a particular social pattern. Frankly I don't know about university education. In 'frontier' societies it is perhaps not a good thing. Most of our writers are really self-

educated. But in a place like France the best way to absorb the past is perhaps by university education. America has no past really.

What led you to start writing?
Some people go to the sea shore and see people swimming and they want to swim too. When I started to read I wanted to write. I had my first story published when I was 14 in a Negro paper. It must have been bad.

Did you consciously take on the responsibility of championing the Negro cause in your writing?
That's a tricky question. I did not consciously feel I was championing any cause. I chose the subject before I realised its importance. It's like a Negro singer who sings the blues and it becomes a part of, an expression of, his whole predicament—his place in society. But he sings for purely personal reasons.

Do you not think that having a social mission is bad for a creative writer?
I would say that Negro subject matter is just as valid as any other. I really think it's for other people to decide if I am didactic or not. If I am fierce in my books it is because I feel fiercely; if I become polemic it is because I am trying to tell the reader something and I am afraid he does not understand.

Hemingway said recently that he had no feeling at the time of belonging to "a lost generation"—do you feel you are a member of a group, a certain "movement" in writing?
I most emphatically deny belonging to any group. What group would I belong to? Not even a Negro group. I suppose it's the critics who put you in those categories but it's nothing to do with me.

Would it have been possible for you to have lived with your white wife in the North reasonably unmolested?
If we had kept within the Black Belt we should not have had too much trouble.

Do you intend taking your children back to the United States?
I don't want to bring them back until they are grown up because of the danger of personality damage.

*When you are renewing your passport here do you not feel some re-
luctance to take the Pledge of Allegiance to the United States which has
caused you so much hardship?*

I don't think it has caused me too much hardship. I live quite com-
fortably. In any case the American Negro is the most vociferous de-
fender of the Constitution. That's exactly what we want: enforcement of
the Constitution.

*Would you not agree that racial discrimination in the North is no
stronger than class snobbery in, let's say, England?*

I don't think racial discrimination can be equated to class snobbery.
Let me put it this way. Anyone is entitled to refuse a man entry into his
house. I did it myself this morning. A fellow rang up and wanted to
come over but I did not want to have him. But not on racial grounds.
. . . [In the original; no omission] When you use the colour of a man's
skin to achieve political ends, there you have racism.

*James Baldwin said that the Southerner suffered under the delusion
that he "understood" the Negro while the Northerner believes he has set
him free. Do you agree with that?*

I agree with Baldwin, partly. But the Northerner can't believe he has
set the Negro free. In the North the Negro lives in a ghetto. The difference in the Negro's situation in the North and South arises out of a difference in societies. In the South it is agrarian, harsher and harder; in
the North, industrial—and there are different kinds of pressure.

Do you think communism will set the Negro free?

I don't believe that communism is something you embrace to set you
free. At that time in Chicago, communism was the only ideology which
made some sense of my experience so I gravitated towards it. I joined
the party. It was a way out of a morass. But in the end it seems to me
that the Communist only treats the Negro well so far as it suits his own
ultimate aims.

*In the introduction to "The Outsider" you said that this was your
"first literary effort projected out of a heart preoccupied with no ideological burdens"; you were "in search of a new attitude to replace
Marxism." Can you claim to have been successful in your search?*

Well . . . [In the original; no omission] the success is, I think, that
one continues to search.

Jazz and Desire

Frank Tenot/1961

From *Cahiers du Jazz,* 4 (April 1961), 53–54. Translated by John DuVal.

In Harlem Richard Wright was familiarly known as "Dick." He was familiar with black music. Frank Tenot interviewed him for Cahiers *a few days before his death.*

F.T.: I see the novelist in you, but through the novelist, the jazz lover.

R.W.: I'm not that interested in jazz, particularly modern jazz. What really interests me and delights me is gospel singing.

F.T.: But isn't modern jazz, after all, influenced by gospel singing?

R.W.: Possibly. I'd like to tell you a theory that's especially dear to me. Protestant ministers have put to religious use the sexual power of convulsive songs and have channeled aphrodisiac music into the spirituals. In Africa the same kind of trance takes place. The witch doctors cry out to their followers when they reach the orgasm which the god plants in their bodies. You can see why it's an easy step from the art of Ray Charles to that of the black preachers. *He* says straight out what *they* couch in more comforting terms.

F.T.: I come back to my first point. Why doesn't modern jazz move you? The Dionysian element is still there.

R.W.: Because modern jazz is for those who have won out, who have integrated themselves into the white world, who have adapted to American society, whereas my concern is with all those who haven't made it and who are caught up in the conflict, and in the drama.

F.T.: Does all Harlem love gospel or jazz?

R.W.: The black bourgeoisie don't like either, because in their anxiety to imitate whites, they consider both to be "primitive" art forms, incapable of expressing lofty, "civilized" sentiments.

F.T.: Well, what kind of music *are* these black bourgeois able to enjoy?

R.W.: Very bad music. Hollywood music. Songs from American musicals. It's sad.

F.T.: So the most important thing is . . . ?

R.W.: Not to be a black bourgeois and to understand that the main gift that jazz has to offer the world today is an affirmation of *desire*. In spirituals and in Ray Charles—I repeat—there's the same erotic exultation. This aspect of black music has been denied for too long. The faith of mystics and of most blacks has a sexual ingredient which well meaning people are too timid to dare admit, but which must be proclaimed.

Index

245